# New Casebooks

## POETRY

WILLIAM BLAKE Edited by David Punter
CHAUCER Edited by Valerie Allen and Aries Axiotis
COLERIDGE, KEATS AND SHELLEY Edited by Peter J. Kitson
JOHN DONNE Edited by Andrew Mousley
SEAMUS HEANEY Edited by Michael Allen
PHILIP LARKIN Edited by Stephen Regan
DYLAN THOMAS Edited by John Goodby and Chris Wigginton
VICTORIAN WOMEN POETS Edited by Joseph Bristow
WORDSWORTH Edited by John Williams
PARADISE LOST Edited by William Zunder

## NOVELS AND PROSE

AUSTEN: *Emma* Edited by David Monaghan
AUSTEN: *Mansfield Park* and *Persuasion* Edited by Judy Simons
AUSTEN: *Sense and Sensibility* and *Pride and Prejudice* Edited by Robert Clark
CHARLOTTE BRONTË: *Jane Eyre* Edited by Heather Glen
CHARLOTTE BRONTË: *Villette* Edited by Pauline Nestor
EMILY BRONTË: *Wuthering Heights* Edited by Patsy Stoneman
ANGELA CARTER Edited by Alison Easton
WILKIE COLLINS Edited by Lyn Pykett
JOSEPH CONRAD Edited by Elaine Jordan
DICKENS: *Bleak House* Edited by Jeremy Tambling
DICKENS: *David Copperfield* and *Hard Times* Edited by John Peck
DICKENS: *Great Expectations* Edited by Roger Sell
ELIOT: *The Mill on the Floss and Silas Marner* Edited by Nahem Yousaf and Andrew Maunder
ELIOT: *Middlemarch* Edited by John Peck
E.M. FORSTER Edited by Jeremy Tambling
HARDY: *Jude the Obscure* Edited by Penny Boumelha
HARDY: *The Mayor of Casterbridge* Edited by Julian Wolfreys
HARDY: *Tess of the D'Urbervilles* Edited by Peter Widdowson
JAMES: *Turn of the Screw* and *What Maisie Knew* Edited by Neil Cornwell and Maggie Malone
LAWRENCE: *Sons and Lovers* Edited by Rick Rylance
TONI MORRISON Edited by Linden Peach
GEORGE ORWELL Edited by Byran Loughrey
SHELLEY: *Frankenstein* Edited by Fred Botting
STOKER: *Dracula* Edited by Glennis Byron
STERNE: *Tristram Shandy* Edited by Melvyn New
WOOLF: *Mrs Dalloway* and *To the Lighthouse* Edited by Su Reid

(continued overleaf)

## DRAMA

BECKETT: *Waiting for Godot* and *Endgame* Edited by Steven Connor
APHRA BEHN Edited by Janet Todd
REVENGE TRAGEDY Edited by Stevie Simkin
SHAKESPEARE: *Antony and Cleopatra* Edited by John Drakakis
SHAKESPEARE: *Hamlet* Edited by Martin Coyle
SHAKESPEARE: *Julius Caesar* Edited by Richard Wilson
SHAKESPEARE: *King Lear* Edited by Kiernan Ryan
SHAKESPEARE: *Macbeth* Edited by Alan Sinfield
SHAKESPEARE: *The Merchant of Venice* Edited by Martin Coyle
SHAKESPEARE: *A Midsummer Night's Dream* Edited by Richard Dutton
SHAKESPEARE: *Much Ado About Nothing* and *The Taming of the Shrew*
  Edited by Marion Wynne-Davies
SHAKESPEARE: *Romeo and Juliet* Edited by R. S. White
SHAKESPEARE: *The Tempest* Edited by R. S. White
SHAKESPEARE: *Twelfth Night* Edited by R. S. White
SHAKESPEARE ON FILM Edited by Robert Shaughnessy
SHAKESPEARE IN PERFORMANCE Edited by Robert Shaughnessy
SHAKESPEARE'S HISTORY PLAYS Edited by Graham Holderness
SHAKESPEARE'S TRAGEDIES Edited by Susan Zimmerman
JOHN WEBSTER: *The Duchess of Malfi* Edited by Dympna Callaghan

## GENERAL THEMES

FEMINIST THEATRE AND THEORY Edited by Helene Keyssar
POST-COLONIAL LITERATURES Edited by Michael Parker and Roger Starkey

---

## New Casebooks Series
### Series Standing Order
**ISBN 0–333–71702–3 hardcover**
**ISBN 0–333–69345–0 paperback**
*(outside North America only)*

You can receive future titles in this series as they are published by placing a standing order. Please contact your bookseller or, in case of difficulty, write to us at the address below with your name and address, the title of the series and the ISBN quoted above.

Customer Services Department, Macmillan Distribution Ltd
Houndmills, Basingstoke, Hampshire RG21 6XS, England

---

*New Casebooks*

# MANSFIELD PARK
and
PERSUASION

EDITED BY JUDY SIMONS

Published by
PALGRAVE
Houndmills, Basingstoke, Hampshire RG21 6XS and
175 Fifth Avenue, New York, N. Y. 10010
Companies and representatives throughout the world

PALGRAVE is the new global academic imprint of
St. Martin's Press LLC Scholarly and Reference Division and
Palgrave Publishers Ltd (formerly Macmillan Press Ltd).

*Outside North America*
ISBN 0–333–63678–3 hardcover
ISBN 0–333–63679–1 paperback

*Inside North America*
ISBN 0–312–17344–X

This book is printed on paper suitable for recycling and
made from fully managed and sustained forest sources.

A catalogue record for this book is available
from the British Library.

A catalogue record for this book is available
from the Library of Congress.

11  10   9   8   7   6   5   4   3
10  09  08  07  06  05  04  03  02

Typeset by EXPO Holdings, Malaysia

Printed and bound in Great Britain by
Antony Rowe Ltd, Eastbourne

# Contents

# Acknowledgements

The editors and publishers wish to thank the following for permission to use copyright material:

Nina Auerbach for 'Jane Austen's Dangerous Charm: Feeling as One Ought About Fanny Price' in *Jane Austen: New Perspectives*, ed. Janet Todd (1983), pp. 208–23. Copyright © by Holmes & Meier Publishers, by permission of Holmes and Meier Publishers, Inc: Marilyn Butler for material from *Jane Austen and the War of Ideas* (1975), pp. 219–36. Copyright © Oxford University Press 1975, by permission of Oxford University Press; Julia Prewitt Brown for material from *Jane Austen's Novels: Social Change and Literary Form* (1979), pp. 128–9, 137–50. Copyright © 1979 by the President and Fellows of Harvard College, by permission of Harvard University Press; Sandra Gilbert and Susan Gubar for material from *The Madwoman in the Attic: the Nineteenth-Century Woman Writer and the Literary Imagination* (1979), pp. 174–83, by permission of Yale University Press; Claudia Johnson for material from *Jane Austen: Women, Politics and the Novel* (1988), pp. 144–8, 158–66, by permission of The University of Chicago Press; D.A. Miller for material from *Narrative and Its Discontents: Problems of Closure in the Traditional Novel* (1981), pp. 77–89. Copyright © 1981 by Princeton University Press, by permission of Princeton University Press; Laura G. Mooneyham for material from *Romance, Language and Education in Jane Austen's Novels* (1988), pp. 146, 162–75, by permission of Macmillan Ltd; Mary Poovey for material from *The Proper Lady and the Woman Writer: Ideology as Style in the Works of Mary Wollstonecraft, Mary Shelley and Jane Austen* (1984), pp. 212–24, by permission of The University of Chicago Press; Edward Said for material from *Culture and Imperialism* (1993), pp. 99–116, Chatto and Windus. Copyright © 1993 by Edward Said, by permission of Random House UK Ltd and The Wylie Agency, Inc. on behalf of the author; Cheryl Ann Weissman for 'Doubleness and Refrain in Jane Austen's *Persuasion*', *The Kenyon Review*, 10, 4 (1988), 87–91. Copyright © 1988 by Kenyon College, by permission of the author; John Wiltshire for material from *Jane Austen and the body* (1993), pp. 159–74, 190–6, by permission of Cambridge University Press; Ruth Bernard Yeazell for 'The Boundaries of *Mansfield Park*', *Representations*, 7 (Summer 1984), 133–52. Copyright © 1984 by the Regents of the University of California, by permission of the University of California Press.

# General Editors' Preface

The purpose of this series of New Casebooks is to reveal some of the ways in which contemporary criticism has changed our understanding of commonly studied texts and writers and, indeed, of the nature of criticism itself. Central to the series is a concern with modern critical theory and its effect on current approaches to the study of literature. Each New Casebook editor has been asked to select a sequence of essays which will introduce the reader to the new critical approaches to the text or texts being discussed in the volume and also illuminate the rich interchange between critical theory and critical practice that characterises so much current writing about literature.

In this focus on modern critical thinking and practice New Casebooks aim not only to inform but also to stimulate, with volumes seeking to reflect both the controversy and the excitement of current criticism. Because much of this criticism is difficult and often employs an unfamiliar critical language, editors have been asked to give the reader as much help as they feel is appropriate, but without simplifying the essays or the issues they raise. Again, editors have been asked to supply a list of further reading which will enable readers to follow up issues raised by the essays in the volume.

The project of New Casebooks, then, is to bring together in an illuminating way those critics who best illustrate the ways in which contemporary criticism has established new methods of analysing texts and who have reinvigorated the important debate about how we 'read' literature. The hope is, of course, that New Casebooks will not only open up this debate to a wider audience, but will also encourage students to extend their own ideas, and think afresh about their responses to the texts they are studying.

*John Peck and Martin Coyle*
*University of Wales, Cardiff*

# Introduction

*JUDY SIMONS*

## I

Joel Weinsheimer has observed that before the nineteen-eighties Austen criticism was highly conservative in tendency and reluctant to venture beyond its traditional confines into new contexts or unfamiliar discourses.[1] The past twenty years have seen a marked shift away from what could be considered this defiantly insular if reassuring position, as poststructuralist, feminist and New Historicist critics have, among others, stated their entitlement to the Austen canon. The selection of essays in this New Casebook is designed to represent the most significant of these recent directions and the impact they have made on the ways in which *Mansfield Park* and *Persuasion* can legitimately be read. If the current state of critical opinion on the novels ultimately emerges as unstable, such instability is perhaps an appropriate reflection of the texts' internal debates as well as of the academic climate which responds to them. It is not a condition, however, which is universally welcomed and it is perhaps salutary to be reminded, however briefly, of this by reference to two studies not included in this collection, but which do help to identify the problems confronting the Austen reader.

The anxiety which modern critical discussions of Austen have engendered is most clearly articulated in Roger Gard's *Jane Austen's Novels: the Art of Clarity* (1992), which states categorically that 'there is no *ambiguity* in Jane Austen'.[2] Gard's book is a direct response to the impact of theory on Austen studies. As a traditionalist critic who wants to return Austen to the 'common reader', Gard argues vigorously for the novels' appeal beyond the literary academy, and supports his contention by using the sales figures of paperback editions of Austen's work as evidence of its market popularity. He suggests that Austen should be returned to her rightful owners, the vast reading public, and to this end his study makes strenuous efforts to demystify the current state of Austen criticism. In reaffirming the role of the writer as central to the relationship between the text and its reader, his thesis implicitly rejects the poststructuralist position which presupposes Roland Barthes' 'death of the author'.[3] Instead, attention is focused on Austen's control over her material and the lucidity of her methods and ideas. Grounded in the belief that, in her ability to communicate directly with an audience, any audience, Jane Austen is a writer who transcends her period, Gard's argument resurrects the assumptions about universal norms that were intrinsic to critical assessments of Austen in the first half of the twentieth century and that helped to establish her as a central figure in the hierarchy of English authors. Although it could be argued that this apparently a-political stance is disingenuous, Gard's work is valuable in reminding us that Austen's novels continue to attract non-specialist readers who have no interest in critical theory, and in attempting to explain the reasons for this he raises important questions regarding artistic value, readability, and audience.

A useful counterpoint to this view is represented by James Thompson's *Between Self and World* (1988), a Marxist study which refutes a-political approaches to reading Austen (such as Gard's) as based on a false premise, that of the texts' innate accessibility and shared cultural convictions. Far from seeing the reading public as a fixed entity with tastes and responses that have remained static over the last two hundred years, Thompson locates reading, just as firmly as writing, within a historical context. Logically, therefore, there can be no consensus about the ways in which texts are received, and no automatic audience response that can be assumed to persist from the eighteenth to the twentieth century. This position provides Thompson with both a linguistic and a historical basis from which to mount his theoretical analysis of Austen's writing. Indeed, for Thompson, literary and cultural theory is an integral component of the critical act, which he perceives as a mode of interrogating the processes of both meaning and interpretation. He suggests that in the past 'what passed for criticism of Austen's fiction is really appreciation, one form or another of explaining how well she writes. If we approach Austen's novels with the aim of showing how good they are, there is little chance that we will ever begin to understand them because we begin by sharing their assumptions.'[4]

These views are worth recording here because of their timing; appearing within five years of one another they represent two opposed critical positions from which modern readers of Jane Austen's fiction can start. Is she a writer whose canonical status is beyond question and whose work operates within a shared system of aesthetic value with which all readers can empathise? Or is she a writer whose very reputation and familiarity erect a formidable barrier which must be demolished before the critical process can take place? At the heart of this debate lies another more wide-reaching issue, that of the nature of the critical enterprise itself: is it, as Gard suggests, the attempt to make a literary work accessible, or is it, in Marxist terminology, the need to 'estrange', so as to read anew? More specifically, who 'owns' Jane Austen? Can her novels be simultaneously common property and the subject of sophisticated theorisation? Or does theory disable both text and reader, and in the process of dismantlement create an exclusive community of theorists, whose language is opaque and who paradoxically re-enshrine Austen's work as an impenetrable nexus of codes and sign systems?

In 1923 Virginia Woolf wrote that 'of all great writers, Jane Austen is the most difficult to catch in the act of greatness'.[5] Yet for virtually fifty years after Woolf's statement most Austen critics were trying to do just that. Taking her 'greatness' for granted, they devoted their attention to the business of examining her artistic method in order to grasp and define the unique quality of her accomplishment. The past twenty years have seen a major shift away from this sort of critical practice, a shift that a critic such as Roger Gard finds disturbing in what he perceives as a disparity between real textual engagement and abstruse theoretical argument. But the two are not necessarily mutually exclusive. For although the essays in this New Casebook collectively might appear to undermine any fixed notion of Jane Austen's writing as a clear and easily defined entity, this does not mean that the critics whose work is reprinted here inevitably lose touch with the individual novel under discussion. A number of the essays retain the meticulous analysis of textual detail that was a fundamental feature of earlier Austen criticism: note, for example, the intensive scrutiny of language in the discussion of *Mansfield Park* by D.A. Miller (essay 2) and of

*Persuasion* by Laura Mooneyham (essay 10).Taken as a whole, however, the collection illuminates the transformation in critical practice as it has developed over the past two decades in relation to Jane Austen, and the consequent intellectual challenge this offers the reader. Instead of analysing the formal properties of the literary text as a self-evident route to an unambiguous meaning, critics such as Miller and Mooneyham see rhetorical devices as key reflectors of multiplex codes of signification, whether linguistic or cultural. These codes and their implications need to be accommodated before a reader can acquire an understanding of conditions which determine textual production and the strands of meaning that are thereby generated. At the same time they indicate the tensions that exist between divergent critical schools, and the consequent debate over interpretation as critics seek to locate Jane Austen's writing within one of a number of possible theoretical contexts.

## II

The particular critical difficulties associated with *Mansfield Park* and *Persuasion* can in part be attributed to the stylistic tensions which characterise both novels, to those ironic shifts and tonal displacements which have proved so disturbing to readers. One of the most important of earlier twentieth-century Austen studies, Marvin Mudrick's *Jane Austen: Irony as Defense and Discovery* (1952), argued persuasively that irony was a technique consciously employed by Austen as a distancing and ultimately self-protective mechanism. In Austen's novels, Mudrick claims, irony becomes a double-edged technical and psychological tool, functioning as a means of retaining authorial control while deliberately inhibiting subjective engagement.[6] Mudrick's study is typical of the New Critical approach of the nineteen-fifties and sixties, which concentrated on the rigorous formal analysis of a text's surface. Later critics are by no means oblivious to the ironies of Austen's texts, but they reconceptualise irony as a means of alerting readers to the different levels of meaning that can co-exist in any work of literature and to alternative interpretations. In this collection, for instance, Julia Prewitt Brown's discussion of *Persuasion* (essay 7) examines the way in which irony emphasises disparity and difference so as to destabilise the reader. The function of the irony can thus be said to foreground the incoherence, which is, for Brown, the hallmark of this novel. Other critics, such as Sandra Gilbert and Susan Gubar (essay 8), go further in seeing irony as a deeply subversive (and characteristically female) weapon, deliberately duplicitous in its construction of contradictory political readings, which appear to endorse the *status quo* while covertly undermining it. Underlying both these discussions is an awareness of conventional formal readings of Austen as a comic novelist and the need to counteract this by drawing attention to the discordant textual features. Whilst arriving at different conclusions about *Persuasion*, both essays alert the reader to the oppositional discourses at work within the novel and the resulting tonal dissonance.

One point on which most earlier critics concur is that *Mansfield Park* and *Persuasion* are Austen's most serious works, works in which the dark comic tone signally lacks the 'light, bright and sparkling' dimension which characterises her early fiction, which dominates *Emma* and which seems to re-emerge in *Sanditon*, Austen's last and incomplete novel. For some readers, however, it is this 'seriousness' that has been a major stumbling block. Critics have found the novels awkward to fit into any neat categorisation of Austen, and perversely resistant to the various critical stereotypes on which Austen's early reputation as moralist or satirist was based. Both works take an isolated heroine as protagonist and in their move towards interiority almost seem to value inaction as an ethical principle. This has resulted in what for some readers are insoluble problems in reception, alienating readers' sympathies so as to render the novels themselves static and impenetrable. Lionel Trilling's famous assertion that 'no one, I believe, has ever found it possible to like the heroine of *Mansfield Park*'[7] and Andor Gomme's complaint that in *Persuasion* 'character is frozen on each first appearance' have met with a general consensus amongst readers who prefer their fictional creations to be vivacious, witty and energetic on the Elizabeth Bennet model.[8] Moreover, in their focus on individual consciousness *Mansfield Park* and *Persuasion* appear to mount a sustained investigation of sensibility (as indeed do other Austen fictions), but it is not clear whether they are celebrating or denouncing Romanticism as a literary or ideological construct. Differing opinions on this issue are provided in the contributions from Marilyn Butler (essay 1), Nina Auerbach (essay 3) and Laura Mooneyham (essay 10) in this volume. Politically too, the novels evade closure. As the essays as a whole demonstrate, both *Mansfield Park* and *Persuasion* can be read in politically

divergent ways, although their refusal to provide a satisfactory resolution to the ideological problems they raise is now accepted as
being one of their most intriguing, even if at times frustrating,
features.

While the critics whose work is included in this collection do not
offer definitive solutions to these problems, they do add consider-
ably to an apprehension of the terms in which the problems themselves are formulated. Nina Auerbach's discussion of *Mansfield
Park* addresses the problem of the hostile reception to Fanny Price
by examining the novel against a tradition of literary Romanticism
that champions the figure of the outcast. Julia Prewitt Brown, on
the other hand, instead of reviewing literary antecedents, as does
Auerbach, for an explanation of Anne Elliot's introspection, looks
ahead to future developments as a basis for her argument that
*Persuasion* anticipates the modern novel of psychological and social
fragmentation. From this perspective Anne's portrayal becomes
effective as one of the first sustained dissections of the alienated
personality. Marilyn Butler, Mary Poovey (essay 5) and Claudia
Johnson (essay 9) read Austen's politics respectively as conservative, radical and progressive, each making a convincing and scholarly case to account for their contrasting interpretations. And whilst
aesthetic criteria no longer predominate in any critic's investigation
of textual strategies, they can inform and underlie discussion, as
Julia Prewitt Brown's conceptualisation of artistic tension in
*Persuasion* makes clear. As all these essays demonstrate, the interrogation of moral or aesthetic absolutes as central to critical discussion of Austen has been replaced by a desire to resituate the
novels in a historical, and often politicised, context whether the perspectives utilised be Marxist, feminist, cultural or linguistic.

A recent literary biography of Jane Austen by Jan Fergus
indicates the nature of the shift away from old-style views of
Austen's work as influenced by her domestic and emotional circumstances to a more culturally oriented interest in the forces that
determine literary production. Fergus depicts Austen as a highly
professional author whose literary career developed in a society
where women were becoming a major force in the publishing industry, and where the conditions for female authorship had never
before been so favourable.[9] This approach, drawing on current
approaches to feminist biography, marks an important stage in
thinking about Jane Austen's writings which forms an antidote to
earlier, more straightforward biographical readings based on

evidence from family memoirs. While the notion of Jane Austen as gifted amateur had already been revised by early Austen scholars such as Mary Lascelles,[10] Fergus goes significantly further in placing Austen firmly in the context of the early nineteenth-century publishing explosion. In examining the changing economic climate and the associated conditions of literary production for women, Fergus makes links between the market economy, authorial independence and the awareness of gender politics with which the narratives of both *Mansfield Park* and *Persuasion* are suffused; she notes, for instance, a sense of power that radiates through *Mansfield Park* and attributes this to Austen's new-found professional confidence.[11] This approach to Austen's life has implications for an understanding of the revolution in Austen studies generally since the nineteen-seventies, a revolution in which sociologically based and feminist critiques have played a crucial part. Indeed, the location of Jane Austen as a writer whose work is transformed when read as indicative of the contemporary political climate and the gender issues which that encodes has been a central determinant in her critical reconstruction. The revisionary impact of this awareness is represented in this volume by essays which in fact come to very different conclusions about Austen, including the contributions from Mary Poovey, Claudia Johnson and John Wiltshire (essay 11).

## III

The most nfluential of all recent studies of Jane Austen and the one which virtually all subsequent Austen commentators in some way acknowledge is Marilyn Butler's seminal work, *Jane Austen and the War of Ideas*, first published in 1975, an extract from which introduces this collection. Butler's work signals and anticipates current critical methodologies in its explicit politicisation of Austen's fiction. It thus provides an appropriate starting point for a volume such as this where the selection of essays foregrounds ideological issues. Butler's historicist approach presents Austen as one of a group of writers who emerged in the seventeen-nineties and whose work is inescapably grounded in the ideological debates of that heated historical moment. In the context of the partisan conservative/radical arguments which dominate not merely government politics of the period but moral and social issues as well, Austen's novels are seen by Butler as representative of the Tory position, staunchly anti-Jacobin in their mistrust of dangerous individualism and uncontrolled sentiment.

Butler's critical methodology forms an effective bridge between past and present readings of Austen. Although the discussion of the fiction is informed by a concept of aesthetic value, this is subordinated to the overriding thesis of the study which forms a repositioning of Austen within a complex scheme of political and social debate, and which was articulated in the period's literature, both fictional and non-fictional. To some extent, as well, Butler's study follows naturally from the sociologically oriented readings of Austen, such as that in Alistair Duckworth's important study, *The Improvement of the Estate* (1971), [12] which avoids expressing any overt political demarcation of Austen, but which insists that the social vision of the novels is inseparable from the precise historical moment of their production. In her revised introduction to the 1987 edition of *Jane Austen and the War of Ideas*, Marilyn Butler explains the genesis of her original work as itself a response to old-style readings of Austen that celebrated her moral and social universality with little regard for the specificity of the application of her ideas. The provision of a fully historicised intellectual scheme, which Butler saw as a prerequisite for an accurate interpretation of a literary text, has now become an accepted starting point for Austen critics, even if their ultimate destinations still seem quite divergent.

Following Marilyn Butler's lead, Julia Prewitt Brown's chapter on *Persuasion* in *Jane Austen's Novels: Social Change and Literary Form* (1979), an extract from which introduces the second half of this volume, locates the novel solidly within a context that takes account of contemporary intellectual and social developments. This does not, however, necessarily lead to a confirmation of Austen as a Christian moralist or a proponent of Tory values on the Butler model. Elsewhere Brown has mounted a vigorous attack on critics who try to impose their own political views on Austen and then take her to task for failing to conform to a preconceived and, in Brown's view, inappropriate ideological position. [13] Her reading of *Persuasion* is at pains to avoid this trap. For instance, her essay examines marriage in Austen's fiction, not as an automatic and unquestioning acceptance of a socially sanctioned institution, but as a fully articulated and even desperate response to a situation which is characterised by uncertainty. The world of *Persuasion* is for Brown one of transition and dislocation, a world where there are no finalities or certainties and where the narrative resolution which Austen provides needs to be contextualised accordingly. Interestingly, this view, and particularly the question of narrative resolution, is decoded from a completely different perspective in the deconstructive readings of Austen provided by D.A. Miller (essay 2) and Cheryl Weissman (essay 12).

Yet another, and in many ways surprising, result of Marilyn Butler's politicisation of Jane Austen has been the strength and variety of the feminist critiques which run counter to her argument. Mary Evans' analysis of *Mansfield Park* in her book *Jane Austen and the State* (1987),[14] not included here for reasons of space, carries with it obvious echoes of Butler's chapter, while challenging its fundamental premise. In Evans' radical reading, Austen emerges as a proponent of liberalism by virtue of the fact that she exposes the ideology of the family as a sham, and lays bare the cracks in the structure of the establishment, thus questioning the aristocracy's fitness for government. Sir Thomas Bertram appears as the exponent of a repressive regime, but as Evans points out, in post-Freudian terms excessive repression merely serves to harbour subversive fantasies and undisciplined desires, and in Sir Thomas's absence, these are allowed to flourish. The metaphor of Mansfield thus reveals a society where the reliance on male authority and the regulation of behaviour lead to anarchy and Evans pursues this to conclude that the society itself, as depicted by Austen, is based on a system of unequal wealth and property distribution, which requires redress. From this perspective, Austen can be seen as belonging to an alternative tradition from the one which Butler describes, one which attacks patriarchal privilege and appeals for democratic access to the processes of government through the figure of Fanny Price. Evans could be accused of wilfully reading the text against the grain here, but her work does reveal the oppositional nature of the debates to which Austen's fiction is subjected in a critical climate which creates space for multiple, and often clashing, interpretative positions.

Not all feminist critics, of course, share the same political agenda, but all start from a common resistance to the assumption that the norms of behaviour are male and that all readers, whatever their class or gender, read in the same way. From this base, however, feminist critical practice has developed to become a rich and pluralist discourse, with its own lively internal debates. Two of its central directions are represented here by the feminist materialist commentaries in Mary Poovey's discussion of *Mansfield Park* and Claudia Johnson's essay on *Persuasion*, and by the gynocritical analysis of *Persuasion* by Sandra Gilbert and Susan Gubar. Feminist materialist criticism of which Evans' book is another excellent example takes its lead from Marxist theory. A prime tenet underlying Marxist theory is the need to examine the relation of literature and of literary criticism to the social and economic conditions of individuals as members of particular cultural, racial or class groupings. For these critics, gender itself is a site of struggle, and the textual representation of women carries political implications that relate to the constructions of society at large. Gynocriticism, on the other hand, concentrates on women in their role as writers and examines their efforts to enter into a literature to which they have traditionally been denied access. Starting from the premise that women write differently from men, these critics, who include Elaine Showalter, Ellen Moers and Margaret Homans as well as Sandra Gilbert and Susan Gubar, examine the distinctive textual and linguistic strategies employed by women authors. Their enterprise is directed towards recovering neglected literary figures of the past and re-reading established canonical figures, such as Jane Austen, against a fresh background of ideas so as to reassess their significance.

In this volume, the contributions from Mary Poovey and Claudia Johnson examine Austen's representation of gender within an interrogative framework that analyses contemporary cultural codes. As they investigate what constitutes the feminine and its associated sign systems, Poovey's and Johnson's critiques find that *Mansfield Park* and *Persuasion* respectively engage in a dialogue about gendered behaviour and sexual difference that was itself a pressing topic for intellectual debate in early nineteenth-century England. It is important not to confuse the concern with the issue of representation that these essays articulate with the studies of 'images of women' which were popular among the nineteen-sixties first wave of feminist literary critics. Neither Poovey nor Johnson, who have differing views about Austen's political stance, is prepared to read the female figures in the novels they discuss as transparent reflections of reality. Rather, they examine configurations of characters and ideas as contributing to a wider debate in which gender carries weight as an important cultural sign, and consequently impacts upon power relations in contemporary society. It is particularly illuminating, for instance, to compare Mary Poovey's treatment of the 'propriety' of Fanny Price from an explicitly feminist perspective with that of Marilyn Butler. Whereas Butler sees the novel as upholding an educational and ethical orthodoxy, Poovey suggests that 'propriety' is a dualistic concept, in which surface and substance divide, and that Austen is consciously utilising the contemporary conduct manual as a negative rather than positive backdrop to her presentation of issues in girls' education.

Claudia Johnson also addresses propriety by relating Anne Elliot's behaviour to her status as an older woman, and as forming a deliberate contrast to the younger heroines of Austen's preceding novels. She sees Anne as located within a network of both positive and negative models of femininity, and argues that these are juxtaposed with prevailing expectations and ideas about gendered conduct. References to current debates about female education are used to throw into relief the schematic nature of the fictional characterisation, and Austen's concern with behavioural codes is presented as conceptual rather than judgemental. Johnson does not suggest that there is any radical hidden agenda here, but rather that in negotiating her way between the polarised opinions which were prevalent at the time, Austen is less doctrinaire than her contemporaries, and in refusing to align herself with either conservative or radical camps, enlarges the progressive middle ground that is the locus for rationalist thinking.

Conversely, the extract from Sandra Gilbert and Susan Gubar's chapter on *Persuasion*, taken from their book, *The Madwoman in the Attic* (1979), bases its analysis of the text according to a gyno-critical theory of authorship which pre-supposes the existence of an unrecognised and undervalued literary tradition.[15] Gilbert and Gubar's revisionary reading of the novel teases out a dramatic subtext of female anger and power from within the superstructure of conformity which the narrative appears to endorse. The tensions they identify between the overt text and the suppressed subtext provide Gilbert and Gubar with a model of female creativity that they apply to Austen as well as to her fictional prototypes. Through her sense of exclusion from a male-dominated society Anne Elliot, they suggest, re-enacts the dilemma and the expressive tactics of her author, resorting to underhand methods of making her feelings known, rather as Jane Austen used a blotter to screen her manuscripts from public view.

*The Madwoman in the Attic* postulates a powerfully seductive thesis which examines nineteenth-century women writers in terms of their reaction to an imaginative cultural history which is essentially patriarchal. It is also a highly provocative work and has been dubbed hysterical on two counts: firstly in its assumption of a single female value system, and secondly for its prioritisation of a romantic ideal of individualistic and rebellious expression over an ethic of rational, if less flamboyant, negotiation.[16] Yet in directing attention to often overlooked details and critically marginalised figures in the narratives they discuss – the re-creation of Mrs Norris in *Mansfield Park* as an authorial surrogate is a particularly stimulating example – Gilbert and Gubar ask readers to reconsider the psychic as well as the political significance of hitherto unperceived tensions, and to enter into a mode of intellectual enquiry which, as it attempts to formulate a feminist poetics, fundamentally reassesses assumptions about literary production. *The Madwoman in the Attic* examines the relationship between textuality and sexuality, and explores ways in which female subjectivities are realised in a world controlled by patriarchal power. Although it does not include the in-depth analysis of contemporary historical source material relating to constructions of femininity, such as is found in Mary Poovey's or Claudia Johnson's studies, it does begin to dissect discourses of power, and in this it shares elements of critical practice with other influential feminist and cultural critics.

Postcolonial critics in particular draw on this understanding of power as a series of structures which are articulated and disseminated through language systems. In its reliance on the discourse of slavery and its foregrounding of a figure who is a property owner both in Britain and in the West Indies, *Mansfield Park* lends itself particularly well to this sort of reading. Edward Said's important essay on the novel (essay 6) consequently offers a very different historical map from that proposed by Marilyn Butler.[17] Said's discussion starts from the Marxist premise that the English and European literary lineage relies on exclusions and regulations for its own self-definition. It argues that the view of history provided in much English literature is consequently flawed because it is incomplete and acknowledges only the principles and events which legitimate its own supremacy. Like Marilyn Butler and Ruth Bernard Yeazell (essay 4), Said recognises the metaphorical significance of space and location in *Mansfield Park*, but whereas Butler discusses the moral impetus, and Yeazell directs attention to the cultural and specifically anthropological force of the spatial metaphor, Said views it in terms of its historical and political dimension. In accordance with the theories of the influential cultural historian, Michel

Foucault, Said argues that discourse can never be analysed as independent of the power structures it both replicates and promotes.[18] Literary texts are not isolated from real events, but are themselves a part of history and should be examined accordingly. As a result, the images of confinement and expansion which pervade *Mansfield Park* take on new meaning in relation to the contemporary debates about slavery and colonialist expansion which form part of the novel's extra-literary contexts. In pointing out how the world of Mansfield that Austen depicts depends for its existence on a network of alternative 'worlds' – both at home and abroad – Said reveals the provocative interplay of discourse and power that is signalled within the text. While providing variant individual interpretations of *Mansfield Park*, both Said's and Yeazell's essays fall within the broadly defined movement known as New Historicism, a school of criticism which insists on recognising how a literary text interacts with and is informed by its non-literary sources. New historicist critics thus break down and indeed blur the traditional boundaries between historical and literary materials, and in the process question the construction of historical truth. In this way the two essays printed here constitute a major departure from the 'official' version of history such as that which underlies Butler's work.

A further illustration of this, which shows evidence of influence from a number of theoretical sources, including Foucauldian, feminist and New Historicist criticism, is the cultural critique of *Persuasion* which is extracted from John Wiltshire's book, *Jane Austen and the body* (1992). The title of this work alone is sufficient to identify it as a product of the nineteen-nineties. Ten years earlier critics were reluctant to concede that Jane Austen's novels even recognised the existence of the body, let alone attributed any great significance to it. In her book, *Sisters in Time* (1989), for instance, Susan Morgan includes a chapter on 'Why There's No Sex in Jane Austen's Fiction', which discusses the reasons for the absence of sexual desire and physicality from Austen's work.[19] Morgan argues that Jane Austen uses comedy to redefine the eighteenth-century understanding of narrative and the possibilities open to the single heroine. In contrast to the Gothic and sentimental fictions of the period with their penchant for victimised heroines, she suggests that Austen's novels deliberately depart from a view of women enshrined within the prevailing preconceptions of gender, in particular that scheme of power relations that represented them only as objects of desire. Morgan's commentary is based on a presupposition that Austen's novels constitute a moral and social analysis which prioritises the intellectual over the physical in the dynamics of personal relations. Wiltshire, however, suggests that the physical and psychological operate in tandem in Austen's intellectual scheme, and that Austen's fiction as a whole reveals a fascination with all aspects of the body, including the codification of sexuality as well as the concern with health and sickness. His analysis of the text is less author-centred than Morgan's and more rooted in the idea of a cultural archive of documentation of which imaginative literature forms one component. To this end his discussion of *Persuasion* draws on contemporary medical treatises, theological tracts, moral philosophy, and social and economic histories of the period so as to show how these infiltrate and determine Austen's artistic reconstruction of her world. A character such as Nurse Rooke acquires fresh significance in a society such as Bath, which is obsessed with disease and physical well-being, and Wiltshire skilfully shows how her role blends in to a cluster of ideas in which nursing, both actual and metaphorical, carries economic, gender and class connotations.

## IV

So far the survey of major initiatives in recent Austen criticism which this introduction has reviewed has concentrated primarily on historicist and cultural critiques, and their concern with the ideological dimensions of Austen's fiction. As noted earlier, much of the intellectual excitement of this work is generated by critics' perception of tensions operative within the texts and by the consequent disclosure of intriguing gaps and slippages which invite exploration. The very premise underlying this enterprise is indicative of the move away from the search for harmony and coherence which characterised Austen criticism of the fifties and sixties to a concept of the problematic as a dynamic site of critical interest. One essay in this volume which deals explicitly with these gaps is Laura Mooneyham's discussion of *Persuasion* (essay 10), extracted from her book, *Romance, Language and Education in Jane Austen's Novels* (1988), a work which takes its orientation from a linguistic rather than a cultural standpoint.

Mooneyham sees *Persuasion* as a study in codes of communication which need to be deciphered. In a society which continually erects barriers in the way of meaning, Anne Elliot is shown to be trapped in a world of suppressed speech, and must negotiate her way through equivocal signals and oblique formal rituals, all of which impede transmission. Mooneyham scrutinises not just the absences and silences in the text, but all sorts of difficulties in communicative acts which result in misinformation, including gestures, letters, overheard conversations and casual gossip which reveals more than it intends. Consequent on this process she shows how language itself is situated at the heart of Austen's interrogation of her society, and the psychic damage suffered by individuals who are excluded from the potency of linguistic control. Mooneyham is by no means the first critic to have focused attention on the importance of the unspoken and its relationship with Anne's personal dilemma, but her discursive analysis is grounded in a sophisticated awareness of Foucauldian linkage between discourse and power, as well as the interest in the overlapping nature of buried texts which merge to produce a complex series of sign systems. Despite the differences in critical strategy, there are interesting parallels between Mooneyham's essay and Wiltshire's, which complement one another in the consideration of romance, gesture and bodily contact between Anne and Wentworth.

A more extreme example of the emphasis on linguistic and textual dissonance is provided by D.A. Miller's analysis of *Mansfield Park*, an essay which also typifies the generally playful nature of deconstructionist practice. Deconstructionist critics are interested in the textual interplay of linguistic and narrative codes, and working on the premise that signifying practices are inherently unstable forms, they draw attention to the inconsistencies and contradictions which ineluctably permeate a work of literature. Deconstruction thus marks a significant departure from the traditional critical activity of seeking a unified meaning in a work of literature. The deconstructionist project rather is to expose the impossibility of such a task and to alert readers to the simultaneous co-existence of polarised strands of meaning which can never be satisfactorily resolved. Miller's essay, for instance, emphasises ways in which the formal narrative ordering of *Mansfield Park* apparently relies on a series of binary oppositions. He also notes, however, the indeterminacies of Mary Crawford's language which undermine a simple polarised structure and thus threaten any stable narrative authority. In drawing attention to the artifice of the novel's ending (an artifice which has also troubled earlier critics in its marked tonal shift from what has gone before), Miller points to the ironies it contains with special reference to Mary's own equivocal position: are we supposed to condemn her or to like her? and are the two responses necessarily mutually exclusive? Mary's own absence from the final section of the novel and her oblique appearance in the last chapters only through reported speech and her own letters reduces her, too, to the status of a text and thus capable of being misinterpreted. Mary Crawford, conventionally seen by critics as a counterbalance in the novel's ideological structure, becomes in Miller's analysis a focus for the dismantling of fixed meaning.

Claudia Johnson, however, has pointed out that Miller's argument presumes that fictional closure encodes some sort of resolution, and that the conclusion of *Mansfield Park*, no less than other of Austen's work, bids good riddance to subversive impulses in the text in order to confirm the authority of a univocal discourse, a return to an authoritative authorial position.[20] She argues that in this respect, Miller, like Marilyn Butler, assumes that *Mansfield Park* is a fundamentally conservative work. Johnson, although she presents a largely convincing case, does not fully account for the highly self-reflexive nature of the novel's closing paragraphs and its self-consciously ludic tone which insists on distancing itself from the characters and situations of the text. As Miller suggests, it is this tonal shift which finally undermines and eludes rather than confirms any sense of 'official' values.

The focus on artistic self-awareness in a text and its consequent recognition of its own fictive status, as seen in both D.A. Miller's and Cheryl Weissman's essays, is one of the basic tenets of a postmodernist consciousness. Jane Austen has been a late candidate for exposure to this type of critique, surprisingly perhaps given the degree of self-reflexiveness and intertextual reference her novels incorporate. Cheryl Weissman's discussion of *Persuasion* does, however, examine the impact of archetypal and fairytale narratives within the novel and probes the disruptive effect of repeated motifs on a variety of levels. It is form and structure as they illuminate content rather than the other way round which is the focus for analysis here. Weissman describes the layering of *Persuasion* as palimpsestic, one text concealing an older, earlier version. The fictional scaffolding is thus exposed and in turn this effectively denaturalises the narrative. Weissman's reading of the palimpsestic nature of the text forms an interesting contrast with Sandra Gilbert and Susan Gubar's determinedly feminist interpretation of the same phenomenon. For Weissman the emphasis on formal motifs and patterns of story-telling also serves to highlight the gaps and absences in those stories which resist a harmonious resolution and make the characters ultimately elusive. This is a striking departure from earlier readings of *Persuasion* which saw character as a fixed and a suitable subject for moral investigation and judgemental analysis.

Weissmann's essay, with its emphasis on the lack of closure in *Persuasion*, Austen's last completed novel, offers an appropriately ironic ending to this collection. For taken as a whole these essays demonstrate not merely the impossibility of arriving at any satisfying resolution to the problems that *Mansfield Park* and *Persuasion* throw into relief, but the apparently inexhaustible supply of questions that can be asked when the texts are exposed to the exhilarating present-day critical climate. Despite claims to the contrary, most insistently coming from feminist critics who see Austen as the first major woman writer fully attuned to feminist politics, the novels continue to resist attempts at critical appropriation, and remain invigorating subjects for the diversity of reading practices current today.

## NOTES

1.  Joel Weinsheimer, in Janet Todd (ed.), *Jane Austen: New Perspectives, Women and Literature Series no. 3* (New York, 1983), p. 257.

2.  Roger Gard, *Jane Austen's Novels: the Art of Clarity* (New Haven, CT and London, 1992), p. 12.

3.  Roland Barthes, 'The death of the author', in *Image–Music–Text*, trans S. Heath (New York and London, 1977).

4.  James Thompson, *Between Self and World: the Novels of Jane Austen* (University Park, TX and London, 1988), p. 6.

5.  Virginia Woolf, 'Jane Austen at Sixty', *The Common Reader* (London, 1925), p. 180.

6.  Marvin Mudrick, *Jane Austen: Irony as Defense and Discovery* (Princeton, NJ, 1952).

7.  Lionel Trilling, 'Jane Austen and *Mansfield Park*', in *The Pelican Guide to English Literature*, ed. Boris Ford (London, 1957), p. 116.

8.  Andor Gomme, 'On Not Being Persuaded', *Essays in Criticism*, XVI (1966), quoted in Malcolm Bradbury, '*Persuasion* Again', *Essays in Criticism*, XVIII (1968), 214.

9. Jan Fergus, *Jane Austen: A Literary Life* (London, 1991).

10. Mary Lascelles, *Jane Austen and her Art* (Oxford, 1939).

11. Fergus, *Jane Austen*, p. 145

12. Alistair M. Duckworth, *Jane Austen's Novels: The Improvement of the Estate* (Baltimore, MD, 1971).

13. Julia Prewitt Brown, 'The Feminist Depreciation of Austen: A Polemical Reading', *Novel* (Spring 1990), 303–13.

14. Mary Evans, *Jane Austen and the State* (London, 1987), pp. 70–5.

15. Sandra Gilbert and Susan Gubar, *The Madwoman in the Attic: The Woman Writer and the Nineteenth Century Literary Imagination* (New Haven, CT, 1979).

16. Julia Prewitt Brown, 'The Feminist Depreciation of Jane Austen', pp. 303–13.

17. In addition to Edward W. Said's essay reprinted here, see Moira Ferguson, '*Mansfield Park*: Slavery, Colonialism and Gender', *Oxford Literary Review*, 13 (1991), 118–39, and Margaret Kirkham, *Jane Austen: Feminism and Fiction* (London, 1986) as examples of successful applications of this approach to *Mansfield Park*.

18. Michel Foucault's theories are articulated in his major works: *Madness and Civilisation* (1961), *The Order of Things* (1966), *Discipline and Punishment* (1975), and *The History of Sexuality* (1976).

19. Susan Morgan, *Sisters in Time: Imaging Gender in 19th Century British Fiction* (Oxford, 1989).

20. Claudia L. Johnson, *Jane Austen: Women, Politics and the Novel* (Chicago and London, 1988), p. 180.

# 1

# *Mansfield Park*: Ideology and Execution

*MARILYN BUTLER*

With the possible exception of *Sense and Sensibility*, *Mansfield Park* is the most visibly ideological of Jane Austen's novels, and as such has a central position in any examination of Jane Austen's philosophy as expressed in her art. It is all the more revealing because here she has progressed far beyond the technical immaturity of the period when *Sense and Sensibility* was conceived, to a position where she can exploit to the full the artistic possibilities of the conservative case; and, at the same time, come face to face with the difficulties it presents. By far the most imaginative and accomplished of received anti-Jacobin novels, *Mansfield Park* reveals all the inherent problems of the genre.

The superb draughtsmanship of the opening chapters of *Mansfield Park* makes it easy to forget that they present a set of themes which are entirely commonplace in the period. Its beginning must have encouraged contemporaries to believe that here was yet another novel by a female about female education.[1] Mrs West's novels, from *The Advantages of Education* (1793) on, had hammered the theme. Mrs Inchbald had dealt with it more elegantly and idiosyncratically in *A Simple Story*, and Fanny Burney had made it a very substantial subsidiary interest in *Camilla*. Since the turn of the century it had retained its place as perhaps the most popular of all themes of women novelists, notable examples being Mrs Opie's *Adeline Mowbray* (1804) and Hannah More's *Coelebs* (1808). Maria Edgeworth, whose literary career was dedicated to the proposition that early education makes the man, had recently given it more extended treatment than ever before in *Patronage* (1814). The last-named novel has indeed innumerable incidental resemblances to *Mansfield Park*, which appeared later in the same year,[2] for not only is its virtuous and well-brought-up heroine, Caroline Percy, compared with her foils, the fashionable Arabella and Georgiana Falconer, who strongly resemble the Bertram girls; but one of the most important sequences concerns the performance of a play, in which Georgiana Falconer displays herself, and Caroline Percy virtuously refuses to take part.

The reader of 1814 thus knew broadly where he, or perhaps more typically she, stood. The novel of female education criticised superficial qualities, particularly accomplishments, which were too narrowly aimed at giving a girl a higher price in the marriage-market: accomplishments and mercenary marriages tended to be coupled together. The debate was linked to, indeed was the female aspect of, that common eighteenth-century topic of educationalists, the inferiority of 'wit' or 'cleverness' to judgement. Hence the relevance of showing that the Bertram girls' education had been spent not only on their appearance and accomplishments, but also on superficial information designed to make them appear clever and well-informed in company – '... the Roman emperors as low as Severus; besides a great deal of the Heathen Mythology, and all the Metals, Semi-Metals, Planets, and distinguished philosophers' (pp. 18–19).

The structure of *Mansfield Park* is as severely built round the contrast between the girls' education and its consequences as the see-saw structure of *A Simple Story* or *Patronage*, though Jane Austen's artistry does much to soften the outlines of the antithesis. (Technically she is now a world away from *Sense and Sensibility*, where the parallels were so much laboured.) The first part of *Mansfield Park*, until Sir Thomas's return facilitates Maria's marriage, is about the entry into life of the two Bertram sisters: their education, their values, and, especially, their inability to resist the worldly baits proffered by the Crawfords. In the second, slightly longer part, Fanny, the exemplary heroine, encounters in her turn the temptation of Henry's love, and Mary's friendship,[3] and prevails. Her endurance sets right the wrongs done at Mansfield by the older girls, just as in the second part of *A Simple Story* Miss Milner's daughter restores the family which was shattered by her mother's lapse from virtue.[4]

Maria Bertram especially is a girl according to the female moralist's common formula. Having demonstrated her vanity and superficiality in adolescence, she grows up with the typical ambition of marrying for money. 'Being now in her twenty-first year, Maria Bertram was beginning to think matrimony a duty; and as marriage with Mr Rushworth would give her the enjoyment of a larger income than her father's, as well as ensure her the house in town, which was now a prime object, it became, by the same rule of moral obligation, her duty to marry Mr Rushworth if she could' (pp. 38–9). This 'duty' is one of the few Maria acknowledges, for as their father's daughter neither she nor her sister Julia feels any obligation. They are not fond of Sir Thomas Bertram, whose role as parent has hitherto been a negative one, and accordingly they feel nothing but a sense of release when he departs for Antigua. 'They were relieved by it from all restraint; and without aiming at one gratification that would probably have been forbidden by Sir Thomas, they felt themselves immediately at their own disposal, and to have every indulgence within their reach' (p. 32).

But, though the Bertram girls resemble other novelists' shallow females, the ideal figure set up in opposition to them is slightly more distinctive. In characterising her heroine, Fanny, Jane Austen illustrates her ideological disagreement with Maria Edgeworth. Caroline Percy of *Patronage*, like Belinda, Leonora, and other Edgeworth model characters, is essentially a rationalist. Fanny Price is a Christian. The clue lies in those characteristics in which the Bertram girls are deficient – 'It is not very wonderful that with all their promising talents and early information, they should be entirely deficient in less common acquirements of self-knowledge, generosity, and humility' (p. 19). Immediately afterwards, Fanny, in conversation with Edmund, is shown to have the qualities her cousins lack. Humility is obviously an appropriate virtue for the Christian heroine; but equally important in Jane Austen's canon is, as always, the impulse towards self-knowledge. Fanny's sense as a Christian of her own frailty, her liability to error, and her need of guidance outside herself, is the opposite of the Bertram girls' complacent self-sufficiency. For Jane Austen 'vanity', the characteristic of the fashionables, is a quality with a distinctly theological colouring. It means both an unduly high opinion of oneself, and a pursuit of worldly goals, 'vanities'. Such an error arises from an inability to place oneself in a larger moral universe, a context in which the self, and the self's short-term gratifications, become insignificant. As an ideal this is wholly different from the Edgeworthian belief in individual self-realisation, leading to greater – not less – personal independence.

The entrance of the Crawfords soon extends and enriches the didactic case. The Crawfords are sophisticated, fully aware disciples of a worldly creed to which the Bertram girls merely veer unconsciously, on account of the vacuum left in their education. Mary Crawford has actually been instructed, by her social circle in general, the marriage of her uncle and aunt in particular, in a wholly sceptical modern philosophy. Her doctrine includes the notion that there are no values but material ones, and that the gratification of the self is the only conceivable goal. Mary's comments about marriage, uttered to her sister Mrs Grant in the first scenes in which we meet her, are obviously meant to be compared with Maria Bertram's reflections about Mr Rushworth. Where Maria is confused as to her values, and barely half aware of the moral implications of what she is doing, Mary sounds, and is, knowingly cynical. 'Everybody should marry as soon as they can do it to advantage .... Everybody is taken in at one period or other .... It is of all transactions the one in which people expect most from others, and are least honest themselves' (pp. 43–6). Even more clearly, Henry Crawford's amoral determination to make the Bertram girls fall in love with him compares with their vague, complacent, and far less formulated readiness to be fallen in love with. The Crawfords, who know precisely what they are doing, are infinitely more dangerous than the Bertrams. More than that, the Bertrams are peculiarly vulnerable to be made the Crawfords' dupes, since their attitudes to life already half incline them to throw off restraint and pursue the self-gratification which the Crawfords' creed allows. It is dangerous to be exposed to worldliness without the worldly-wisdom which goes with it.

The triple contrast, of three kinds of education, three kinds of moral attitude, is maintained in every early scene. The cynical Crawfords, planning their pleasures with cold selfishness; the Bertram girls, equally selfish but more naïve; Fanny, who alone after a few days retains enough insight and objectivity to see that Henry Crawford is still plain. Whatever the topic of dialogue, the moral landscape of the various characters is what really receives attention. Mary, for instance, brings up the question of whether Fanny is 'out' or 'not out', so that Jane Austen can contrast two widely diverging ideals of young womanhood. Edmund considers whether, out or not out, young women act with any real modesty; Mary, whether they act in accordance with convention (p. 50). Similarly, when Mary borrows Fanny's horse, the thoughts and actions of three principals, Edmund, Fanny, and Mary, can be examined in turn. Edmund, who has always been considerate of Fanny, is now seduced by his physical delight in Mary into forgetting her. Fanny, after detecting her own jealousy, and struggling with motives of which she is suspicious,[5] can at least display some genuinely objective concern for the horse. Mary correctly ascribes her own behaviour to selfishness, so gaily that she proves the vice has little meaning for her.

*Mansfield Park* is the first Austen novel to be conceived as well as executed after the appearance of Maria Edgeworth's social comedies.[6] Jane Austen had deployed lesser characters in a stylised pattern around her heroine before, but she had not exploited in any sustained way the typical Edgeworth intellectual comedy. The brilliant dialogue in *Pride and Prejudice* is the natural culmination of a technique Jane Austen had used since *Catharine*: it gives the reader and heroine simultaneously an objective insight into character. In the first part of *Mansfield Park* a new element is added: the subject-matter of a conversation becomes as important as the insight it offers into character, because conservation becomes the occasion for the clash of distinct systems of value. Three key topics recur, all of them often found in anti-Jacobin novels of the 1790s. The first is Nature, and is illustrated by contrasting the attitudes of different characters towards living in the country. All late-eighteenth-century moralists of whatever colouring prefer the country to the town,[7] but Jane Austen's Fanny does so as a typical conservative: because she associates it with a community, in which individuals have well-defined duties towards the group, and because physically it reminds her of the wider ordered universe to which the lesser community belongs. Urban life, on the other hand, has given Mary selfish values: she betrays her egotism when she laughs at the farmers who will not let her have a wagon to move her harp, and her materialism when she comments that in London money buys anything. The second issue that will recur in conversation in the novel, though sometimes allusively in association with Nature, is religion; the third is marriage. All three come to the fore in the sequence that provides an ideological key to the book, the visit to Sotherton.

The Crawfords' indifferent and even destructive attitude to the country emerges when the visit to Sotherton is first projected, for they go there as improvers. Essentially their feelings are negative about the external scene they propose to deal with. Utility is not a criterion which concerns them.[8] Nor do they respond to the sentimental connotations of a feature of landscape, the link with the past provided by Sotherton's heavy, ancient avenue of trees. It is actually Mary who first voices the idea that change must temporarily at least mean disequilibrium: she remembers the time when her uncle improved his cottage at Twickenham as a period of anarchy. But she is restless for novelty, and improvements are fashionable; in the arbitrary name of fashion she urges Mr Rushworth to employ a landscape artist such as Repton. It does not occur to her, as it does to Fanny, to regret the destruction of the trees, since she is scarcely aware of inanimate nature, or the wider physical universe beyond herself and the few people she cares for. Sotherton itself is, or ought to be, a Burkean symbol of human lives led among natural surroundings, man contiguous with nature and continuous with his own past. Fanny finds it both these things, when she sees the grounds and begins to walk around the house. But Mary is bored and even hostile (p. 85).

In interpreting the meaning of the house within its grounds, and the chapel within the house, the two minds are joined by a third, Mrs Rushworth's. She has learnt her speech parrot-fashion from the housekeeper, and her interest is far more in the grandeur of the outward appurtenances than in the quality of the life lived. Her casual remarks about the chapel – that the seat-covers were once less tasteful than they are now, and that it was her husband who discontinued the religious services – show clearly enough how superficial her values are. '"Every generation has its improvements",' remarks Mary: and between Rushworth senior, who gutted the house in the interests of modernity, and Rushworth junior, who with Henry Crawford's help proposes to do the same for the grounds, there is morally little to choose.

The scene in the chapel, where Mary is offensive about clergymen, brings out for the first time in full the gulf between the Crawfords and religious orthodoxy. In discussing the suspension of chapel services, Mary thinks only of the immediate convenience to individuals who might have had to attend; while Fanny and Edmund have two concerns – the well-being of the individual, *sub specie aeternitatis*, and the social validity of established forms of worship:

'It is a pity', cried Fanny, 'that the custom should have been discontinued. It was a valuable part of former times. There is something
in a chapel and chaplain so much in character with a great house,
with one's ideas of what such a household should be! A whole family
assembling regularly for the purpose of prayer, is fine!'

Mary in her individualism cannot even begin to apprehend the
social value Fanny sees in religion:

'At any rate, it is safer to leave people to their own devices on such
subjects. Every body likes to go their own way – to choose their own
manner and time of devotion. The obligation of attendance, the formality, the restraint, the length of time – altogether it is a formidable
thing, and what nobody likes....'

Such an argument demands to be answered in terms of the individual, and Edmund does answer it:

'... We must all feel *at times* the difficulty of fixing our thoughts as
we could wish; but if you are supposing it a frequent thing, that is to
say, a weakness grown into a habit from neglect, what could be
expected from the *private* devotions of such persons? Do you think
the minds which are suffered, which are indulged in wanderings in a
chapel, would be more collected in a closet?'

(pp. 86–7)

The double function which Fanny and Edmund see religion as
serving is important in the novel, and is developed more fully in
subsequent conversations between Fanny, Edmund and Mary. In
the wilderness Edmund speaks of the social role of the country
clergyman, his influence by example and precept on the minds of
his parishioners (pp. 92–3). Later, when Fanny discusses Dr Grant
with Mary, it is she who raises the more private, spiritual aspect:

'I cannot but suppose that whatever there may be to wish otherwise
in Dr Grant, would have been in greater danger of becoming worse
in a more active and worldly profession, where he would have had
less time and obligation – where he might have escaped that knowledge of himself, the *frequency*, at least, of that knowledge which it is
impossible he should escape as he is now.'

(pp. 111–12)

Mary is clearly equally indifferent both to the social aspect of
religion ('duty' and 'morals'), and to its spiritual demand of

self-knowledge, since she accepts no reality outside her own sens-
ations. But to Fanny and Edmund the two meanings of religion
are interdependent, and 'knowledge of the self' and knowledge of a
reality outside the self cannot be disassociated from one another.[9]

The theme of marriage is first glanced at in the chapel when Julia
spitefully refers to Maria's coming marriage to Mr Rushworth. In
the hollow sham of a chapel the full emptiness of the proposed ceremony is felt. Afterwards, in the strangely diagrammatic sequence in
the wilderness, we see sketched out the shadowy future, or at least
tendency, of the various sexual relationships which are developing
in the novel. Edmund and Mary walk up and down, supposedly for
a finite time, and within the wilderness; but Edmund, not for the
first or last time, forgets his promise to Fanny and strays further
than he meant. Henry and Maria arrive with Mr Rushworth at the
gate, and while he (their future dupe) is away fetching the key, they
escape through the palisade into the liberty of the park. Julia, who
acts with the same impatience of restraint as they, and to the same
end, is less guilty because she is not escaping from an acknowledged
fiancé in the company of a desired lover. And so on. In any other
novel such a miming of future events would seem an intolerable contrivance; but, extreme though it is, in *Mansfield Park* it does not
seem illegitimate. The action of the novel is so entirely bound up
with the value-systems of the various characters that they are always
to a greater or lesser extent illustrating, acting out, their beliefs.

The sequence in the grounds, with Fanny still and alone on the
seat, the others walking about, is especially expressive in terms of
their relative roles. The worldly characters are the real subject of
the first half, and Jane Austen is ingenious in letting them occupy
the centre of the stage while Fanny as yet remains in the wings. Her
consciousness is deliberately left slightly childish and unformed.
Instinctively she tries to tell right from wrong, but as yet she lacks
the ability; by contrast the Bertram sisters have the decision that
comes with greater assurance and maturity, but they have no moral
discrimination. Fanny's turn to act is to come, but her role of
wondering observer of her cousins' doings is in itself expressive,
suggesting as it does the virtuous person's struggle towards judgement and knowledge that is being neglected by the active characters.
She has the role which often carries so much prestige in eighteenth-
century literature, that of the thoughtful bystander. Like Gibbon's
'philosopher', she strives to interpret, to make some sense out of the
superficial chaos of events. However unformed her opinion and in-

articulate her expression of it, her anxious vigil on the bench in the park is enough in itself to remind the reader of a long tradition of men who have been wise in retirement, whose ascendancy lay in detachment from the actors and the common scene.

The conclusions Jane Austen tries to direct her reader's attention to are encouraged by Fanny's demeanour, yet not dictated by her at all. Jane Austen is not interested in impressions conveyed by subjective identification with a heroine. While Sterne or Mackenzie induce the reader to act the part of the man of feeling,[10] she casts the reader as a moral arbiter. If there must be identification, it is with Fanny's role, not with her individual responses, which (at least as they affect Edmund) are depicted with ironic detachment. Meanwhile the reader's judgements are guided by other, more objective means. References to familiar issues are no doubt among the most important. But equally interesting, and in actual practice more original, is the extremely detailed presentation of what, after all, Jane Austen wants us to value. For the first time she gives her external world a solidity and scale which eventually belittles individual characters.

Although the scene at Sotherton is stylised, it is also very natural – in its setting, as far as concerns the house and grounds, and in the sense it conveys of the day as a rather unsuccessful outing, an occasion felt in mixed and on the whole uncomfortable ways by the many people involved. The result of this curious blend of stylisation and naturalism is to give flesh to the conservative case as no one else had done except Burke. As in the *Reflections on the French Revolution*, with its reiterated references to hearths, homes and families, so in the scene at Sotherton society takes on visible shapes.[11] The house and grounds are old, impressive, handsome, but under the rule of the Rushworths hollow, without the core of belief (symbolised by the chapel) which could give meaning to so much pompous grandeur. The cynical Crawfords have appeared, like Satan in the Garden of Eden, hostile to the old ethos of the place and bent on destruction. Every detail of what they say and do suggests their self-willed lawlessness: Mary, irrationally challenging the dimensions of the wilderness because she happens to feel tired; Henry, defying the restraint imposed by the limits of the ground and the locked gate. Yet the Crawfords' encroachment at Sotherton, dangerous though it seems, remains in the end curiously ineffective – for, like Burke, Jane Austen not only locates the enemy but diminishes him. In the Bertram sisters and in Henry there is an odd, wilful capacity for self-destruction. They are more likely to reject a momentary restraint than to attack restraints systematically. In escaping into the park, Henry, Maria, and Julia go off in a different direction from their supposed objective, the avenue of oaks; which accordingly survives the threat they originally offered it. Sotherton, although an empty shell, remains intact. By the end of the story it is only individuals, Maria and to a lesser extent Henry, who have destroyed themselves. A little through direct description, more through our sense of the weariness of the characters, we retain an impression of the heaviness, the largeness, but also the age and endurance of Sotherton, which is an important part of the moral framework for what follows.

Although some of its meaning has become obscured by purely historical difficulties of interpretation, the play-sequence remains the most masterly part of *Mansfield Park*. Unlike the account of Sotherton, where the naturalism and the scheme sometimes jar, it is equally fine on its many levels. Best of all is the presentation of that distinctive technique of the first volume of *Mansfield Park*, the serial treatment of several consciousnesses. At the beginning of volume i, chapter xii, for example, we enter successively the minds of Mary Crawford, the Bertram sisters, Henry Crawford, and Fanny. The next chapter, the thirteenth, takes us into and out of the consciousness of Mr Yates; through the views of all the characters involved, first directly in dialogue and then in reported speech; to the silencing of Edmund when Mary joins in, and the happy concurrence of Mrs Norris. There is no other comparable sequence of a Jane Austen novel so independent of the heroine. It is as though the movement of the sentimental period, towards distinguishing the central character by special insight into his inner life, has been put into reverse. The characters in this part of *Mansfield Park* each have their speeches, their scenes, like characters in a drama.

This, since it is a play they are rehearsing, is wholly appropriate. But what amuses Jane Austen – and even amuses Fanny – is that each actor continues to be selfishly absorbed by personal feelings, in spite of the corporate activity they are engaged in. Fanny is 'not unamused to observe the selfishness which, more or less disguised, seemed to govern them all' (p. 131). Many of the actors – Mr Yates, Tom, and Mr Rushworth, for example – clearly think in terms of the effect they will make in acting their own parts. Maria and Henry, though not motivated by the vanity of the actor, are bent on self-gratification of an even more culpable kind. Mary, and even Edmund, focus intently upon the significance to them of their own scenes. Apparently comic dialogues, in which plays and parts are argued over – and the selfishness of the actors revealed – have simultaneously a serious level of meaning. Not one of the actors, not even Edmund, has a proper sense of what it is as a whole that they are doing. When issues of propriety arise, even the more intelligent of them persist in looking at their own speeches: Mary admits that some of hers should be cut, Edmund is embarrassed by his. Only Fanny, the detached bystander, reads the play through and reacts to it as a whole.

Fanny's most important function here is that she alone perceives something pitiful and wrong in solipsism. 'Fanny saw and pitied much of this in Julia; but there was no outward fellowship between them. Julia made no communication, and Fanny took no liberties. They were two solitary sufferers, or connected only by Fanny's consciousness' (p. 163). As at Sotherton, she never directs the reader's opinions in detail: her watchfulness gives the necessary clue. When it comes to discussion of the general issue, to act or not to act, she can seem maddeningly inarticulate. Her general opinion about the play is the bald conclusion, 'everything of consequence was against it'. Pressed to take part herself, she is merely depicted showing the outward signs of confusion and distress (p. 146). Later, when she is alone in the East room, the reader has his first real insight into her attempts to sift right from wrong. But these do not in fact throw much light on the general issue. What is important about Fanny's cogitations is that they involve scrupulous self-examination, the critical mental process that everyone else in the novel neglects.

For a general judgement of the play-acting, therefore, the reader must not rely on Fanny's articulation but on an independent understanding of the issue, informed as at Sotherton by a subtle network of allusion. The reader's efforts to understand are expected to parallel Fanny's, but to be more mature, more experienced about the world and its pitfalls. There seems to be no doubt, for example, that Jane Austen takes as read our familiarity with the common contemporary arguments against amateur acting, even though no one in the novel alludes to them plainly. By 1814 the increasingly strong Evangelical movement had sufficiently publicised the link between upper-class immorality and its rage for private theatricals.[12] A common and important leading objection is that play-acting tempts girls especially into an unseemly kind of personal display. In his *Enquiry into the Duties of the Female Sex*, 1797, which Jane Austen read with approval in 1805, Thomas Gisborne declares that acting is 'almost certain to prove injurious to the female sex'.[13] Even granted that the chosen play 'will be in its language and conduct always irreprehensible' (a condition certainly not met by *Lovers' Vows*), Gisborne believes that acting will harm a young woman through encouraging vanity and destroying diffidence 'by the unrestrained familiarity with the other sex, which inevitably results from being joined with them in the drama'.[14] Fanny's principal doubts seem to relate to the women's parts of Amelia and Agatha (p. 137). Unquestionably Jane Austen expects us to see the play as a step in Maria Bertram's road to ruin.

For the four principals, Maria and Henry, Mary and Edmund, the play represents an elaborate exercise in 'encouraging vanity' and 'destroying diffidence'. Unlike Mr Rushworth or Mr Yates, not one is vain in the trivial sense of seeking self-display; but all are after the kind of worldly 'vanity' that concerns Jane Austen in *Mansfield Park*, since all equate the pretended stage love-making with real love-making. *Lovers' Vows* gives them a licence for what would normally be entirely improper. Their scenes together permit physical contact between the sexes (as when Henry holds Maria's hand) and a bold freedom of speech altogether outside the constraint imposed by social norms. Lionel Trilling has ingeniously but anachronistically suggested that Jane Austen objects to the insincerity involved in acting a role.[15] This is surely near the opposite of the truth. In touching one another or making love to one another on the stage these four are not adopting a pose, but are, on the contrary, expressing their real feelings. The impropriety lies in the fact that they are *not* acting, but are finding an indirect means to gratify desires which are illicit, and should have been contained. The unbridled passions revealed by the play-acting are part of the uninhibited selfishness which it has been the purpose of the sequence to bring out. The point is underlined by the casting, for the actors play exaggerated versions of themselves. Mr Rushworth plays Count Cassel, a foolish and rejected suitor. Mary plays the forward and free-thinking Amelia. Edmund plays a lovelorn clergyman. Maria plays a fallen woman. The stage roles of all these imply not insincerity, but liberation.

The imagined free world which comes into being on stage is a comprehensible entity, the clearest image in all Jane Austen's novels of what she is opposed to. And meanwhile the 'real' world of

Mansfield, which is suddenly neglected and at risk, also begins to take on solidity. As at Sotherton, the most eager disciples of the dangerous activity – there it was improving, here play-acting – are those who should be the guardians of the place. Tom is the play's producer, while Mrs Norris happily (and economically) presides over the physical damage caused to Sir Thomas's property. Yet at Mansfield Park, as at Sotherton, the really dangerous figures are the Crawfords: a fact which we see fully only if, like Fanny, we look at the play as a whole.

Ideologically, the choice of play is crucial. Kotzebue's *Lovers' Vows* counterpoints what the rehearsals have revealed of the actors' selfishness and reckless quest for self-gratification, since its message is the goodness of man, the legitimacy of his claims to quality, and the sanctity of his instincts as a guide to conduct. It is, in fact, the dangerous foreign reading-matter which so often appears in anti-Jacobin novels, though wonderfully naturalised. Nor could any literate reader of the period be unaware of the connotation of the play. Quite apart from its successful runs at Covent Garden, Bath, the Haymarket, and Drury Lane between 1798 and 1802, the name of Kotzebue, by far the most popular, or notorious, of German playwrights in England at this period, was quite enough to indicate what *Lovers' Vows* was likely to be about.[16] He was the most sanguine of optimists about the beauty and innocence of human nature left to follow its own instincts. One of his heroines[17] marries her brother and has children by him, until her happiness is unnecessarily destroyed by the revelations of a meddlesome priest. Another innately virtuous victim of prejudice is the pregnant nun sentenced to death by an alliance of king and priestly hierarchy (in *The Virgin of the Sun*); she is made touchingly innocent, and her persecutors either cowardly or bigoted. This play was not well known in England, but Sheridan scored a tremendous success with the less controversial sequel, *Pizarro*, in 1799. A third Kotzebue play as often seen as *Lovers' Vows*, and even more notorious, was *The Stranger*, in which the heroine is a guilty runaway wife, who is (rightly, the play makes clear) forgiven and reinstated by her husband. There could thus be no doubt in the minds of Jane Austen and most of her readers that the name of Kotzebue was synonymous with everything most sinister in German literature of the period. A sanguine believer in the fundamental goodness and innocence of human nature, the apostle of intuition over convention, indeed of sexual liberty over every type of restraint, he is a one-sided propagandist for every position which the anti-Jacobin novelist abhors.[18] Unless the modern reader feels, like Fanny, the anarchic connotation of the whole play – rather than, like Edmund and Mary, the daring of individual speeches – he is in no position to understand its significance in relation to Mansfield Park and its owner, Sir Thomas.

Like other plays in the Kotzebue canon, *Lovers' Vows* attacks the conventions by which marriage upholds existing rank, and exalts instead the liaison based on feeling. In the main action Baron Wildenhaim, who has endured years of loneliness and remorse since refusing to marry the peasant girl whom he seduced, is persuaded to think more rightly by their illegitimate son, Frederick. In the subplot the Baron's daughter, Amelia, persuades the clergyman, Anhalt, to overlook the fact that she is a woman – by convention passive – and a noble – by convention debarred from marrying a bourgeois; her argument is that in defiance of convention they should obey their impulse.[19] Thus Frederick and Amelia are the two characters in the play who expound Kotzebue's message of freedom in sexual matters, and defiance of traditional restraints. They are played by the Crawfords, who thus again in their play-acting adopt not an assumed role but a real one. During the rehearsals they have often seemed almost diffident. It is only in relation to their parts in the play that they are revealed once more as the advocates of social and moral anarchy.

The affront felt by Sir Thomas has puzzled some observers more than it should. He returns home to find some material damage to his house, and his study in confusion. After discovering this, he steps out on to the stage for an irresistibly comic moment, his startled confrontation with the ranting Mr Yates. Because our insight into the scene is through Tom's eyes, we interpret it as Tom does – in the spirit of pure comedy – and are liable to miss the underlying point of the meeting. The head of the house, upholder in the novel of family, of rank, and of the existing order, is confronted at the heart of his own terrain by a mouthing puppet who represents a grotesque inversion of himself: the dignified baronet meets the 'Baron' whose play-function is to abandon his dignity and to legitimise his mistress. Sir Thomas and Baron Wildenhaim are the heads of their respective worlds, and the sudden meeting emphasises their significant relationship. In the future, the fact that Sir Thomas both resembles and differs from the Baron appears even more ironically, for he is called upon to deal with Maria's real-life lapse from virtue. At the time it is sufficient that a character who is central to the play's ethos makes a direct challenge to the house and its owner. Even the Crawfords, who have abstained from general discussion of the propriety of acting, know immediately that this father will not permit the play to go on. They retreat, as at Sotherton. And, though, as at Sotherton, they appear at first to have done little harm, this time they have made more significant inroads than ever before into the fabric of the Bertram family. The individuals who have sampled what the play means, who have thrown off restraint, are the more likely to do the same again. Much later, after Maria's flight with Henry, Tom describes the 'dangerous intimacy of his unjustifiable theatre' as an ancillary cause of his sister's fall (p. 462).

But this is not the story of the whole book. After the climax created by Sir Thomas's return early in the second volume, a major change occurs. The cast narrows dramatically: Maria and Mr Rushworth, Julia, Mr Yates, and Tom depart, leaving a much quieter world, and a smaller scene. From being a bystander, Fanny becomes the active heroine. Henry turns his attention from the Bertram sisters to her, and the rest of the book requires her to make a positive stand: to discern the true nature of evil, to choose the future course of her life, and, through a period of total loneliness, like a true Christian, to endure.

From Marilyn Butler, *Jane Austen and the War of Ideas* (Oxford, 1975), pp. 219–36.

## NOTES

[Marilyn Butler's discussion of *Mansfield Park* is taken from her highly influential study, *Jane Austen and the War of Ideas*, a work which has been largely responsible for the modern historicising of Austen as a writer whose fiction is informed by and contributed to the intellectual debates of her time. In this extract, Butler locates *Mansfield Park* within the contemporary literary tradition of the novel of female education and its moral directives. She demonstrates how *Mansfield Park* both draws on this tradition in its presupposition of readers' familiarity with its norms, and departs from it in significant ways: notably through the presentation of Fanny Price as the oppositional counterpart to the moral deficiencies of the Bertrams and the Crawfords. Butler argues that Austen's representation of Fanny's Christianity and its implications (with reference to education, marriage and religion) amounts to an endorsement of a politically conservative stance. The extract examines the visit to Sotherton as an episode which functions as an ideological key to the novel's meaning. Butler suggests that although the episode is an intellectual *tour de force*, it should be considered an artistic failure: the argument of the text is presented so schematically that the dramatisation of Fanny's consciousness only exhibits her human failings without succeeding in making her more likeable.

Butler's reading shows Jane Austen setting out the terms of a debate which reflects contemporary anxieties about the threat of materialism and the associated erosion of moral hierarchies. While in many ways responsible for bringing Austen's work to late twentieth-century critical notice, it also serves to expose the textual vulnerability of the novel. References to *Mansfield Park* are to the edition by R.W. Chapman (Oxford, 1923). Ed.]

[All references to the novel are given in parentheses in the text. Ed.]

1.  See Marilyn Butler, *Jane Austen and the War of Ideas* (Oxford, 1975), pp. 54–5.

2.  *Patronage* was published in December 1813, although 1814 appears on the title page; *Mansfield Park* about five months later (it was advertised in the *Morning Chronicle* on 23 and 24 May). *Mansfield Park* was finished in the summer of 1813, and was not influenced by *Patronage*.

3.  For the frequent reappearance of the lover and the sentimental friend as tempters, see Mrs West's novels and Jane Austen's *Catharine* and *Northanger Abbey*.

4.  See Butler, *War of Ideas*, p. 54.

5.  As usual in Jane Austen, an awareness that one is influenced by ulterior motives is a sign of grace, not weakness. See the discussion of Elinor in Butler, *War of Ideas*, pp. 199–200.

6.  But cf. Mrs Q.D. Leavis, 'A Critical Theory of Jane Austen's Writings', *Scrunity*, X (1942) and XII (1942).

7.  See Butler, *War of Ideas*, pp. 97–8 and 110. The Rousseauist of course preferred the country for very different reasons, because it enabled him to be morally independent and left him free to cultivate the self.

8.  Cf. Henry's later cavalier dismissal of the farmyard at Thornton Lacey, *Mansfield Park*, p. 242.

9.  The question of Fanny's religion is generally dealt with indirectly, for reasons of taste. The nearest suggestion to a religious *experience* is the occasion when she contemplates the stars and reflects that there would be less evil and sorrow in the world if 'people were carried more out of themselves by contemplating such a scene' (p. 113).

10. See Butler, *War of Ideas*, p. 19.

11. For a more detailed discussion of Jane Austen's handling of her two great houses in *Mansfield Park*, and the implicit parallel with Burke, cf. Alistair M. Duckworth, *The Improvement of the Estate* (Baltimore, MD, 1971), pp. 46 ff.; and Avrom Fleishman, *A Reading of Mansfield Park* (Minneapolis, 1967), p. 23.

12. David Spring, 'Aristocracy, Social Structure and Religion in the Early Victorian Period', *Victorian Studies*, VI (1962–3), 263–80. Some critics see special significance in the fact that by acting the Betrams are aping the aristocratic friends of the Hon. Mr Yates – himself a typically profligate representative of his class. The case against acting as given within the novel is an example of Jane Austen's Tory preference for the sober *mores* of the gentry against those of the Whig aristocracy. See D.J. Greene, 'Jane Austen and the Peerage', *PMLA*, LXIII (1953), 1017–31, and Fleishman, *A Reading of Mansfield Park*, p. 29.

13. Quoted by Frank W. Bradbook, *Jane Austen and her Predecessors* (Cambridge, 1966), p. 36. Cf. *Jane Austen's Letters* (Oxford, 1979), ed. R.W. Chapman, p. 169. In two of the best known novels of the same year as *Mansfield Park*, Fanny Burney's *The Wanderer* and Maria Edgeworth's *Patronage*, the heroine also has scruples about acting for reasons similar to those given by Gisborne.

14. Quoted by Bradbrook, *Jane Austen and her Predecessors*, p. 39.

15. Lionel Trilling, 'Mansfield Park', *The Opposing Self* (New York, 1955), pp. 218–19.

16. For an allusion to the plot of *Lovers' Vows* which assumes that the public still knows it well in 1812, see Butler, *War of Ideas*, p. 93. Information about performances of the play is given in Walter Sellier's unpublished German thesis, 'Kotzebue in England' (Leipzig, 1901), pp. 19–20.

17. In *Adelaide von Wulfingen*, trans. B. Thompson, London, 1801.

18. For discussion of the relationship of Jane Austen's novel with Kotzebue's play, cf. E.M. Butler, 'Mansfield Park and Lovers' Vows', *Modern Language Review* (July 1933), and the reply by H. Winifred Husbands, *MLR* (April 1934); and William Reitzel, 'Mansfield Park and Lovers' Vows', *Review of English Studies* (October, 1933). On the whole critics have concentrated on whether the reader of *Mansfield Park* is expected by Jane Austen to know the roles of individual characters in *Lovers' Vows*. I believe, and have tried to show, that some passages in the novel are enriched by our perceiving a connection between play characters and novel characters, yet it seems to me that Austen does not *rely* on our knowing so much.

What she does expect (more reasonably) is that we will have a general impression of the ideology of the play.

19.   For a summary of the play's attack on rank, see Crane Brinton, *The Political Ideas of the English Romanticists* (London, 1926), p. 39: 'Society – cultivated society – is always wrong. The individual who has courage to act against it is always right.'

# 2

# Good Riddance: Closure in *Mansfield Park*

*D.A. MILLER*

'Let other pens dwell on guilt and misery. I quit such odious subjects as soon as I can, impatient to restore every body, not greatly at
fault themselves, to tolerable comfort, and to have done with all
the rest' (*Mansfield Park*, p. 461). A moral decorum informs the
narrator's pose. Just as perfect ladies know to let certain subjects
drop, the perfect lady who is also a novelist (strictly: who is about
to cease being a novelist) needs to 'have done' with certain subjects,
on which, on whom it is not proper to 'dwell'. Jane Austen defines
her conception of the operation of closure in a nutshell: a restora-
tion of 'comfort' proceeding by an exclusion of what made things
uncomfortable. Most obviously, what has to be got rid of are
certain characters – mainly the Crawfords, but also Maria Bertram
and Mrs Norris. To get rid of certain characters, however, is
perhaps only a broad way of getting rid of *what characterised the
text* under their sponsorship, an insufficiently purposeful or
wrongly opaque language.

Inevitably, we single out Mary Crawford, whose language has
made up so much of the text. What has most interestingly characterised her in the novel, as we have seen, is the uncertainty she promotes – in herself as well as in others – about how to take her
discourse, how to take the subjects it treats and the subject who
utters it. Unlike her brother, who 'loves to be doing' and hence
creates 'a public disturbance at last' (pp. 57, 163), Mary never
commits an act that polite society can quasi-automatically take for

a clarification of her real character. A seamlessness and a reserve mark her speeches, despite their articulateness and their volubility. It is hard not to feel that something is being withheld in them, and easy not to know where, precisely, one motive or trait overlaps with another. For a time even the narrator respects the reticence of Mary's self-presentation. Our fascination with Mary Crawford springs from the absence of full terms to grasp her, much like Edmund's and even Fanny's fascination with her (p. 208), or Mary's own fascination with herself. ('Ignorance', Barthes suggests, 'is the main characteristic of fascination.'[1]) To *know* Mary must be the work of an active interpretation, reconstruing the ignorance that she ironically propagates into a valid cognition. Derived from a set of terms that Mary does little to provide, this interpretation must always be forced, in the sense of being incommensurable with its object. As if to underline the gap between Mary as she is and Mary as she will come to be known, the novel develops the 'knowledge of her real character' (p. 459) along a different track from the one that she herself sponsors: in the conversations between Edmund and Fanny, reviewing her character and revising it on the basis of moral principles that she does not intrinsically share. Here is the first of them, suggesting the operation involved as well as what menaces its success:

> 'Well Fanny, and how do you like Miss Crawford *now?*' said Edmund the next day, after thinking some time on the subject himself. 'How did you like her yesterday?'
>
> 'Very well – very much. I like to hear her talk. She entertains me; and she is so extremely pretty, that I have great pleasure in looking at her.'
>
> 'It is her countenance that is so attractive. She has a wonderful play of feature! But was there nothing in her conversation that struck you Fanny, as not quite right?'
>
> 'Oh! yes, she ought not to have spoken of her uncle as she did. I was quite astonished. An uncle with whom she has been living so many years, and who, whatever his faults may be, is so very fond of her brother, treating him, they say, quite like a son. I could not have believed it!'
>
> 'I thought you would be struck. It was very wrong – very indecorous.'
>
> 'And very ungrateful, I think.'
>
> 'Ungrateful is a strong word. I do not know that her uncle has any claim to her *gratitude*; his wife certainly had; and it is the warmth of her respect for her aunt's memory which misleads her here. She is

awkwardly circumstanced. With such warm feelings and lively spirits it must be difficult to do justice to her affection for Mrs Crawford, without throwing a shade on the admiral. I do not pretend to know which was most to blame in their disagreements, though the admiral's present conduct might incline one to the side of his wife: but it is natural and amiable that Miss Crawford should acquit her aunt entirely. I do not censure her *opinions*; but there certainly *is* impropriety in making them public.'

'Do not you think,' said Fanny, after a little consideration, 'that this impropriety is a reflection itself upon Mrs Crawford, as her niece has been entirely brought up by her? She cannot have given her right notions of what was due to the admiral.'

'That is a fair remark. Yes, we must suppose the faults of the niece to have been those of the aunt; and it makes one more sensible of the disadvantages she has been under. But I think her present home must do her good. Mrs Grant's manners are just what they ought to be. She speaks of her brother with a very pleasing affection.'

'Yes, except as to his writing her such short letters. She made me almost laugh; but I cannot rate so very highly the love or good nature of a brother, who will not give himself the trouble of writing any thing worth reading, to his sisters, when they are separated. I am sure William would never have used *me* so, under any circumstances. And what right had she to suppose, that *you* would not write long letters when you were absent?'

'The right of a lively mind, Fanny, seizing whatever may contribute to its own amusement or that of others; perfectly allowable, when untinctured by ill humour or roughness; and there is not a shadow of either in the countenance or manner of Miss Crawford, nothing sharp, or loud, or coarse. She is perfectly feminine, except in the instances we have been speaking of. *There* she cannot be justified. I am glad you saw it all as I did.'

(pp. 63–4)

This is Edmund's crucial first step – in knowing Miss Crawford and in failing to know her. That he chooses to hold this retrospective with Fanny suggests that he recognises a need for it, and his division of Mary's conduct into improprieties and allowable amusements is a preliminary attempt to sort out their confusion in Mary herself. The very scrupulosity of his analysis can seem to pay tribute to a highly proper flexibility, a moralist's sensitivity to the nuances of his case. However, it also seems a symptom of an unexorcised fascination that, far from making his principles more flexible, threatens to bend them out of shape. Edmund's incipient moral knowledge of Mary tends repeatedly to collapse back into the sheer fascination of his empirical response to her ('She has a wonderful play of feature ... such warm feelings and lively spirits ... a very pleasing affection ... not a shadow of [ill humour or roughness] in [her] countenance or manner'). Implicitly, Jane Austen insists on what Edmund does not realise – that a moral knowledge (if it is to have cognitive status) must reconstitute the empirical phenomena brought before it according to its own principles; and that a rigorously maintained distance from the empirical is therefore a condition of its possibility. A moral knowledge of Mary Crawford will never take her up as she appears, for her appearances are designed to undermine such knowledge. It can only take her up when she has been 'converted' (in the sense that currency is converted from one unit to another): reconstituted as its own object. Behind Edmund's error of judgement stands the full unabandoned wealth of his actual response to her, and he turns her own categories of self-presentation (irony, ambiguity, fascination) into a pseudo-knowledge camouflaging the desires that these arouse in him.

> 'I heard enough of what she said to you last night, to understand her unwillingness to be acting with a stranger; and as she probably engaged in the part with different expectations – perhaps, without considering the subject enough to know what was likely to be, it would be ungenerous, it would be really wrong to expose her to it.'
>
> (pp. 154–5)

Dismayed at 'Edmund so inconsistent', Fanny correctly sees Miss Crawford's 'influence in every speech' (p. 156). Or again:

> 'Miss Crawford ... has great discernment. I know nobody who distinguishes characters better. – For so young a woman it is remarkable! She certainly understands *you* better than you are understood by the greater part of those who have known you for so long; and with regard to some others, I can perceive, from occasional lively hints, the unguarded expressions of the moment, that she could define *many* as accurately, did not delicacy forbid it. I wonder what she thinks of my father! She must admire him as a fine looking man, with most gentleman-like, dignified, consistent manners; but perhaps having seen him so seldom, his reserve may be a little repulsive. Could they be much together I feel sure of their liking each other. He would enjoy her liveliness – and she has talents to value his powers. I wish they met more frequently!'
>
> (pp. 198–9)

What we see, through the blinds of Edmund's narrative *incon-science*, is the suggestive ambiguity of Mary's performance: how unguarded are her unguarded expressions? and who are the people whom delicacy forbids her to define accurately? Stuart Tave thinks it likely that 'Sir Thomas is the one character she is forbidding herself'.[2] He is one character, certainly – that is the obvious joke – but hardly *the* one. Surely, the point of the passage comes in the contrast between what must have been Mary's ambiguously under-stated and not quite decidable meaning and Edmund's duped eagerness to confer on it the easy legibility of his desires. As usual, Mary has suggested a mystery of there being more to her than she cares to reveal, which Edmund – not even recognising it as a mystery – resolves as he likes. The instance of Mary Crawford makes it a particularly urgent matter to maintain the gap between the empirical and the cognitive orders; and to collapse the two, as Edmund is always doing, subverts the autonomy of a genuine moral knowledge – brings it back under Mary's corrupting 'influence'.

This is probably dotting too many i's, but the point, however one wishes to put it, is an important one. Jane Austen's novels implicitly draw this distinction between the empirical and the known, defining it by a conterminous distinction between the poly-valent language of the novelistic (oriented toward the signifier) and the univocal language of the ideological (oriented toward the signified). The novelist wants to end with full and definitive knowl-edge, in part because such knowledge (whether we compare it to the conclusion of a Socratic dialogue or a detective story) traditionally marks the enclosure of discourse. By dramatising the shift from one order to another, however, by making this shift the *agon* of her novels, Jane Austen lays her cards on the table, as perhaps only a novelist extremely confident in the validity of her ideology can do. There is no hiding the fact that the imposition of knowledge necessarily coincides with a depletion of empirical reality, or that the closural meaning depends on a purgation of excess signifiers.

In the last hundred or so pages of *Mansfield Park*, Mary Crawford disappears from direct view. She is represented only by her letters to Fanny and by Edmund's report of his last meeting with her. It is as though the novelist could work toward Mary's expulsion from the Mansfield scene only by giving her a preliminary vacation – as though Mary had to be distanced before being known and dismissed. In a sense, it ought to be a nice proof of our reading of Mary's character that she finally becomes – within the novel's representation itself – only a text: the text of her letters, the text of her conversation as Edmund reports it. Just as a letter bespeaks the absence of its writer, so Mary's thoughts and speeches have always seemed to juggle away the presence of a central self that could be fixed in knowledge and truth. One might be tempted to say that, when represented by her written texts alone, Mary becomes quintessentially herself – that is, a self whose whereabouts (in every but the geographical sense) are in question. Fanny's response to one of her early letters – written before Tom's illness or Henry's elopement – tends to confirm this view:

> This was a letter to be run through eagerly, to be read deliberately, to supply matter for much reflection, and to leave every thing in greater suspense than ever. The only certainty to be drawn from it was, that nothing decisive had yet taken place. Edmund had not yet spoken. How Miss Crawford really felt – how she meant to act, or might act without or against her meaning – whether his importance to her were quite what it had been before the last separation – whether if lessened it were likely to lessen more, or to recover itself, were subjects for endless conjecture, and to be thought of on that day and many days to come, without producing any conclusion.
>
> (p. 417)

In fact, however, Mary's letters come to be much less equivocal and (like those of Lady Susan) more positively wicked than her speeches and reported thoughts had ever been. 'The influence of the fashionable world' and 'the influence of London', of course, provide a blanket motivation for this sudden self-simplification (pp. 421, 433), but it can also be accounted for in terms of a restructured interplay of textual styles. One might say that the context in which Mary's irony is viewed has changed. While the novel was itself in a state of suspension, Mary's ironical discourse seemed attractively (if also somewhat dangerously) to embody the narratable moment. In the closural context of crisis and decision (brought about by Edmund's ordination, Tom's illness, Henry's elopement), the relative weight of this discourse has altered, and Mary's typical response now seems almost a failure to respond at all to the importance and the urgency of what has happened. Dominated by the novel's newly reinforced earnestness, Mary's characteristic liveliness now seems a hardened sarcasm, a thoroughly corrupted cynicism.

Alternatively, one might say that Mary's irony itself has defaulted under the pressure of crisis, which forces the basic desires that her irony has tamed into playfulness to reassert themselves sharply. The language of her later letters comes surprisingly close to direct assertiveness:

> I really am quite agitated on the subject [of Tom Bertram's illness]. Fanny, Fanny, I see you smile, and look cunning, but upon my honour, I never bribed a physician in my life. Poor young man! – If he is to die, there will be *two* poor young men less in the world; and with a fearless face and bold voice would I say to any one, that wealth and consequence could fall into no hands more deserving of them.
>
> (p. 434)

When Mary was present at Mansfield, all the strategies of her discourse tended to throw dust in everyone's eyes – to make her inaccessible to a direct purchase, or to exceed such a purchase (like Fanny's) by more complexity than it was able to grasp. Now that she is absent from Mansfield, the margin of uncertainty that her irony had needed to introduce is all too fully provided for; and it is as if Mary were compensating for the inaccessibility built into her situation by an increasing directness of desire, which can now be revealed, decisively, as desire of the wrong kind.

All along, however, the suggestiveness and implied incompleteness of Mary's discourse have made it liable to being construed in less suggestive and more complete ways. To the extent that it has posed a scandal to oversimple notions of legibility (such as Edmund and Fanny tempt readers to entertain), it is – like most scandals – susceptible to being tamed. Edmund is ready to blame himself 'for a too harsh construction of a playful manner' (p. 421); and though he is right, I think, about his construction being 'too harsh' (so is Fanny's [p. 367]), this seems to be called for by the requirements of closure. Here is our last dramatic view of Mary Crawford in the novel, presented through Edmund's haunted recollection. He has expressed his disappointment at her response to the elopement.

> 'She turned extremely red. I imagined I saw a mixture of many feelings – a great, though short struggle – half a wish of yielding to truths, half a sense of shame – but habit, habit carried it. She would have laughed if she could. It was a sort of laugh, as she answered, "A pretty good lecture upon my word. Was it part of your last sermon? At any rate, you will soon reform every body at Mansfield and

Thornton Lacey; and when I hear of you next, it may be as a celebrated preacher in some great society of Methodists, or as a missionary in foreign parts." She tried to speak carelessly; but she was not so careless as she wanted to appear. I only said in reply, that from my heart I wished her well, and earnestly hoped that she might soon learn to think more justly, and not owe the most valuable knowledge we could any of us acquire – the knowledge of ourselves and of our duty, to the lessons of affliction – and immediately left the room. I had gone a few steps, Fanny, when I heard the door open behind me. "Mr Bertram," said she, with a smile – but it was a smile ill-suited to the conversation that had passed, a saucy playful smile, seeming to invite, in order to subdue me; at least so it appeared to me. I resisted; it was the impulse of the moment to resist, and still walked on.'

(pp. 458–9)

The entire scene is the last climax of the novel, but it is an untypical last climax for a Jane Austen novel to have. In the other novels, the last climactic scene is the one in which Mr Right – usually with a proposal – confirms his attachment to his lady. Sufficiently freed and illumined, the desires of each fix on the other. In *Mansfield Park*, that scene is reduced to a paragraph or so of summary in the windup of the last chapter (as in 'Edmund did cease to care about Miss Crawford, and became as anxious to marry Fanny, as Fanny herself could desire' [p. 470]). Instead, in its rightful place, comes this scene in which an attachment is disconfirmed, broken off. Mary is given the typical structural position of a heroine, without a heroine's typical good luck. In the context of all the novels taken together, the *hapax* here underlines the importance of Mary Crawford's appeal (much more than that of an ordinary rival like Lucy Steele or Harriet Smith) and the consequent strain of expelling her from Edmund's life. It is telling, too, that Jane Austen gives us the scene through a character's narration of it – that is, from a point of view that she has never fully embraced. Edmund's narration is charged with emotional revulsion and disgust, bespeaking by negation his attraction and desire. Seen by his anxious fears of her powers of performance, Mary turns into a vulgar Delilah, openly gesturing sexual solicitation. One must wonder whether such a perspective does not invite us – on the evidence of its own self-betraying bias – to imagine a different version of the scene, more ambiguous and less obvious than Edmund's. (It is hard to envision Mary's smile – or any smile this side of a leer – yielding so full a

sense as 'seeming to invite, in order to subdue me'.) But the necessity of Edmund's point of view becomes clear when Fanny comes to
its support: 'Fanny, now at liberty to speak openly, felt more than
justified in adding to his knowledge of [Miss Crawford's] real
character, by some hint of what share his brother's state of health
might be supposed to have in her wish for a complete reconciliation' (p. 459). Who wants Mary's 'real character', or the strategies
of irony, ambiguity, and fascination that have been part of its self-
composition, when what is now needed is the *knowledge* of her real
character? (Is Mary removed from the foreground of the novel so
that this may be more easily secured – behind her back, as it were?)
If the categories of moral knowledge are to be brought to bear on
her effectively, then the linguistic polyvalency that has made up her
empirical reality in the novel must be forcibly reduced. The closure
that Mary is subjected to involves a necessary simplification of her
discourse and the implications that it has sustained.

Yet after this closure has taken place, fixing Mary as essentially
mercenary and meretricious, she is curiously allowed to recover (in
the narrator's final wrap-up) some of her earlier complexity.

> Mary, though perfectly resolved against ever attaching herself to a
> younger brother again, was long in finding among the dashing repre-
> sentatives, or idle heir apparents, who were at the command of her
> beauty, and her £20,000 any one who could satisfy the better taste
> she had acquired at Mansfield, whose character and manners could
> authorise a hope of the domestic happiness she had there learnt to
> estimate, or put Edmund Bertram sufficiently out of her head.
>
> (p. 469)

The tones of Mary's self-irony have once more been allowed to
infiltrate the narrator's discourse about her. 'Perfectly resolved ...'
seems a more exaggerated formulation than the state of her feelings
probably warrants, and hyperbole has been a typical mode of
Mary's self-camouflage ('the *never* of conversation' [p. 92]).
'Dashing representatives, or idle heir apparents' recalls the mock
romancing of her diction ('the former belles of the house of
Rushworth' [p. 87]). And the deliberate understating of her inability to 'put Edmund Bertram sufficiently out of her head' suggests
her own style much more than it does the narrator's (compare her
comment to Fanny, '[Edmund] gets into my head more than does
me good' [p. 416]). Even in this closing summation, Mary recovers

her capacity to unsettle the judgement made on her. It is clear that there is a discrepancy between this Mary and the Mary that Edmund and Fanny have just expelled from their lives. What keeps this Mary 'long in choosing' is precisely 'the better taste' that they have condemned that Mary for wanting. (Mary has acquired her better taste, moreover, 'at Mansfield'; it is not, therefore, the belated fruit of repentant exile.)

The discrepancy points up the subtractive nature of Edmund's and Fanny's proceedings. Mary can add up to the siren and adventuress that they see in her only if something has been taken away – namely, everything that does not so add up. Only reduction and rescaling will produce a decisive knowledge of Mary Crawford (that is, one with closural force); but once a closure has thus been guaranteed and Mary become an effectively closed book (a 'bad' character), then the novelist can put back some of what had to be taken away for closure and expulsion to take place. Of course, the novelist is in deep sympathy with what Edmund and Fanny do; but her text gives full dramatic weight to the fact that it is *they* who do it. A narrator whose point of view cannot be identified with theirs simply watches on, as it were, not hostile to their activities, but neither wholly committed to them. The consequences of this construction are interestingly double. On the one hand, the interpretation that Edmund and Fanny impose on Mary secures the enclosure of the form; it provides the form with an alibi for its own rounded termination. On the other hand, this closure is made to issue from claims on our awareness (those represented by the crises of Edmund and Fanny) whose limited and partial scope has been repeatedly defined: by the status of Edmund and Fanny as characters, deprived of a fully authoritative overview; by the separate track on which they have conducted their discussions about Mary; by the narrator's point of view, different from theirs; and finally, by the complex modes of portraying Mary in the novel. Closure is thus effective, rounding off the novel, bringing this sequence and that development to an end; but its efficacy is shown to depend on a suppression, a simplification, a sort of blindness. This is what is theoretically recognised in the difference between the narrator's last view of Mary and that of Edmund and Fanny. Can the theoretical recognition be made because, in practice, it operates in benign interests? Jane Austen would seem to be saying: 'Moral knowledge, of the kind Edmund and Fanny impose, *is* "unfair"; it does involve a reduction of Mary's complexity. But this reduction is the necessary price of settlement. If one needs knowledge and settlement badly enough, as Edmund and Fanny do, the cost of obtaining them is rightly paid.' At the moment it takes place, the closure practised on Mary Crawford voids the text of a certain linguistic richness, but the riddance is felt to operate in the interest of the good. Nonetheless, to dramatise the movement of closure as it works to translate the polyvalent into the univocal is also (in however back-handed a way) to recognise the intrinsic incapacity of such a closural system ever to totalise the novel, or to absorb the full dimensions of its signifiers within an ostensible meaning. To this limited extent, the richness of, say, Mary Crawford is given back to us once we recognise the self-enclosed nature of the closural system, which closes only what *can* be closed (what has been remade into its own object) and has done with 'all the rest'.

From D.A. Miller, *Narrative and Its Discontents: Problems of Closure in the Traditional Novel* (Princeton, NJ, 1981), pp. 79–89.

## NOTES

[In this somewhat playful discussion of *Mansfield Park*, D.A. Miller explodes the principles which underlie conventional interpretations of the novel's meaning by showing how meaning itself can be reduced to little more than a game of reading signs. The excerpt is taken from a wider study which examines narrative strategies in general and addresses the whole issue of what Miller terms the 'non-narratable' in fiction, that is what is implicit as well as explicit in the dynamics of storytelling. In particular, Miller is interested in how the closing episodes which authors select for their stories reinforce an understanding of what is formally appropriate in order to bring about a satisfying narrative resolution.

Miller subjects textual discourse to close scrutiny to reveal how this process allows meaning to evaporate rather than solidify. In his analysis, the ending of *Mansfield Park*, an ending that has intrigued many critics in the past, opposes and undercuts the deliberately authoritative narrative voice of earlier scenes and draws attention to its own status as a fictive construct. He points out that Mary Crawford, who has been so central to the polarities of meaning which the novel has seemed to examine, suddenly disappears from the closing episodes, and becomes merely another sign introduced into the already confusing world of sign systems confronting the reader. Miller concludes that she is an uncomfortable presence which would prevent the satisfying closure of the novel and that by removing her

Jane Austen shows her recognition of the intrinsic limitations of the fictional form in conveying meaning. References and citations to Austen's work are from *The Novels of Jane Austen*, ed. R.W. Chapman, 5 vols, 3rd edn (London, 1932–4). Ed.]

[All references to the novel are given in parentheses in the text. Ed.]

1.   *Roland Barthes par Roland Barthes* (Paris, Seuil, 1975), p. 5.

2.   Stuart Tave, *Some Words of Jane Austen* (Chicago, 1973), p. 164.

# 3

# Jane Austen's Dangerous Charm

*NINA AUERBACH*

Alone among masters of fiction, Jane Austen commands the woman's art of making herself loved. She knows how to enchant us with conversational sparkle, to charm our assent with a glow of description, to entice our smiles with the coquette's practised glee. No major novelist is such an adept at charming. Samuel Richardson, her greatest predecessor, disdained gentlemanly amenities in his revelations of the mind's interminable, intractable mixture of motives when it engages itself in duels of love; George Eliot, her mightiest successor, rejected charm as an opiate distracting us from the harsh realities her knobby, convoluted books explore. These majestic truthtellers could not write winningly if they tried, for they are too dismally aware of the dark side of enchantment; while even in her harshest revelations, Jane Austen is a maestro at pleasing.

Yet, from the cacophony of marriages with which it begins, to the depressed union which ends it, *Mansfield Park* is unlikable. When so knowing a charmer abrades her reader, her withdrawal from our pleasure must be deliberate. She herself studied the gradations of liking *Mansfield Park* inspired, something she had not troubled to do with her earlier books, as we know from her meticulously compiled 'Opinions of *Mansfield Park*': 'My Mother – not liked it so well as P. & P. – Thought Fanny insipid. – Enjoyed Mrs Norris. – ... Miss Burdett – Did not like it so well as P. & P. Mrs James Tilson – Liked it better than P. & P.',[1] and so on. We do not know whether these carefully measured dollops of liking amused Jane Austen or annoyed her, but we do know that she was intrigued by the degree to which her unlikable novel was liked. Her apparent withdrawal from the reader's fellowship suggests a departure from the community and the conventions of realistic fiction toward a Romantic and a dissonant perspective. If we examine this difficult novel, with its particularly unaccommodating heroine, in relation to contemporaneous genres beyond the boundaries of realism, we may better understand Jane Austen's withdrawal from a commonality of delight.

The silent, stubborn Fanny Price appeals less than any of Austen's heroines. Perhaps because of this, she captivates more critics than they. 'Nobody, I believe, has ever found it possible to like the heroine of *Mansfield Park*',[2] Lionel Trilling intoned in 1955, and few would contradict this epitaph today. Yet Trilling goes on to apotheosise this literary wallflower, transfiguring her into a culturally fraught emblem who bears on her scant shoulders all the aches of modern secularism. Such later interpreters as Avrom Fleishman[3] similarly embrace Fanny as emblem if not woman, wan transmitter of intricate cultural ideals. It seems that once a heroine is divested of the power to please, she is granted an import beyond her apparently modest sphere, for, unlike Jane Austen's other, more immediately appealing heroines, Fanny has been said to possess our entire spiritual history as it shapes itself through her in historical time. Elizabeth and Emma live for readers as personal presences, but never as the Romantic, the Victorian, or the Modern *Zeitgeist*. Failing to charm, Fanny is allowed in compensation to embody worlds.

But readers who have been trained to respect the culturally fraught Fanny still shy away from her as a character. Living in uncomfortable intimacy with her as we do when we read the novel, we recall Kingsley Amis's taunt that an evening with Fanny and her clergyman husband 'would not be lightly undertaken'.[4] We may understand our heritage through Fanny Price, but ought we to want to dine with her? The question is important because, for theorists like George Levine, the more bravely realism departs from the commonality of fellowship, the more radically it tilts towards a monstrosity that undermines the realistic community itself.[5] In the very staunchness of her virtue Fanny Price seems to me to invoke the monsters that deny the charmed circle of realistic fiction. Though she uses the word 'ought' with unyielding authority, she evokes uncertainty and unease. Though we learn more about her life, and participate more intimately in her consciousness, than we do with Jane Austen's other heroines, the bothering question remains: How ought we to feel about Fanny Price?

*Mansfield Park* tilts away from commonality in part because it breaks the code established by Jane Austen's other novels. Few of us could read *Pride and Prejudice, Persuasion*, or even *Emma*, without liking the heroines enough to 'travel with them', in Wayne Booth's charming phrase.[6] *Mansfield Park* embodies a wryer literary perception, one especially congenial to Jane Austen's poetic contemporaries: the creator of Fanny Price assumes that one may live with a character one doesn't like. One motive power of Romantic poetry is the fascination of the uncongenial. In 'Resolution and Independence', Wordsworth can be possessed by a deformed and virtually non-human leech-gatherer, although the poet is too remote from the old man to absorb a word of his exhortation; an unkempt sinner, Coleridge's Ancient Mariner can snatch our imagination from a wedding, that great congenial sacrament of human community. These gnarled figures lure us out of fellowship to adopt the perspective of the monstrous and the marginal.

Fanny captures our imaginations in this same Romantic way, by welcoming the reader into her solitary animosity against the intricacies of the normal: 'Fanny was again left to her solitude, and with no increase of pleasant feelings, for she was sorry for almost all that she had seen and heard, astonished at Miss Bertram, and angry with Mr Crawford'.[7] The compelling, blighting power of Fanny's spectatorship at Sotherton is characteristic: morality dissolves into angry and unpleasant feelings whose intensity is an alternative to community. For while Fanny's Romanticism suggests itself in her isolating sensibility, her stylised effusions to nature, she is most Romantic in that, like Wordsworth's leech-gatherer or Coleridge's Mariner, there is something horrible about her, something that deprives the imagination of its appetite for ordinary life and compels it toward the deformed, the dispossessed.

This elevation of one's private bad feelings into a power alternate to social life associates Fanny not merely with early Romantic outcasts, but with such dashingly misanthropic hero-villains as Byron's Childe Harold, Mary Shelley's Frankenstein, and Maturin's Melmoth. Their flamboyant wilfulness may seem utterly alien to this frail, clinging, and seemingly passive girl who annoys above all by her shyness, but like them, she is magnetically unconvivial, a spoiler of ceremonies. During the excursion to Sotherton, the

rehearsals of *Lovers' Vows*, the game of Speculation, her baleful
solitude overwhelms the company, perhaps because it expresses and
exudes their own buried rancour. In families ranging from Sir
Thomas Bertram's stately authoritarianism to the casual disorder
of her father's house, Fanny exists like Frankenstein as a silent,
censorious pall. Her denying spirit defines itself best in assertive
negatives: 'No, indeed, I cannot act' (p. 168).

Fanny's credo resonates beyond her particular disapproval of
staging *Lovers' Vows*, for, even when the play is not in question,
Fanny refuses to act. Instead, and consistently, she counteracts; a
creed which seems a high-minded elevation of her own honesty
against the dangerous deceit of role-playing is also resistance to the
comic, collective rhythms of realistic fiction itself. The joyless
exercises of her delicate body tacitly condemn not only acting, but
activity in general; Mary Crawford's elation at horseback riding is
as antagonistic to Fanny as is her flair for acting. At Sotherton,
Fanny stations herself beside the dangerous ha-ha as a still bulwark
against the mutual serpentine pursuit of the other characters;
playing Speculation, she alone will not take the initiative that will
advance the game. Fanny's refusal to act is a criticism not just of
art, but of life as well. Her timidly resolute denial of acting includes
activity and play, those impulses of comedy which bring us together
in ceremonial motions where fellowship seems all. Her refusals are
her countercharm against the corporate and genial charm with
which Jane Austen's comedies win love.

Fanny's role as counteractive genius and spirit of anti-play is
anomalous in a romantic heroine, but not in a hero-villain. Like
Frankenstein and his monster, those spirits of solitude, Fanny is a
killjoy, a blighter of ceremonies and divider of families. It is precisely this opposition to the traditional patterns of romantic comedy
that lends her her disturbing strength. Her misery amid the bustle of
the play is the stigma of her power:

> She was full of jealousy and agitation. Miss Crawford came with
> looks of gaiety which seemed an insult, with friendly expressions
> towards herself which she could hardly answer calmly. Every body
> around her was gay and busy, prosperous and important, each had
> their object of interest, their part, their dress, their favourite scene,
> their friends and confederates, all were finding employment in
> consultations and comparisons, or diversion in the playful conceits
> they suggested. She alone was sad and insignificant; she had no share
> in any thing; she might go or stay, she might be in the midst of their

noise, or retreat from it to the solitude of the East room, without being seen or missed.

(p. 180)

But though she is stricken in the midst of play, unable and unwilling to act, Fanny never retreats from activity. Finally, her 'jealousy and agitation' seem to take concrete shape in the angry intruder, Sir Thomas Bertram, who lends authority to Fanny's bad feelings and ends the play. Sir Thomas's interruption seems only the culmination of Fanny's silent, withering power over performance, for before he appears she has already drawn control to her watching self. Backstage, she alone is in possession of each actor's secret grievance; watching and prompting from her isolation, she alone knows everybody's lines. A centre of fierce inactivity, Fanny broods jealously over the play until she masters both its script and the secret designs of its actors, at which point Sir Thomas's return vindicates her silent obstructive power. Fanny abdicates from stardom to assume a more potent control over the action: she appropriates to her solitude the controlling omniscience of the rapt audience.

As her novel's sole and constant watcher, the controlling spirit of anti-play, Fanny relinquishes performing heroism to become the jealous reader, whose solitary imagination resurrects the action and keeps it alive. In her own delicately assertive phrase, 'I was quiet, but I was not blind' (p. 358). As quietly seeing spectator of others' activities, Fanny plays a role as ambiguous as the reader's own: like Fanny, we vivify the action by our imaginative participation in it, while we hold as well the power to obstruct it by our censure. The anomalous position of the watcher more than justifies Mary Crawford's perplexed question: 'Pray, is she out, or is she not?' (p. 81). Withholding herself from play, Fanny ingests the play of everyone she silently sees. As omniscient spectator of all private and public performances, Fanny remains 'out' of the action, while her knowledge seeps into its subtlest permutations. Our discomfort at her, then, may incorporate our discomfort at our own silent voyeurism; as a portrait of the reader as a young woman, she is our unflattering if indelible reflection. Her fierce spectatorship forces our reluctant identification.

As omniscient watcher and anti-comic spirit linked in uncomfortable community to the solitary reader, Fanny possesses a subtler power than we find in brighter and livelier heroines of fiction. That dynamic misreader Emma Woodhouse is forced by her own misconstructions into the limited position of actor in the comedy she is trying to control from without, while Fanny's role as omniscient outsider thrives on her continued abstention. In her role as controlling, anti-comic watcher, Fanny moves beyond the sphere of traditional heroinism to associate herself with a host of dashing British villains. Like them, this denying girl will not, perhaps cannot, eat; her abstinence makes her a spectral presence at the communal feast. Reunited with her family at Portsmouth, instead of feasting with them, as any of Dickens' or Charlotte Brontë's waifs would gladly do, she is repelled by the very suggestion of food, by 'the tea-board never thoroughly cleaned, the cups and saucers wiped in streaks, the milk a mixture of motes floating in thin blue, and the bread and butter growing every minute more greasy than even Rebecca's hands had first produced it' (p. 428). Family food induces only a strangely modern nausea. Fanny's revulsion against food, along with her psychic feasting on the activities of others, crystallises her somewhat sinister position as outsider who strangely and silently moves into the interior. Her starved incapacity to eat familial food is suggestive of that winsome predator the vampire, an equally solitary and melancholy figure who haunts British literature in his dual role as dark abstainer from a comic dailiness of which he is secretly in possession. Like Fanny, the vampire cannot eat the common nourishment of daily life, but he feasts secretly upon human vitality in the dark.

In adopting the role of traditional literary villains, Fanny infects our imaginations in a way that no merely virtuous heroine could do. Her hungry exclusion seems unappeasable and triumphant. In so far as she draws sustenance from her role as omniscient outsider at family, excursion, wedding, play, or feast, she stands with some venerable monsters in the English canon. Not only does she share the role of Mary Shelley's creature, that gloomy exile from family whose vocation is to control families and destroy them, but there is a shadow on her even of the melancholy Grendel in the Anglo-Saxon epic *Beowulf*. An exile from common feasting, Grendel peers jealously through the window of a lighted banquet hall. He defines his identity as outsider by appropriating the interior; he invades the lighted hall and begins to eat the eaters. At the end of *Mansfield Park*, Fanny too has won a somewhat predatory victory, moving from outsider in to guiding spirit of the humbled Bertram family. Fanny's cannibalistic invasion of the lighted, spacious estate of Mansfield is genteel and purely symbolic, but, like the primitive

Grendel, she replaces common and convivial feasting with a solitary and subtler hunger that possesses its object. In this evocation of an earlier literary tradition, Fanny is Jane Austen's most Romantic heroine, for she is part of a literature newly awakened to ancient forms and fascinated by the monstrous and marginal. In the subtle streak of perversity that still disturbs readers today, she shows us the monsters within Jane Austen's realism, ineffable presences who allow the novels to participate in the darker moods of their age.[8]

Fanny's jealous hunger, which can be assuaged only by private, psychic feasting, isolates her in comedy while it associates her with such venerable predators as the Ancient Mariner, the vampire, the Byronic hero-villain, and, in a far-off echo, *Beowulf*'s Grendel. Her initiation is not that of the usual heroine, whose marriage reconciles us to the choreography of comedy; instead, like the hero-villain, she proclaims her uniqueness through possessive spectatorship. The implications of Fanny's refusal to act are more richly glossed in Romantic poetry and fiction than in early nineteenth-century realism, but Romantic criticism also illuminates the complex genesis of a Fanny Price: her stubborn creed, 'I cannot act', recalls some problematic characters of Shakespeare, in whom such critics as Coleridge and Hazlitt discovered new significance.

Like *Mansfield Park*, Shakespearean drama characteristically pivots upon the performance of a play within a play; like Jane Austen, Shakespeare increasingly pushes to centre stage the character who refuses to act. Thus, in his early *A Midsummer Night's Dream*, all the rustics lumber through their parts in the thoroughly comic 'Pyramus and Thisbe', but by the time we reach *Twelfth Night*, the play is marred: the austere Malvolio is made to perform in a cruel drama not of his making, posturing for the delectation of the raucous plotters just as he thinks he is being most sincere. This humiliation of an upright, if unlikable, character by the cruelty of play anticipates the complex tone of *Mansfield Park*, though Fanny's sharper eye for traps forbids her seduction by the players.

Malvolio abandons his part in outrage, bellowing as he exits, 'I'll be revenged on the whole pack of you!' Perhaps in his revenge he returns as Hamlet, our most famous star who refuses to act. Like Fanny, Hamlet casts himself as a jealous and melancholy death's head in a gay, if false, company. His stern creed – 'Madam, I know not seems' – epitomises, like hers, refusal to act. Non-active in the complex political drama of his family life, Hamlet likewise takes no part in the microcosmic play within the play, though, like Fanny, he hovers hungrily around its periphery, knowing all the parts. His avid spectatorship ultimately upstages the actors and spoils the performance, replacing communal play with rage and slaughter; at the end of her novel, Fanny too reigns at Mansfield in consequence of a family havoc begun at the ruin of the play.

Of course, Fanny is not Hamlet, nor was she meant to be. She is not a doomed prince, but a pauper, a woman, and a survivor; she neither rages nor soliloquises, revealing her power and her plans only haltingly and indirectly. Still, in her complex relation to the play which epitomises her novel's action, Fanny has more in common with Hamlet than she does with the helpless women he excoriates when they cross his path. For Hamlet is Shakespeare's supreme anti-actor and counteractor, the avid and omniscient spectator of the game, who fascinates us as Fanny does because he expresses his virtue by the characteristics of conventional villainy. Jane Austen's contemporaries were obsessed by this troubling sort of hero: Samuel Taylor Coleridge reconceived Hamlet as a paragon of non-activity, deifying for the modern age a character too pure to act, whose doom and calling are the destruction of play. Fanny Price may be one feminised expression of this new, Romantic fascination with Hamlet as a modern type. As Jane Austen's Hamlet, scourge and minister of a corrupted world, the perfection of the character who won't play, Fanny Price in her unyielding opposition, her longing for a purified and contracted world, gains majesty if not charm. She is as sternly denying as Hamlet, banishing in turn her cousins Maria and Julia, her parents, and the rakish, witty Crawfords from her own finer sphere. These multiple banishments align her with one type of Romantic hero, while denying her the warmth readers want in a heroine. Confronted with so richly disturbing a figure, we would insult her to sentimentalise her when *Mansfield Park* itself does not. For, as we shall see, Fanny's anti-human qualities are stressed in the text of the novel as well as in its contexts. In her progress toward power, her charmlessness only increases her efficacy as Mansfield's scourge and minister.

'Nobody falls in love with Fanny Price', Tony Tanner warns us [see Introduction in Tanner (ed.), *Mansfield Park* (Harmondsworth, 1966), p. 8]. We have seen that few readers have done so; Jane Austen further confounds our emotions by making clear that none of the characters within the novel falls in love with her either, though most heroines exist to win love. She wins neither the affect-

ion nor the interest of her parents, though they are not always un-
responsive; the charm of a Henry Crawford evokes an answering
charm in them, but when Fanny's penitential visit to Portsmouth is
over at last, her parents seem as relieved to see her leave as she is to
go. Kinship is equally unappetising to all.

Within Mansfield, the gracious adoptive family to which Fanny
returns with such ardour, she wins love in proportion to her
cousins' shame, receiving emotional interest they failed to earn.
Fanny, despised by all, is embraced as a last resource when Sir
Thomas's natural children disgrace themselves in turn. Jane Austen
is coolly explicit about the cannibalistic undercurrents of this, and
perhaps of all, requited love:

> My Fanny indeed at this very time, I have the satisfaction of
> knowing, must have been happy in spite of every thing. She must
> have been a happy creature in spite of all that she felt or thought she
> felt, for the distress of those around her … and happy as all this must
> make her, she would still have been happy without any of it, for
> Edmund was no longer the dupe of Miss Crawford.
>
> It is true, that Edmund was very far from happy himself. He was
> suffering from disappointment and regret, grieving over what was,
> and wishing for what could never be. She knew it was so, and was
> sorry; but it was with a sorrow so founded on satisfaction, so
> tending to ease, and so much in harmony with every dearest sensa-
> tion, that there are few who might not have been glad to exchange
> their greatest gaiety for it.
>
> (p. 446)

In this redemption from her usual depression, Fanny's only available happy ending is the predator's comedy; surely there is deliberate irony in Jane Austen's pitiless repetition of 'happy' amid this
household of collapsed hopes. Never in the canon is the happy
ending so reliant upon the wounds and disappointments of others;
though we leave Fanny ministering avidly to these wounds, they
will never heal. The love she wins from her adoptive family is not a
free tribute to her beauty, her character, or her judgement, but the
last tender impulse of a stricken household.

The love of her two suitors, Henry and Edmund, is similarly un-
dermined. Everything about Henry Crawford, that mobile and consummate actor, calls his sincerity into question. He stages his love
scenes before select audiences, all carefully chosen to put the greatest possible pressure on Fanny, only to humiliate her flamboyantly
by his elopement with Maria once she has begun to respond. As

Fanny and we know, his passion for her repeats more grandly his pattern of behaviour with her silly cousins, so that only the most sentimentally credulous reader could find this new performance credible. The watcher Fanny knows his love is play, and thus by definition the medium of her humiliation; but in exposing the ardour of the romantic hero as a sadistic game, Jane Austen undermines the reader's own impulse to fall in love with Fanny by undermining love itself.

Readers of *Sense and Sensibility, Pride and Prejudice,* and *Emma* expect Edmund Bertram, Fanny's proper husband and sober soulmate, to redress the balance; the probity of this good suitor's love should define the sham of Henry's. But if for Henry love is another variant of private theatricals, a series of ritual attitudes staged for an audience, Edmund's love is so restrained as to be imperceptible. Like Mr Knightley, he is exemplary as Fanny's tender mentor, proud of his pupil's right feelings and right attitudes, but he has none of Mr Knightley's life as an incipient lover. Sexual jealousy fuels the latter's sternly protective manner and his indignant disapproval of Frank Churchill, while Edmund hints of no passions beyond what we see, showing not a glimmer of jealousy when Henry Crawford makes demonstrative love to Fanny. Edmund's impeccably clerical conscience interprets his future wife's prospective marriage as a convenience to facilitate his own engagement to Henry's seductive sister. Jane Austen is a sharp observer of men struggling with powerful feelings; like Knightley, Darcy and Wentworth fight to repress, through prudence or anger, a love that proves too strong for them; but she withholds from Edmund Bertram any feelings worth denying. The unlocated and undramatised conversion that leads to his marriage carries as little emotional weight as it could do: 'I only intreat every body to believe that exactly at the time when it was quite natural that it should be so, and not a week earlier, Edmund did cease to care about Mary Crawford, and became as anxious to marry Fanny, as Fanny herself could desire' (p. 454).

This clipped, perfunctory summary, together with the fact that no earlier hints have prepared us for an outbreak of passion on Edmund's part, seems deliberately designed to banish love from our thoughts. The final marriage is as stately and inevitable as Edmund's ordination will be; the ritual is performed, though neither love nor guardianship quite joins the marrying couple. The narrator's reiterated appeal to nature – 'what could be more natural than the change?' – is a further symptom of the hopelessness of love, for, as we shall see below, nature is a feeble contender in the manipulated world of *Mansfield Park*. Though Edmund marries the woman he ought, the stern hope he husbands is a loveless strength.

A romance from a writer of marriage comedies that so unremittingly denies love to its heroine is a brave novel indeed, particularly when this heroine is ready to love both her emotionally desiccated suitors. If two wooing men cannot manage to love Fanny, with the true suitor proving as hollow as the false, then surely the reader never will. Austerely alone in a community of fictional heroines for whom love is their chief talent and reward, Fanny is further isolated from affection by her radical homelessness. This waiflike attribute may lead us to associate *Mansfield Park* with such Victorian orphan-myths as *Jane Eyre*: Jane, like Fanny, is an unprepossessing orphan, 'a discord' in her corrupted foster family, who grows into an iron-willed little saviour. But like most of her orphaned analogues in Victorian fiction, Jane is baptised into strength by the recovery of family: it is not her love for Rochester, but her healing interlude with her recovered cousins, the Rivers family, that allows her identity and her destiny to cohere.[9] The more radical Fanny similarly recovers her family during a romantic crisis, only to discover her total absence of kin. Her ideal home is her utter homelessness. She belongs everywhere she is not: 'When she had been coming to Portsmouth, she had loved to call it her home, had been fond of saying that she was going home; the word had been very dear to her; and so it still was, but it must be applied to Mansfield. *That* was now the home. Portsmouth was Portsmouth; Mansfield was home' (pp. 420–1).

The word may be very dear, but the thing eludes her as she eludes it. Victorian orphan-fiction typically begins with the loss of home and ends with its recovery, but here, home is palpable to Fanny only by its absence. Mansfield itself is no true home. The vacuum at its heart is evident not only in the flights of all its members except the supine Lady Bertram, but in the chilling ease with which it can be transformed into a theatre. Upon her return, Fanny compels the gutted Mansfield to be her home by an act of will, but in its shrunken regenerate state it bears little resemblance to the place in which she grew up. Fanny's dual returns, to her natural and then to her adoptive origins, prove only the impossibility of self-discovery through return. Thus, though she may resemble later orphan-heroes, Fanny is a more indigestible figure than these wistful waifs, for whom embracing their kin is secular salvation. In the tenacity with which she adheres to an identity validated by no family, home, or love, she denies the vulnerability of the waif for the unlovable toughness of the authentic transplant. Her fragility cloaks the will to live without the traditional sanctions for life. Underlying her pious rigidity is a dispossession so fundamental that, among nineteenth-century English novelists, only the tact of a Jane Austen could dare reveal it in a lady.

Readers are right, then, to find Fanny a relentlessly uncomfortable figure in a domestic romance and to wonder nervously where Jane Austen's comedy went. This uncompromising novel never dissolves its heroine's isolation; she merely passes from the isolation of the outcast to that of the conqueror. Her solitude is rarely alleviated by pathos; instead, she hones it into a spectator's perspective from which she can observe her world and invade it. In this above all, she is closer to the Romantic hero than to the heroine of romance: her solitude is her condition, not a state from which the marriage comedy will save her. In her relentless spectatorship, Fanny may be Jane Austen's domestic answer to Byron's more flamboyant and venturesome Childe Harold, exile from his kind, passing eternally through foreign civilisations in order to create elegies to their ruins. Though Fanny travels only to Sotherton and Portsmouth, her role too is alien and elegiac, as it is at Mansfield itself; like Byron's persona, she is a hero because she is sufficiently detached to see the death of worlds. Fabricating an identity from uprootedness, she conquers the normal world that acts, plays, and marries, through her alienation from it. In the text of her novel, she is a being without kin, but in its context, she exudes a quiet kinship with the strangers and the monsters of her age.

Like other literary monsters, Fanny is a creature without kin who longs for a mate of her own kind. The pain of her difference explains a longing in *Mansfield Park* that is common to much Romantic literature and that, in its obsessed exclusiveness, may look to modern readers unnervingly like incest: the hunger of sibling for sibling, of kin for kind. Seen in its time, the ecstatic, possessive passion Fanny divides between her brother William and her foster brother Edmund, her horror at the Crawfords' attempt to invade her emotions, seem less relevant to the Freudian family romance than to the monster's agonised attempts to alleviate his monstrosity. Mary Shelley's monster asks only that Frankenstein create for him a sister-wife; Bram Stoker's Dracula experiences his triumphant climax when turning his victims into fellow members of the Undead, thus making of them sisters as well as spouses. Fanny yearns similarly in isolation for a brother-mate, repelling the Crawfords above all because they are so different as to constitute virtually another species: 'We are so totally unlike ... we are so very, very different in all our inclinations and ways, that I consider it as quite impossible we should ever be tolerably happy together, even if I *could* like him. There never were two people more dissimilar. We have not one taste in common. We should be miserable' (p. 345).

This rage of self-removal extends itself to Mary Crawford as well, above all perhaps in the emotional spaciousness with which Mary reaches out to Fanny as her 'sister'.[10] Mary's quest for sisters of gender rather than family, her uncomfortably outspoken championship of abused wives, her sexual initiative, and her unsettling habit of calling things by their names, all suggest the pioneering sensibility of her contemporary, Mary Wollstonecraft; but Fanny cannot endure so universal an embrace, clutching only the shreds of kinship. The novel ends as it ought, with Mary's expulsion into a wider and sadder world, while Fanny, still isolated, clings jealously to her conquered family.

Fanny as Romantic monster does not dispel our discomfort in reading *Mansfield Park*, but may explain some of it. Until recently, critics have limited their recognition of the monsters that underlie Jane Austen's realism to the peripheral figures whose unreason threatens the heroine, while the heroine herself remains solidly human.[11] Yet Fanny excites the same mixture of sympathy and aversion as does Frankenstein's loveless, homeless creature, and the pattern of her adventures is similar to his. Frankenstein's monster begins as a jealous outcast, peering in at family and civic joys. His rage for inclusion makes him the hunted prey of those he envies, and he ends as the conqueror of families. Fanny too is a jealous outcast in the first volume. In the second, she is besieged by the family that excluded her in the form of Henry Crawford's lethal marriage proposal; finally her lair, the chilly East room, is hunted down like Grendel's and invaded by Sir Thomas himself. In the third volume, Fanny, like Mary Shelley's monster, becomes the solitary conqueror of a gutted family. This movement from outcast within a charmed circle to one who is hunted by it and then conqueror of it aligns Jane Austen's most Romantic, least loved heroine with the kin she so wretchedly seeks.

Modern readers may shun Fanny as a static, solitary predator, but in the world of *Mansfield Park* her very consistency and tenacity are bulwarks against a newly opening space that is dangerous in its very fluidity: even Sir Thomas Bertram's solid home is made vulnerable by economic fluctuations in far-off Antigua.[12] Though the large and loveless house that gives it its name has made many readers feel that *Mansfield Park* is Jane Austen's most oppressive novel, its dominant emotional atmosphere induces a certain vertigo, evident in the apparent rocklike solidity, but the true and hopeless elusiveness, of the word 'ought'. 'Ought' tolls constantly, its very sound bringing a knell of absolutism, and nobody uses it with more assurance than the hero and heroine. Fanny can dismiss Henry Crawford simply because 'he can feel nothing as he ought', while Edmund freights the word with religious and national authority: 'as the clergy are, or are not what they ought to be, so are the rest of the nation' (p. 121). As a barometer of feelings, morals, and institutions, the word seems an immutable touchstone, but in fact it has no objective validation. Its authority in the novel is entirely, and alarmingly, self-generated. The great houses Mansfield and Sotherton scarcely institutionalise the 'ought' that resounds in the novel's language; the Portsmouth of the Prices and the London of the Crawfords are equally ignorant of its weight. It has no echo in the world of households and institutions.

Yet this lack of official authority does not prevent the novel's misguided characters from using the word with the same assurance as Fanny and Edmund do. Sir Thomas says of a Fanny who is brewing rebellion, 'She appears to feel as she ought' (p. 230); for Mary, the party with which Maria Rushworth inaugurates her miserable marriage finds everything 'just as it ought to be' (p. 406); Maria herself avoids only the word in seeing her mercenary marriage as 'a duty' (p. 72). Even Edmund, who has transmitted its value to Fanny, abuses the word throughout the novel, beginning with his myopic pressure on Fanny to live with her hated Aunt Norris: 'She is choosing a friend and companion exactly where she ought' (p. 60). The incoherence underlying Edmund's authoritative vocabulary tells us that the word recurs anarchically, for there is no objective code to endow it with consistency. Fanny, for example, longs for a loving reunion with her indifferent mother, hoping that 'they should soon be what mother and daughter ought to be to each other' (p. 366), but as usual the novel provides no objective image of this 'ought': in *Mansfield Park* and throughout Jane Austen's canon, mothers and daughters are at best indifferent and at worst antagonistic, depriving the commanding word of validation. Fanny is repeatedly hymned as the only character who feels consistently as she ought, but in a world where the word changes its meaning so incessantly, her role as a walking 'ought' merely isolates her further. Whatever authority Fanny has comes magically from herself alone. Though she can control the inchoate outside world, it is too lacking in definition to claim kinship with her.

For though Fanny possesses a quasi-magical power over the action, she represents less a moral than a shaping principle, assuming the author's prerogatives along with the reader's: the novel's action happens as she wills, and so her emotions become our only standard of right. In its essence, the world of *Mansfield Park* is terrifyingly malleable. Jane Austen detaches herself from her Romantic contemporaries to reveal both inner and outer nature as pitifully ineffectual compared to what can be made. Mrs Price grows listless toward Fanny because the 'instinct of nature was soon satisfied, and Mrs Price's attachment had no other source' (p. 382). The gap between Mrs Price and Mrs Bertram can never heal because 'where nature had made so little difference, circumstances [had] made so much' (p. 400). Mary Crawford's nature, like Maria's and Julia's, is similarly helpless against the constructive, or the deconstructive, power of her medium: 'For where, Fanny, shall we find a woman whom nature had so richly endowed? – Spoilt, spoilt! –' (p. 441). By contrast, we know that Susan Price will survive, not because of her natural qualities, but because she is 'a girl so capable of being made, every thing good' (p. 409). Nature's insufficiency may explain the deadness of Fanny's effusions to stars, trees, and 'verdure', for though she laments improvements, Fanny is the most potent of the novel's improving characters. In so malleable and so defective a world, Fanny is polite to the stars, but she turns her most potent attention on the vulnerable, that which is 'capable of being made'.

In Mary Shelley's *Frankenstein* as well, family, nature, and even the Alps pall before the monster who is capable of being made. The monstrosity of *Mansfield Park* as a whole is one manifestation of its repelled fascination with acting, with education, and with landscape and estate improvements: the novel imagines a fluid world, one with no fixed principles, capable of awesome, endless, and dangerous manipulation. The unconvivial stiffness of its hero and heroine is their triumph: by the end, they are so successfully 'made' by each other that he is her creature as completely as she has always been his. The mobility and malleability of *Mansfield Park* is a dark realisation of an essentially Romantic vision, of which Fanny Price represents both the horror and the best hope. Only in *Mansfield Park* does Jane Austen force us to experience the discomfort of a Romantic universe presided over by the potent charm of a charmless heroine who was not made to be loved.[13]

From Janet Todd (ed.), *Jane Austen: New Perspectives* (New York, 1983), pp. 208–23.

## NOTES

[Nina Auerbach's discussion of Fanny Price offers an ingenious solution to the problem of the text's hostile reception (a problem which Marilyn Butler also identifies) by taking as her starting point her own unease with a charmless heroine. Referring to a well-established tradition of literary configurations of the isolated observer from Beowulf to Shakespearean drama, Auerbach points out that such figures carried special resonance for the Romantic writers who were Austen's contemporaries. She compares Fanny to a Romantic outcast, an exile from the domestic comedy which surrounds her, and finds surprising analogies between Fanny and the monster in Mary Shelley's *Frankenstein*, a work published four years later. In its emphasis on solitude, inactivity and a negative sensibility, *Mansfield Park's* depiction of Fanny Price is thus seen as a perfect reflection of the preoccupations of the period.

Auerbach's is a cogent and provocative thesis which concentrates on the dark elements in the novel as supportive of Jane Austen's vision of a Romantic universe: it is because it ultimately disallows the possibility of domestic harmony that the text consequently generates discomfort among its readers. In suggesting that such discomfort is an integral feature of the Romantic vision, Auerbach provides a very different literary context for *Mansfield Park* from that of Marilyn Butler and also offers an alternative approach to the issue of narrative 'discontent' with which D.A. Miller also engages. References to Jane Austen's work are to *Minor Works*, ed. R.W. Chapman (London, rpt. 1969) and to *Mansfield Park* (Harmondsworth, 1966). Ed.]

1. Jane Austen, *Minor Works*, ed. R.W. Chapman (1954; rpt. London, 1969), p. 432.

2. Lionel Trilling, '*Mansfield Park*', rpt. in Ian Watt (ed.), *Jane Austen: A Collection of Critical Essays* (Englewood Cliffs, NJ, 1963), p. 128.

3. Avrom Fleishman, *A Reading of Mansfield Park* (1967; rpt. Baltimore, MD, 1970), pp. 57–69.

4. Kingsley Amis, 'Whatever Became of Jane Austen?' (1957), rpt. in Watt, *Jane Austen*, p. 142.

5. 'Keeping the monster at bay is one part of the realist enterprise. The other is to keep him, or her, alive', George Levine, *The Realistic Imagination: English Fiction from Frankenstein to Lady Chatterley* (Chicago, 1981), p. 80. Judith Wilt, *Ghosts of the Gothic: Austen, Eliot, and Lawrence* (Princeton, NJ, 1980), pp. 121–72, provides an eerily suggestive discussion of the terror that infuses Jane Austen's vision of commonality.

6. Wayne Booth, *A Rhetoric of Fiction* (Chicago, 1961), p. 245.

7. Jane Austen, *Mansfield Park* (1814; rpt. Harmondsworth, 1966), p. 127. Future references to this edition will appear in the text.

8. George Levine speculates about the monstrous potential of Jane Austen's more inquisitive heroines, though he assumes, overhastily in my opinion, that Fanny's passivity exempts her from monstrosity (p. 41). Sandra M. Gilbert and Susan Gubar are more catholic in their definition: '[Austen's] heroines, it seems, are not born like people, but manufactured like monsters, and also like monsters they seem fated to self-destruct', Gilbert and Gubar, *The Madwoman in the Attic: The Woman Writer and the Nineteenth-Century Literary Imagination* (New Haven, CT, 1979), p. 129. For more capacious examinations of Jane Austen's dark Romanticism, see Wilt, *Ghosts of the Gothic*, pp. 121–72, and Nina Auerbach, 'Jane Austen and Romantic Imprisonment', in *Jane Austen in a Social Context*, ed. David Monaghan (London, 1981), pp. 9–27.

9. See Maurianne Adams, '*Jane Eyre*: Woman's Estate', in Arlyn Diamond and Lee R. Edwards (eds), *The Authority of Experience: Essays in Feminist Criticism* (Amherst, MA, 1977), pp. 137–59; and Fleishman, *A Reading of Mansfield Park*, p. 72, for more discussion of Fanny as orphan. For a broader discussion of the subversive implications of fictional orphanhood, see Nina Auerbach, 'Incarnations of the Orphan', *English Literary History*, 42 (Fall 1975), 395–419.

10. See Janet Todd, *Women's Friendship in Literature* (New York, 1980), pp. 246–74, for a provocative analysis of Fanny's, and Jane Austen's, rejection of female friendship and the radical autonomy it provides.

11. See, for instance, Donald Greene, 'Jane Austen's Monsters', in John Halperin (ed.), *Jane Austen: Bicentenary Essays* (Cambridge, 1975), pp. 262–78. Amis, in Watt, *Jane Austen*, p. 144, and Julia Prewitt Brown, in *Jane Austen's Novels: Social Change and Literary Form* (Cambridge, MA, 1979), p. 100, do in passing call Fanny Price a

monster, but this appellation seems more a cry of horror than an expression of sustained literary interest.

12. See Fleishman, *A Reading of Mansfield Park*, pp. 36–42.

13. A somewhat shorter version of this paper was presented as the keynote address of the 1980 meeting of the Jane Austen Society. Their kind invitation to speak made me wonder for the first time how I ought to feel about Fanny Price.

# 4

# The Boundaries of *Mansfield Park*

*RUTH BERNARD YEAZELL*

## THE DIRT AT PORTSMOUTH

Immediately before the climax of *Mansfield Park*, in the last chapter of Fanny Price's exile at Portsmouth, comes a passage extraordinary for Jane Austen – extraordinary both in the concreteness of its details and in the sense of revulsion it records:

> She felt that she had, indeed, been three months there: and the sun's rays falling strongly into the parlour, instead of cheering, made her still more melancholy; for sun-shine appeared to her a totally different thing in a town and in the country. Here, its power was only a glare, a stifling, sickly glare, serving but to bring forward stains and dirt that might otherwise have slept. There was neither health nor gaiety in sun-shine in a town. She sat in a blaze of oppressive heat, in a cloud of moving dust; and her eyes could only wander from the walls marked by her father's head, to the table cut and knotched by her brothers, where stood the tea-board never thoroughly cleaned, the cups and saucers wiped in streaks, the milk a mixture of motes floating in thin blue, and the bread and butter growing every minute more greasy than even Rebecca's hands had first produced it....
>
> (p. 439)

The vulgar confusion that Fanny has registered ever since her arrival at Portsmouth is here brought vividly into focus. From the walls marked by the oil of her father's head to the unclean utensils on the table marred by her brothers, the motes in the milk and the greasy bread, Austen's heroine sees her family home as stained and polluted. Fanny may have been too long pampered at Mansfield Park, or Austen may have been tempted to indulge in some conventional disparagement of town life. But neither explanation accounts for the intensity of this consciousness of dirt – nor for its surfacing at this particular moment, as if prescient of the moral revulsion about to come. The passage continues:

> Her father read his newspaper, and her mother lamented over the ragged carpet as usual, while the tea was in preparation – and wished Rebecca would mend it; and Fanny was first roused by his calling out to her, after humphing and considering over a particular paragraph – 'What's the name of your great cousins in town, Fan?'
>    A moment's recollection enabled her to say, 'Rushworth, Sir'.
>    'And don't they live in Wimpole Street?'
>    'Yes, Sir.'
>    'Then, there's the devil to pay among them, that's all.'
>
> (p. 439)

Fanny's disgusted perception of dirt and spoilage among her immediate kin at Portsmouth thus directly anticipates her shocked verdict on the 'too horrible ... confusion of guilt' among her great cousins in London.[1] The squalor of Mrs Price's housekeeping is inevitably swallowed up in the horror of Mrs Rushworth's adultery, and the scandalised Fanny is soon summoned back to Mansfield and away from the mess on the family table. Guilty confusion commands more attention than the homely Portsmouth kind, especially in a world so insistently moralised as Austen's: distracted by the climactic revelations, the rush back to familiar characters and to moral judgement, the reader, too, tends to forget the dirt. But the sense of pollution recorded here is characteristic of the design of Austen's most troublesome novel.

Dirt, Mary Douglas has suggested, is not so much an idea in itself as a function of the need for order – 'a kind of compendium category for all events which blur, smudge, contradict, or otherwise confuse accepted classifications'.[2] If pollution ideas come strongly to the fore whenever the lines of a social system are especially precarious or threatened, as Douglas argues,[3] it is not surprising that in this interval of heightened anxiety and suspense, Fanny Price should see dirt. The sojourn at Portsmouth has been characterised from its beginning by peculiar tension and disquiet. To be at 'home' for the heroine of this novel is in fact to be in exile, displaced from the only ground to which her history has truly attached her. '*That* was now the home. Portsmouth was Portsmouth' (p. 431). No firm period has been fixed for her stay, and in the days before the scandal breaks, the term of her banishment threatens to lengthen indefinitely. The noise and disorder of her father's house have not prompted in Fanny the wish to be mistress of Everingham, as Sir Thomas had hoped, but Henry Crawford's persistent courtship of her at Portsmouth has proved unsettling. Without any serious change of heart, she is nonetheless disarmed by his apparent sincerity and embarrassed by the consciousness of all that distinguishes him from her vulgar relations. To walk upon the High Street with Henry and encounter her father is to bring 'pain upon pain, confusion upon confusion' (p. 401). Between her shame at her family and her wavering assessment of Henry's capacity for change, Fanny Price has never before seemed so subject to confusion, her state of mind so vulnerably suspended. Worried and estranged, she must at the same time wait helplessly for the resolution of Edmund's own unsettled state, the outcome of his protracted, indecisive courtship of Mary. Her anxiety has already been further compounded by the news of Tom's illness when the mail brings yet another alarming letter, a hasty note from Mary Crawford, with its disturbing allusions to a scandal she does not name. The troubled suspense that has marked Fanny's entire stay at Portsmouth culminates in still another day of waiting before Mr Price's newspaper unexpectedly confirms the scandal, and anxiety gives way to 'the shock of conviction' (p. 440).

Fanny's revulsion at the news is vehement and absolute. 'She passed only from feelings of sickness to shuddering of horror. ...' And the origin of the sickness is the discovery of people dangerously out of place, of accustomed categories blurred and confounded:

> The event was so shocking, that there were moments even when her heart revolted from it as impossible – when she thought it could not be. A woman married only six months ago, a man professing himself devoted, even *engaged*, to another – that other her near relation – the whole family, both families connected as they were by tie upon tie, all friends, all intimate together! – it was too horrible a confusion of guilt, too gross a complication of evil, for human nature, not in a state of utter barbarism, to be capable of – yet her judgment told her it was so.
>
> (p. 441)

As D.A. Miller has noted, 'Fanny's curious disbelief and excessive disgust are inadequately served by the moral terms in which they are accounted for'.[4] 'Too gross a complication of evil' is closer to the 'stains and dirt' in the Prices' parlour than it is to considered judgement. Fanny's revolt from the very event as impossible, her conclusion that 'the greatest blessing to every one of kindred with Mrs Rushworth would be instant annihilation' (p. 442), are only climactic instances of the tendency to organise experience by drawing sharp lines of exclusion. Though Fanny is the principal vehicle of such thinking, the novel as a whole reveals a similar impulse to draw a world divided by clear spatial and ontological boundaries – to envision sunshine as 'a totally different thing in a town and in the country'. Anxiety about transitional states and ambiguous social relations is repeatedly countered in *Mansfield Park* by this categorical sorting of things into the clean and the dirty, the sacred and the profane.

To approach *Mansfield Park* in so anthropological a spirit may well seem perverse. The inhabitants of the Park are hardly the natives of a distant culture, and few fictional languages would ordinarily seem less translatable into the anthropologist's terms than the subtle discriminations of Jane Austen. But the fact remains that modern readers have persistently felt *Mansfield Park* as somehow alien and remote, and that alone of all her novels, it seems to require special pleading. Indeed a latent tendency to think anthropologically, or at least to associate *Mansfield Park* with the 'primitive', can be detected in a number of the novel's critics. Lionel Trilling's attempt to explain 'the great fuss that is made over the amateur theatricals' by allusion to 'a traditional, almost primitive, feeling about dramatic impersonation' represents probably the most familiar case.[5] Trilling's contention that there is something Platonic about the novel's distrust of acting has been much disputed,[6] but he is not alone in reaching for such analogies, nor in responding to what he elsewhere terms the 'archaic ethos' of the text.[7] Even a critic so sensitively attuned to the particulars of cultural history as Alistair Duckworth finds himself supplementing his effective use of Edmund Burke by reference to Lévi-Strauss – suggesting that the feeling for local ground at Mansfield might instructively be compared to the Bororo Indians' profound attachment to the circular arrangement of their huts.[8] The frequent association of Fanny Price with Cinderella, sometimes surrounded by vague allusions to 'archetype' and 'myth', may also arise from the sense that this is the closest of Austen's novels to older forms of story-telling, and that it operates by more primitive laws.[9]

Readings of *Mansfield Park* have repeatedly tried to bring the novel into accord with the rest of Austen's canon and to justify the values that govern it.[10] But even the most acute and learned of such efforts do not quite satisfy – in part, I would suggest, because they must labour under the strain of rationalising what is not finally rational. Stuart Tave's patient attempt to explain the disapproval of the theatricals is a case in point. Arguing that the issue is not the theatricals in themselves, but 'these people in these circumstances', he carefully articulates the 'whole series of objections, increasing in specificity and force' which are levelled against the scheme, all the while evading the deep anxiety conveyed by this very need to spin out one objection after another.[11] Like other gestures of rejection in *Mansfield Park*, the drive to condemn the theatricals still seems greater than the sum of these reasonable parts. What is missing from such a beautifully rationalised account is the fundamental sense of taint and pollution that seems to underlie so many of the novel's moral judgements. When other critics observe that the passion for theatricals spreads to Mansfield like a 'germ', call Mary Crawford's correspondence 'tainted', or allude to the 'fear of contamination' that pervades the novel,[12] they come closer to what is at once deepest and most troubling in *Mansfield Park*. Even those unappreciative readers who disgustedly reject the book as corrupt and repellent are perhaps more directly in sympathy with the novel's own impulses to sort and discard.[13]

## THE PURGATION OF MANSFIELD PARK

When Sir Thomas Bertram returns from Antigua to discover that the 'infection' of acting has 'spread' from Ecclesford to Mansfield (p. 184), he undertakes to combat that infection by energetically cleaning house. The theatre that has been temporarily erected in his billiard room is dismantled, the scene painter dismissed, and 'Sir Thomas was in hopes that another day or two would suffice to wipe away every outward memento of what had been, even to the destruction of every unbound copy of "Lovers' Vows" in the house, for he was burning all that met his eye' (p. 191). It takes just 'another day or two' before Mr Yates, the stranger who has carried the infection to Mansfield, voluntarily quits the house: 'Sir Thomas hoped, in seeing him out of it, to be rid of the worst object connected with the scheme, and the last that must be inevitably reminding him of its existence' (pp. 194–5). By wiping away every sign of the theatricals, even burning the books, Sir Thomas does not merely put an end to his children's acting scheme but ritually purges Mansfield of its dangers. Sir Thomas wants 'a home that shuts out noisy pleasures' (p. 186), and his gesture firmly re-establishes those boundaries that 'shut out', restoring a space that had been profaned.

The risks of play-acting at Mansfield have been intensified from the start by circumstances in which boundaries are already significantly threatened, by states of uncertain passage and transition. 'In a *general* light, private theatricals are open to some objections', Edmund argues, 'but as *we* are circumstanced, I must think it would be highly injudicious, and more than injudicious, to attempt any thing of the kind. It would show great want of feeling on my father's account, absent as he is, and in some degree of constant danger: and it would be imprudent, I think, with regard to Maria, whose situation is a very delicate one, considering every thing, extremely delicate' (p. 125). Note that it is not merely Sir Thomas's absence from home that is at issue, but the fact that his travels expose him to 'constant danger' – that his perilous journey renders him the object of suspense and anxiety. The anxieties prompted by Maria's 'delicate situation' are superficially quite different – the risks she confronts are purely social and psychological, not physical; yet she, too, is embarked on a dangerous passage. Any engagement marks a period of transition, but Maria's social place is further unsettled by the fact that she has been pledged to Mr Rushworth while her father is absent; engaged, yet not quite engaged, she is even more precariously suspended than is customary between her father's domain and that of her future husband. If acting 'is almost certain to prove ... injurious' to the female sex, as Thomas Gisborne's 1797 *Enquiry* on that sex's duties insisted, then Maria's ambiguous position renders her especially vulnerable. The perils that Gisborne associated with any theatrical performance by a woman – the risks of 'unrestrained familiarity with persons of the other sex, which inevitably results from being joined with them in the drama'[14] – can only be heightened for one who is tempted to flirt with the relative freedom of a committed woman, even while she lacks the very protection that firm commitment affords. With its own shifting identities, its toying with sexual licence and transgression, *Lovers' Vows* is hardly the play to minimise such dangers.

The traditional distrust of the actor's role-playing is never directly articulated in *Mansfield Park*, but the anxiety of boundary-confusion is everywhere felt. Edmund suggests that the theatre has its place, in fact, but there is something more than the love of talent behind his preference for 'good hardened real acting' over the amateur's kind (p. 124): hardened actors presumably have a more calloused sense of their own boundaries, are less in danger of too fluidly surrendering to their dramatised selves. When Mary Crawford realises that she must 'harden' herself by private rehearsals with Fanny before she can dare to speak Amelia's lines (p. 168), what she seeks to avoid is the embarrassing consciousness that her dramatic role may be confused with her real one – an embarrassment all the greater because Amelia's immodest speeches themselves transgress the limits appropriate to her sex. Fanny's reluctant attempt to read the part of Anhalt, in contrast, is accompanied 'with looks and voice so truly feminine, as to be no very good picture of a man' (p. 169). Her utter incapacity to act, especially to act across gender-lines, emblematically confirms her integrity: Fanny can represent no one but herself.

The fuss over the theatricals reaches its comic climax when Sir Thomas enters his billiard room only to find himself upon a stage, unwittingly cast opposite Yates's 'ranting young man'. Trivial as the removal of Sir Thomas's billiard table may seem, the 'general air of confusion in the furniture' (p. 182) that he discovers on his return is the sign of a more profound disturbance, as the uneasy consciousness of his children confirms. While their father has been in danger, they have thoughtlessly invaded and violated his 'own dear room' (p. 181). One violation opens the way to others, and the 'confusion of guilt' in London eventually follows. When Edmund grudgingly agreed to act himself rather than open Mansfield to yet more strangers, on the other hand, he characteristically sought 'to confine the representation within a much smaller circle' (p. 155) – to narrow and tighten the borders. Here as elsewhere in the novel, anxiety manifests itself in a heightened attention to the sanctity of domestic space.

*Mansfield Park* may be the most openly Christian of Jane Austen's novels,[15] but the Christianity of its saving remnant is a peculiarly domestic religion. The only place of worship we see the characters enter is a household chapel, and the novel's theological debate begins when Fanny laments the discontinued custom of family prayer: 'There is something in a chapel and chaplain so much in character with a great house, with one's ideas of what such a household should be!' (p. 86). Fanny's sense of the sacred is typically rooted in domestic ground, and to her way of thinking, the collective disciplines of large households and of religious practice are naturally linked. As Sir Thomas's later defence of the resident clergy also suggests, religion seems to flourish best in a fixed and local space. Nineteenth-century anthropologists might sharply distinguish the modern, universalist impulses of Christianity from the ancients' worship of family, place, and local gods, but the spiritual emotions with which Fanny and Edmund are associated have much in common with that ancient faith.[16] Of course it is precisely because the current generation at Sotherton no longer frequents the household chapel that Fanny has been moved to invoke the older ways; the awareness of change typically prompts the celebration of domestic ritual. Mary Crawford, in contrast, presumably gives voice to the restless, individualistic spirit of Sotherton's contemporary inhabitants when she replies that 'it is safer to leave people to their own devices on such subjects. Every body likes to go their own way. ...' (p. 87). Mary speaks for the modern temper; but Fanny, like the novel as a whole, sets herself against the tide of history – almost, in fact, against the very idea of time and change.

Paul Tillich's suggestion that 'a non-historical interpretation of history, even if arising in Christian countries, must return to paganism in the long run',[17] may help to explain why the Christianity of *Mansfield Park* so oddly resembles the domestic religion of ancient Rome. Commentators on the novel have often been troubled by what seems to them Sir Thomas's decidedly un-Christian response to his daughter Maria's fall. For the crime of adultery with Henry Crawford, Mrs Rushworth is apparently to be exiled from Mansfield Park forever. Though Mrs Norris 'would have had her received at home, and countenanced by them all', Sir Thomas 'would not hear of it'. Mrs Norris characteristically assumes that the problem is Fanny, but Sir Thomas

> very solemnly assured her, that had there been no young woman in question, had there been no young person of either sex belonging to him, to be endangered by the society, or hurt by the character of Mrs Rushworth, he would never have offered so great an insult to the neighbourhood, as to expect it to notice her. As a daughter – he hoped a penitent one – she should be protected by him, and secured in every comfort, and supported by every encouragement to do right,

which their relative situations admitted; but farther than *that*, he would not go. Maria had destroyed her own character, and he would not by a vain attempt to restore what never could be restored, be affording sanction to vice, or in seeking to lessen its disgrace, be anywise accessory to introducing such misery in another man's family, as he had known himself.

(pp. 464–5)

As Julia Brown has astutely noted,[18] this has a disquieting resemblance to the paternal conduct recommended by Mr Collins in *Pride and Prejudice*, when that cleric advises Mr Bennet on the elopement of Lydia and Wickham: 'You ought certainly to forgive them as a Christian, but never to admit them in your sight, or allow their names to be mentioned in your hearing.' The idea of permanently banishing one of the Bennet girls seems both menacing and absurd, but the exile of Sir Thomas's child is a sober necessity. Mr Bennet pointedly mocks Mr Collins's 'notion of christian forgiveness', and Elizabeth knows 'what curiosities his letters always were' even before she reads his solemn verdict that 'the death of your daughter would have been a blessing in comparison of this'.[19] But the comedy of Fanny Price's similarly drastic response to the 'disgrace' of Maria is far less clear: 'it appeared to her, that as far as this world alone was concerned, the greatest blessing to every one of kindred with Mrs Rushworth would be instant annihilation' (p. 442). The qualifying clause makes an orthodox concession, but as far as this world alone is concerned, Fanny's code of honour seems more Roman than Christian.

Of course Maria has committed adultery, not merely fornication; if her punishment is more severe than Lydia Bennet's, so is her crime. A different system of relations governs the later novel: *Mansfield Park* draws its boundaries more tightly than does *Pride and Prejudice*, and the transgressions it postulates are correspondingly more extreme. Indeed in a world dominated by worship of the family, adultery is the greatest of crimes, the most threatening violation of domestic purity.[20] Lydia Bennet can return to Longbourn a bride, her guilt at least papered over by marriage, but Maria Bertram must be exiled from home forever – lest 'a vain attempt to restore what never could be restored' only give further sanction to vice. Though Mary Crawford suggests that Maria might recover partial respectability through a second marriage to her seducer, Edmund indignantly dismisses such an alliance. But if domestic religion requires a strict ban on adultery, the corollary of that rule is a certain bias toward incest:[21] at the end of the novel, Fanny quickly passes from Edmund's 'only sister' (p. 444) to his wife. While Elizabeth Bennet comes to love and win a once-proud stranger, *Mansfield Park* rejects such cheerfully exogamous impulses in favour of an insistent endogamy. Anticipating both Fanny's marriage to Henry and her own to Edmund, the misguided Mary Crawford feels that she and Fanny 'are born to be connected' and will one day be 'sisters' (p. 359). But the novel's design is with Fanny, who has no intention of mingling Crawfords and Bertrams. 'Edmund, you do not know *me*', she silently addresses her absent cousin; 'the families would never be connected, if you did not connect them' (p. 424). Once they learn of the adultery, both Fanny and Edmund take for granted that no further connection between the families is possible. 'That Edmund must be for ever divided from Miss Crawford, did not admit of a doubt with Fanny ...' (p. 453). As for Edmund, though he formally repudiates Mary only when she attempts to gloss over 'the dreadful crime' (p. 457), he already arrives at their meeting 'regarding it as what was meant to be the last, last interview of friendship, and investing her with all the feelings of shame and wretchedness which Crawford's sister ought to have known ...' (p. 454).

It is precisely with such feelings of irremediable shame that Lydia Bennet's sister conducts what she imagines is her last interview with Darcy, tainted as she is by 'such a proof of family weakness, such an assurance of the deepest disgrace' as must divide her from her former suitor forever. But the plot of *Pride and Prejudice* operates by more accommodating laws, and the sibling's 'infamy' there works to unite the lovers, not to sever them. Elizabeth's very conviction that she has utterly lost Darcy forces her to recognise the strength of her feeling and prepares for his second proposal: 'never had she so honestly felt that she could have loved him, as now, when all love must be vain.'[22] Darcy's memory of his own sister's narrow escape from Lydia's disgrace, his realisation that his pride has kept him from warning others of the danger, prompt him to acknowledge an implicit kinship in the Bennets' shame – and to demonstrate his honour and his devotion by arranging for Lydia's marriage. Lady Catherine may fear that if her nephew in turn makes a sister-in-law of '*such* a girl', the shades of Pemberley will be 'polluted', but the chief function of her final pronouncements is to render all objections to the lovers' union absurd. In the closing paragraphs of the novel the narrator informs us that Lady

Catherine 'condescended' to visit the Darcys at Pemberley 'in spite of that pollution which its woods had received'.[23] Though Lady Bertram is also a figure of comedy, no such irony attends her view of Mansfield's vulnerability to pollution and the need of permanently barring her tainted daughter from the house. 'Guided by Sir Thomas', the narrator assures us, 'she thought justly on all important points' – one of which appears to be that Maria's disgrace can never be 'wiped off' (p. 449).


## MODEST FEMININE LOATHINGS

Fanny Price is the only one of Austen's heroines to have a childhood, and the account of her growing up extends over Austen's longest period of narrated time. Yet the Austen novel that most resembles a *Bildungsroman* proves the novel least open to real development and change.[24] When Fanny first arrives at Mansfield, her cousins make much of her deficient education; while they profess shock that she cannot name the principal rivers in Russia, the obvious irony will be that it is Fanny who has the least to learn. She may gain in assurance as she gets older, and we have Sir Thomas as a witness to her increasing beauty, but in character and judgement she is essentially formed from the start. Edmund receives credit as her mentor, yet theirs is a very different balance of wisdom from that between Henry Tilney and Catherine Morland or between Knightley and Emma. On all the most critical questions, whether of engaging in theatricals or of falling in love, it is Edmund rather than Fanny who must discover his mistakes. As he himself says after the catastrophe of *Lovers' Vows*, 'Fanny is the only one who has judged rightly throughout, who has been consistent' (p. 187). And in nothing is she more consistent than in her attachment to Edmund: Austen's narratives typically turn on the heroine's education in love, yet Fanny's romantic emotions virtually have no history. Her choice of Edmund seems fixed before such matters are ever consciously at issue, and it remains steadfast throughout.[25] Even when she is assiduously wooed by the novel's charming young man, it is not Fanny but Sir Thomas and Edmund who are nearly seduced by the performance. Like the flirtations of Willoughby, Wickham, and Frank Churchill, Henry Crawford's pursuit of the heroine serves as a lesson in proper judgement, but in this case the heroine herself requires no enlightenment.

Only while she is indefinitely suspended from Mansfield does
Fanny's firm verdict on Henry's character seem to waver, and the
novel as a whole appear to flirt with the possibility of significant
change. 'I believe *now* he has changed his mind as to foreseeing the
end', Austen wrote of her own brother Henry when he was in the
midst of the novel's third volume; 'he said yesterday at least, that he
defied anybody to say whether H.C. would be reformed, or would
forget Fanny in a fortnight.'[26] Yet this suspense does not yield to
new knowledge, but to acts that painfully confirm the old, and the
anxieties of time are abruptly concluded by the renewed marking of
exclusive space. The report of the adultery may nonetheless come to
the reader as something of a shock – but just because such plotting
so harshly insists that the promise of change was an illusion. Events
do not compel the heroine to grow; they simply drive others to
recognise what she has always been.

When Mansfield welcomes Fanny back, it is no longer to the
humble east room with its chilly hearth; the wicked aunt is van-
quished, the two older girls disgraced, and 'the lowest and last'
(p. 221) assumes her rightful place in the house. If Fanny resembles
Cinderella, as many have sensed, she is perhaps most Cinderella-
like in this – that hers is not so much a story of growing up as a
myth of recognition, a fantasy of being at last acknowledged for
the princess one truly is. In most versions of the fairy tale, the
heroine begins as an only and much-loved child; her rags and ashes
are a temporary debasement, signs of the humiliation she is forced
to endure when a stepmother and stepsisters invade her father's
house. At the crucial moment of transformation, degraded appearances are cast off as dirt, and the heroine reveals herself to be
worthy of a prince. Magic may transform rats into coachmen and
dirty rags into dresses of gold, but hers is the inherent virtue and
loveliness – and the small feet. When the glass slipper fits, even her
stepsisters are compelled to recognise Cinderella as the beautiful
lady of the ball. Cinderella may have dwelled among ashes, but the
dirt has not really touched her; in retrospect, she seems to have
been simply waiting to be discovered, her essential purity undefiled.
Indeed in a curious footnote to his lengthy discussion of the tale,
Bruno Bettelheim laments that by mistranslating the French
'Cendrillon', the English name for the heroine incorrectly associates
her with cinders rather than ashes – the latter being a 'very clean
powdery substance' and not 'the quite dirty remnants of an incomplete combustion'.[27] Though Bettelheim's etymology contradicts his

earlier stress on the importance of dirt in the tale, his insistence that the genuine Cinderella was never really dirty at all suggests how deep are the longings her story addresses.

Like 'Cinderella', *Mansfield Park* associates its heroine with dirt only to deny the force of the association. But unlike the fairy tale, the novel establishes her purity not by an outward, symbolic transformation but by an inner response, the experience of revulsion. Fanny visits her parents' home and finds it unclean – discovers, in effect, that she is not her parents' child. She cannot even stomach the food of this 'home', but must send out, covertly, for chaster fare: 'She was so little equal to Rebecca's puddings, and Rebecca's hashes, brought to table as they all were, with such accompaniments of half-cleaned plates, and not half-cleaned knives and forks, that she was very often constrained to defer her heartiest meal, till she could send her brothers in the evening for biscuits and buns.' As to whether nature or nurture has prompted such disgust, the text seems unable to decide. 'After being nursed up at Mansfield', the narrator observes on the matter of the puddings and the hashes, 'it was too late in the day to be hardened at Portsmouth' (p. 413). But only a chapter earlier, Fanny had felt a 'thrill of horror' when her father invited Henry Crawford to partake of the family mutton, since '*she* was nice only from natural delicacy, but *he* had been brought up in a school of luxury and epicurism' (pp. 406–7). The structure of the novel has made it impossible to determine whether Fanny could ever have thrived at the family table: though Fanny's Portsmouth origins were reported, her represented history only began at Mansfield, and it was at Mansfield that her appetites and affections were given narrative life. Even mother-love has long been displaced: embracing Mrs Price for the first time, Fanny sees features which she 'loved the more, because they brought her aunt Bertram's before her' (p. 377)!

By returning Fanny to her parents' house only when it is clear that she does not belong there, the narrative elides the most problematic interval in a daughter's history, that anxious period in which she gradually shifts her allegiance from one family to another. Fanny never really has to negotiate the passage that proves so dangerous for Maria Bertram; though she literally journeys back and forth between two houses, the sense of movement is largely an illusion. The transfer of its daughters' loyalties poses a difficult problem for any patriarchy, but the more the family is itself the locus of worship, the more critical is the transition, since to enter a new family is to adopt new gods. In the ancient world a bride did not officially cross the threshold of her husband's dwelling until she had first returned home to participate in a solemn rite of passage, a ceremony in which her father formally separated her from the paternal hearth.[28] The preference for Bertrams over Prices is also partly a spiritual choice, but when Fanny returns to Portsmouth, the anxieties of change are evaded by the foregone conclusion. Mr Price greets his daughter with 'an acknowledgement that he had quite forgot her' – and 'having given her a cordial hug, and observed that she was grown into a woman, and he supposed would be wanting a husband soon, seemed very much inclined to forget her again'. Fanny, for her part, 'shrunk back to her seat, with feelings sadly pained by his language and his smell of spirits' (p. 380). At Mansfield, Fanny had imagined that 'to be at home again, would heal every pain that had since grown out of the separation' (p. 370), yet no sooner is she confronted by the vulgar words and odours of Portsmouth than she automatically imitates Mansfield's gestures of exclusion. For all the naturalistic comedy of the scene, the division between father and daughter is scarcely less abrupt and absolute than in the ancient ritual. In fact this daughter's story has been so arranged that the normal separation on coming of age will never occur, since she was taken from her parents while still a child and will marry into the very family by which she has been raised. The Portsmouth chapters do not offer a history of the heroine's separation from her family of origin, merely repeated demarcations of a space that already divides them.

Though Sir Thomas deliberately tries to unsettle her, Fanny's instinctive revulsions continue to guard her from contamination. She may temporarily soften in her judgement of Henry Crawford, but she is hardly more tempted by his attractions than by Rebecca's hashes. Indeed the lines drawn by Fanny's delicacy are finally more to be trusted than the boundaries of Mansfield Park itself. The house and its inhabitants prove vulnerable to change and corruption, but the distinctions that should ideally be defined by its borders are grounded more securely in the consciousness of the heroine. If the limits of that consciousness may also occasionally be breached, the offending thought can be immediately swept out – as Fanny hastens to do when she once finds herself entertaining dangerous ideas of Edmund:

> To think of him as Miss Crawford might be justified in thinking, would in her be insanity. To her, he could be nothing under any

circumstances – nothing dearer than a friend. Why did such an idea occur to her even enough to be reprobated and forbidden? It ought not to have touched on the confines of her imagination.

(pp. 264–5)

The idea that has thus transgressed – that Edmund might be 'dearer than a friend' – has broken in only under the cover of negation, but the alert mental housekeeper has nonetheless quickly spotted it and rushed to remove it. 'It ought not to have touched on the confines of her imagination': like other spaces, consciousness maintains its own purity by shutting things out.

Those internalised lines in the heroine's consciousness, the limiting confines of her imagination, are most evident when she is contrasted with Mary Crawford, as Fanny's own meditation suggests. With the Crawfords' arrival, there are in effect two marriageable young women for the Bertram brothers, but Fanny believes that only Mary may be 'justified' in thinking herself so. As for Mary, she no sooner arrives at Mansfield than she begins to weigh the relative attractions of the elder and younger sons – and to assess the status of the potential competition:

> 'I begin now to understand you all, except Miss Price', said Miss Crawford, as she was walking with the Mr Bertrams. 'Pray, is she out, or is she not? – I am puzzled. – She dined at the parsonage, with the rest of you, which seemed like being *out*; and yet she says so little, that I can hardly suppose she *is*.'
>
> (p. 48)

Mary's question prompts an extended discussion of the etiquette of 'coming out', as the three young people consciously examine the problematic conventions governing female coming-of-age in their culture. As to the 'outs and the not outs', as Edmund somewhat impatiently terms them (p. 49), there would seem no question where Mary herself stands, having boldly introduced the subject in her very first recorded conversation with the Bertram bachelors. Indeed 'till now', Mary declares, she 'could not have supposed it possible to be mistaken as to a girl's being out or not', since 'manners as well as appearance are ... so totally different', and the moment many a girl crosses that imaginary threshold she abruptly abandons all previous reserve (p. 49). Tom Bertram offers in evidence his own embarrassments with a certain Miss Anderson, whose stony silence at one meeting had given way to boisterous aggression at the next. Though Mary deplores the awkwardness of such sudden transitions, she confesses herself unable to determine 'where the error lies'. But Edmund responds that 'the error is plain enough ... such girls are ill brought up. ... They are always acting upon motives of vanity – and there is no more real modesty in their behaviour *before* they appear in public than afterwards.' If modesty can be thrown off, apparently, it is not 'real': true modesty is a form of consciousness, not merely of behaviour, and the test of its existence is that it does not change. The genuinely modest woman would have no wish to behave immodestly even if she were free to do so – nor would she have any idea how to begin. Mary, however, significantly fails to understand him:

> 'I do not know', replied Miss Crawford hesitatingly. 'Yes, I cannot agree with you there. It is certainly the modestest part of the business. It is much worse to have girls *not out*, give themselves the same airs and take the same liberties as if they were, which I *have* seen done. *That* is worse than any thing – quite disgusting!'
>
> (p. 50)

By presuming that the only alternative to the girl who abruptly alters her behaviour when she comes out is the girl who acts immodestly from the start, Mary unwittingly reveals that she finds a modest consciousness unimaginable. All she can recognise is the difference in manners and appearance, the distinction between acting with or without restraint. Inner boundaries do not exist for her, and when she insists on returning to the problem of Fanny at the close of the conversation, it is only to settle the question in the most conventionally external of terms: 'Does she go to balls? Does she dine out every where, as well as at my sister's?' The answer to both queries being negative, 'the point' for Miss Crawford 'is clear': 'Miss Price is *not* out' (p. 51).

At the close of Edmund Bertram's last conversation with Mary Crawford, he turns to look back at her as she smilingly calls after him from a London doorway – 'but it was a smile', as he later tells Fanny, 'ill-suited to the conversation that had passed, a saucy playful smile, seeming to invite, in order to subdue me ...' (p. 459). Edmund walks on, and gives no sign. If it is perhaps too much to say that the scene suggests a prostitute soliciting a client, there is no question that Mary's equivocal placement and expression are the final emblems of her impurity, and that the impulse by which Edmund cuts her seems a momentary instinct of revulsion, an effort to avoid contamination.[29] By her willingness to call seduction and adultery mere 'folly' (p. 454), by her hope that the guilty pair might still join in marriage, even live down the scandal with 'good dinners, and large parties' (p. 457), she has betrayed her tolerance for unclean mixtures, the casual promiscuity of her mind.

What finally condemns Mary Crawford is no deed of her own, but the fact that her 'delicacy' is 'blunted' (p. 456) – which is to say that her consciousness fails to draw sharp lines of revulsion:

> 'She reprobated her brother's folly in being drawn on by a woman whom he had never cared for, to do what must lose him the woman he adored; but still more the folly of – poor Maria, in sacrificing such a situation, plunging into such difficulties, under the idea of being really loved by a man who had long ago made his indifference clear. Guess what I must have felt. To hear the woman whom – no harsher name than folly given! – So voluntarily, so freely, so coolly to canvass it! – No reluctance, no horror, no feminine – shall I say? no modest loathings!'
>
> (pp. 454–5)

Edmund's broken syntax, his hesitation to 'say', conveys its own modest reluctance. To allude to 'poor Maria's' crime is difficult enough, but the guilt of the adultress seems dwarfed by the failure of Mary Crawford to condemn her. What Edmund most hesitates to name is Mary's lack, that absence of 'modest loathings' which has left her mind 'corrupted, vitiated' (p. 456). Mary is 'spoilt, spoilt!' (p. 455) – or 'at least,' as Edmund conscientiously adds when he describes that last dangerously seductive smile, 'it appeared so to me' (p. 459). How Mary actually looked at him and how Edmund needed to see her cannot in the end be distinguished. Like the narrator's ironic allusion to Edmund's going over the story with Fanny again and again, that detail suggests something of the anxiety that may motivate such a vision, the very uneasiness that prompts one to see and reject the unclean.

## HOUSEKEEPING LESSONS

The most notorious crossing of a boundary in *Mansfield Park* occurs at Sotherton, the Rushworths' estate, past an iron gate that blocks a way from the wood into the park beyond. Mr Rushworth, betrothed to Maria Bertram, awkwardly returns to the house for the key to the gate, leaving Maria and Henry Crawford alone with the quietly seated Fanny to await his return. (Mary Crawford and

Edmund have already departed for a further walk through the wood.) Subject to the combined effects of Henry Crawford's stimulating flattery and Fanny's silent observation, Maria quickly grows restive. 'If you really wished to be more at large, and could allow yourself to think it not prohibited', Henry obligingly suggests, 'you might with little difficulty pass round the edge of the gate, here, with my assistance.' With an 'I certainly can get out that way, and I will', Maria plunges over and away, beyond the reach of Fanny's cautious protests (p. 99). The ingenious management of the scene has been much admired, as Jane Austen makes her imaginary estate the grounds of a lively allegory about female abandonment and restraint. But it is of course still more difficult to represent prohibitions – or to honour them – without the gates, walls, or ha-has which a Sotherton so readily yields. The true test of virtue in the novel is the internalised boundary, and the true heroine polices even 'the confines of her imagination'.

Such spatial frameworks, in all imaginings, tend to suppress or supplant temporal ordering. Thus the conversation of Mary Crawford with Tom and Edmund Bertram about a young woman's coming-of-age automatically becomes an exchange about the 'outs' and the 'not outs' – the speakers conventionally adopting a language which already translates temporal changes into metaphorical positions in space. This emphasis on space, and the boundaries of spaces, is finally what we mean when we think of *Mansfield Park* as 'primitive'. The parodic *Northanger Abbey* and the unfinished *Sanditon* are also fictions named for a special place, but no other novel of Jane Austen's calls such attention to its boundaries, emphasises so strenuously the line between the in and the out, the acceptable and the unclean. The opportunity of presenting a child's development and adaptation to new experience it vigorously converts into an opportunity for revulsion and drawing distinctions. The most religious of Jane Austen's novels – if that term can be used – is not as Christian as the vocation of its hero would lead one to believe. *Mansfield Park* concentrates not on salvation or final ends, but on place and guarded female consciousness. It lacks a Christian sense of history.

*Mansfield Park* has been called Jane Austen's 'Victorian' novel,[30] and I would like to suggest that what makes it seem Victorian, paradoxically, is just this archaic strain in its thinking. The domestic religion of the Victorians, the culture's anxious insistence on feminine modesty and even 'loathing', may be more general instances of Mary Douglas's rule that pollution ideas come to the fore whenever the lines of a social system are especially precarious and threatened. Austen's novel is worth comparing in this connection to a representation of a different kind, from the following generation in England. Sarah Stickney Ellis's *The Women of England* is another descriptive work that is filled with prescriptions. Like *Mansfield Park*, it offers 'familiar scenes of domestic life', but without the continuous action and specified group of characters of a novel. It is also professedly Christian, though the author apologises in her preface 'for having written a book on the subject of morals, without having made it strictly religious'.[31] Despite its avowals, that is to say, *The Women of England* is not so much an argument for Christian values as for cleanliness and order in the home and 'retiring shyness' and 'purity of mind' in the housekeeper. Associating 'good household management' with the 'wall of scruples' by which English women are guarded, Ellis characteristically links one form of cleanliness with the other, her language metaphorically identifying female purity and the sharp demarcations of domestic space. Women preserve the sanctity of the home, and that sanctity is above all a matter of boundaries: 'In short, the customs of English society have so constituted women the guardians of the comfort of their homes, that, like the Vestals of old, they cannot allow the lamp they cherish to be extinguished, or to fail for want of oil, without an equal share of degradation attaching to their names.' With a flourish of Podsnappery, she declares that 'in other countries' women 'resort to the opera, or the public festival' and carelessly neglect their homes, those other countries being 'necessarily ignorant' of England's 'science of good household management'.[32]

Ellis explicitly addresses those women who have only one to four servants and 'no pretension to family rank', but the domestic order she celebrates seems hopelessly beyond the reach of Mrs Price and her two servants; Ellis's household ideal is much closer to that 'cheerful orderliness' which Fanny, confronted by the chaos of Portsmouth and Rebecca, nostalgically attributes to Mansfield Park (p. 392). Though she would presumably have no more taste for Rebecca's cooking than does Fanny, Ellis has nothing but scorn for those homemakers who prefer the kitchen to the drawing-room and firmly disapproves of 'the constant bustle of providing for mere animal appetite'. The emphasis of *The Women of England* is on order, both outward and inward: 'Not only must an appearance of outward order and comfort be kept up, but around every domestic scene there must be a strong wall of confidence, which no internal suspicion can undermine, no external enemy break through.' What marks off the sanctity of home from the unclean world beyond is not so much a wall of stone or brick – or a gate of iron – as 'the boundary-line of safety, beyond which no true friend of woman ever tempted her to pass'.[33]

*The Women of England* has much to say of women's influence, their education, dress, manners, conversation, consideration and kindness, but it is virtually silent on the most obvious concern of all: women's role in childbirth and the rearing of children. The women of England play critical roles in the family – but primarily as sisters, daughters, and wives, rather than as mothers. So unequivocally do the walls of home exclude time, along with the unclean, that married women seem to have become sacred virgins, vestals to whom childbearing is apparently unknown. Nothing violates space like children, unfortunately – as Jane Austen, with her host of nieces and nephews and her relatively cramped quarters, must have been well aware. 'The house seemed to have all the comforts of little Children, dirt & litter', she commented sharply to her sister, after returning from the home of one particularly fertile couple; 'Mr Dyson as usual looked wild, & Mrs Dyson as usual looked big.'[34] And nothing more readily carries the imagination backward and forward in time as childrearing: to introduce children into the world is inevitably to confront the pressures of history. Like *The Women of England*, Austen's novels keep out children, especially from a heroine's future, and this exclusion is particularly apparent in *Mansfield Park*. The house at Mansfield has its 'old nurseries' next to Fanny's attic (p. 9), but there is no evidence that they will ever be put to further use. All the children of the novel, of course, are back at Portsmouth, where Mrs Price was experiencing 'her ninth lying-in' when 'her eldest was a boy of ten years old' (p. 5). Such a brood puts the dirt at Portsmouth in perspective.

'Poor Woman!' as Austen wrote to her sister of a similarly prolific acquaintance, 'how can she be honestly breeding again?' 'Poor Animal', another letter sounds the note of revulsion, 'she will be worn out before she is thirty. ... I am quite tired of so many Children.'[35] Children remind us that we are 'poor animals' caught in time, and whatever Jane Austen's private feelings about parturition, the form of *Mansfield Park* represents a response to anxieties that were not Austen's alone. Such anxieties are in some measure always with us, but the England of Sarah Ellis felt them with a particular intensity. The 'boundary-line of safety' around the women of England shuts out the 'field of competition' in which the men of England are engaged, that arena in which 'their whole being is becoming swallowed up in efforts and calculations relating to their pecuniary success' and in which 'to slacken in exertion, is altogether to fail'. In Ellis's sterilised version of sexual sacrifice, man needs 'all' of woman's 'sisterly services, and, under the pressure of the present times, he needs them more than ever', for sisterly services foster in him 'that higher tone of feeling, without which he can enjoy nothing beyond a kind of animal existence'.[36] Free of an 'animal existence' and its natural consequences, the relation of sister and brother is a purely structural as opposed to a temporal connection between the sexes – or at least offers the illusion of such a possibility. It is not surprising that the final marriage at Mansfield Park should assume this form. Edmund Bertram brings back to Mansfield 'my only sister – my only comfort now' (p. 444).

From *Representations*, 7 (Summer 1984), 133–52.


## NOTES

[The essentially anthropological model which forms the basis for Ruth Bernard Yeazell's approach complements the other sociologically oriented readings of Jane Austen in this collection. Like Edward Said's essay, Yeazell's discussion focuses on the spatial imagery which dominates *Mansfield Park* and concentrates in particular on the anxieties surrounding boundaries, both actual and symbolic, and the consequent moral implications of emblematic divisions. In this reading, the Christian world of rational argument, which critics such as Marilyn Butler identify as central to the novel's meaning, is reassessed against what Yeazell sees as an implicit paganism, which appeals to deep-seated, ritualised codes of behaviour, and which accounts for a fear of pollution. The examination of the imagery of dirt and disease relates the narrative tropes of the text both to archetypal narrative patterns and to contemporary social imperatives, and together these establish a framework for Yeazell's analysis of transgression. The discussion has elements in common not only with Said's essay but with the structuralist reading of *Persuasion* in Cheryl Ann Weissman's contribution to this volume, which also notes the correspondences between Austen's narratives and the structures and motifs of traditional fairytales. References to *Mansfield Park* are to the edition by R.W. Chapman, 3rd edn (London, 1934). Ed.]

1. Jane Austen, *Mansfield Park*, ed. R.W. Chapman (1934: rpt. London, 1960), pp. 439, 441. All further references to this work will be included parenthetically in the text.

2. Mary Douglas, *Implicit Meanings: Essays in Anthropology* (London, 1975), p. 51. The third chapter of this book, 'Pollution' (pp. 47–59), extends and refines the ideas advanced in Douglas's earlier *Purity and Danger: An Analysis of Concepts of Pollution and Taboo* (London, 1966).

3. *Purity and Danger*, p. 139.

4. D.A. Miller, *Narrative and Its Discontents: Problems of Closure in the Traditional Novel* (Princeton, NJ, 1981), p. 58.

5. Lionel Trilling, *The Opposing Self: Nine Essays in Criticism* (1955: rpt. New York, 1959), p. 218.

6. See in particular David Lodge's verdict – 'Jane Austen was neither a Platonist nor a primitive ...' – in *Language of Fiction: Essays in Criticism and Verbal Analysis of the English Novel* (London, 1966), p. 98; and Stuart M. Tave's extended discussion of the problem of the theatricals in *Some Words of Jane Austen* (Chicago, 1973), pp. 183–94. Tony Tanner, however, pursues the Platonic comparison in his Introduction to the Penguin edition of the novel (Harmondsworth, 1966), pp. 26–31. It might be noted that those who object to the allusion to Plato are critics especially attuned to the verbal texture of Austen's novels, while those who exploit the connection are more concerned with what might be termed the novels' deep structures.

7. Lionel Trilling, *Sincerity and Authenticity* (1971; rpt. Cambridge, MA, 1974), p. 76.

8. Alistair M. Duckworth, *The Improvement of the Estate: A Study of Jane Austen's Novels* (Baltimore and London, 1971), p. 57.

9. For Fanny as Cinderella, see D.W. Harding, 'Regulated Hatred: An Aspect of the Work of Jane Austen' (1940), rpt. in *Jane Austen: A Collection of Critical Essays*, ed. Ian Watt (Englewood Cliffs, NJ, 1963), pp. 173–9; C.S. Lewis, 'A Note on Jane Austen' (1954), rpt. in Watt, pp. 29–30; and Avrom Fleishman, *A Reading of Mansfield Park: An Essay in Critical Synthesis* (Minneapolis, 1967), pp. 57–69. Both Lewis (p. 29) and Fleishman (pp. 66–8) allude to 'archetypes'. Fleishman's entire chapter, which is called 'The Structure of the Myth', also evokes the work of Lévi-Strauss.

10. In addition to Duckworth, *Improvement of the Estate*, pp. 36–80, and Tave, *Some Words of Jane Austen*, pp. 158–204, I would single out Marilyn Butler's chapter on the novel in *Jane Austen and the War of Ideas* (Oxford, 1975), pp. 219–49.

11.  Stuart Tave, *Some Words of Jane Austen*, p. 185.

12.  Tony Tanner, Introduction to *Mansfield Park*, p. 27; Thomas R. Edwards, Jr, 'The Difficult Beauty of *Mansfield Park*', *Nineteenth-Century Fiction*, 20 (1965), 59; Julia Prewitt Brown, *Jane Austen's Novels: Social Change and Literary Form* (Cambridge, MA and London, 1979), p. 87.

13.  See, for instance, Kingsley Amis's notorious pronouncement that *Mansfield Park* is 'an immoral book' and evidence of Austen's 'corruption' in 'What Became of Jane Austen? [*Mansfield Park*]' (1957), rpt. in Watt, pp. 141–4. See also Marvin Mudrick's more subtle but nonetheless severely critical treatment of the novel's 'inflexible and deadening moral dogma' (p. 180) in *Jane Austen: Irony as Defense and Discovery* (Princeton, NJ, 1952), pp. 155–80. 'What imagination will not quail before the thought of a Saturday night at the Edmund Bertrams, after the prayer-books have been put away?' (p. 179).

14.  Thomas Gisborne, *An Enquiry into the Duties of the Female Sex* (London: T. Cadell, Jr and W. Davies, 1797), p. 174: p. 175. Jane Austen seems to have read 'Gisborne', as she called it; in a letter to Cassandra of 30 August [1805] she thanked her sister for recommending it and pronounced herself 'pleased with it'. See *Jane Austen's Letters to her sister Cassandra and others*, ed. R.W. Chapman, 2nd edn (Oxford, 1979), p. 169. Both Frank W. Bradbrook, *Jane Austen and Her Predecessors* (Cambridge, 1966), p. 36; and Marilyn Butler, *Jane Austen and the War of Ideas*, pp. 231–2, cite Gisborne's comments in connection with *Mansfield Park*.

15.  That *Mansfield Park* is the most religious of Austen's novels is widely taken for granted, despite the fact that many commentators no longer interpret her famous letter to Cassandra (29 January [1813]) as announcing that the subject of the novel was to be 'ordination' (*Letters*, p. 298). Several offhand, and frustratingly contradictory allusions to the Evangelicals in her letters have also helped to fuel much controversy over the novel's denominational sympathies. On the 'ordination' debate, see Charles E. Edge, '*Mansfield Park* and Ordination', *Nineteenth-Century Fiction*, 16 (1961), 269–74; Joseph W. Donohue, Jr, 'Ordination and the Divided House at Mansfield Park', *English Literary History* 32 (1965), 169–78; and letters to the editor of the *Times Literary Supplement* from Hugh Brogan, Brian Southam, Margaret Kirkham, Denis Donoghue and Mary Lascelles (19 Dec. 1968; 2, 9, 16, and 30 Jan. 1969). For discussions of the novel's relation to Evangelicism, see Avrom Fleishman, *A Reading of Mansfield Park*, pp. 19–40; Marilyn Butler, *Jane Austen and the War of Ideas*, pp. 242–5; and David Monaghan, '*Mansfield Park* and Evangelicism: A Reassessment', *Nineteenth-Century Fiction*, 33 (1978), 215–30.

16. See Numa Denis Fustel de Coulanges, *The Ancient City: A Study on the Religion, Laws, and Institutions of Greece and Rome* (1956: rpt. Baltimore and London, 1980): 'For us the house is merely a domicile – a shelter; we leave it, and forget it with little trouble; or, if we are attached to it, this is merely by the force of habit and of recollections; because, for us, religion is not there; our God is the God of the universe, and we find him everywhere. It was entirely different among the ancients; they found their principal divinity within the house. ... Then a man loved his house as he now loves his church' (p. 91). *La Cité antique* first appeared in France in 1864; though the publishers do not say so, the Hopkins edition reprints Willard Small's original English translation of 1873. It is difficult to imagine a nineteenth-century Englishman so casually dismissing the house as 'merely a domicile – a shelter'.

17. Paul Tillich, *The Protestant Era*, trans. James Luther Adams (Chicago, 1948), p. 20.

18. Julia Prewitt Brown, *Jane Austen's Novels*, p. 97.

19. Jane Austen, *Pride and Prejudice*, ed. R.W. Chapman (1932: rpt. London, 1959), p. 364; pp. 296–7.

20. Fustel de Coulanges, *The Ancient City*, p. 89.

21. Ibid., n. 7: 'Though this primitive morality condemned adultery, it did not reprove incest; religion authorised it. The prohibitions relative to marriage were the reverse of ours. One might marry his sister ... but it was forbidden, as a principle, to marry a woman of another city.'

22. Jane Austen, *Pride and Prejudice*, pp. 278, 279, 278.

23. Ibid., pp. 357 and 388.

24. Avrom Fleishman misleadingly insists on the need to recognise the novel as a *Bildungsroman*. See *A Reading of Mansfield Park*, pp. 71–3. Cf. A. Walton Litz, *Jane Austen: A Study of Her Artistic Development* (New York, 1965): 'Jane Austen took for the heroine of *Mansfield Park* a girl who is essentially passive and uninteresting, and in so doing she deliberately rejected the principle of growth and change which animates most English fiction' (p. 129). See also Lionel Trilling's resonant remarks in *Sincerity and Authenticity*: '*Mansfield Park* ruthlessly rejects the dialectical mode and seeks to impose the categorical constraints the more firmly upon us. It does not confirm our characteristic modern intuition that the enlightened and generous mind can discern right and wrong and good and bad only under the aspect of process and development, of futurity and the interplay and resolution of contradictions. ... It is antipathetic to the temporality of the dialectical mode; the only moment of judgement it acknowledges is *now*: it is in the exigent present that things are what they really are,

not in the unfolding future.' Trilling significantly terms this 'an archaic thought' (pp. 79–80).

25. Only Elinor Dashwood perhaps approaches such steadfast devotion, but in *Sense and Sensibility* Elinor's fixed position is counterbalanced by Marianne's dramatic capacity for emotional error and change.

26. Letter to Cassandra Austen (5 March [1814]), *Letters*, p. 381.

27. Bruno Bettelheim, *The Uses of Enchantment: The Meaning and Importance of Fairy Tales* (New York, 1977), pp. 253–4n. See also his subsequent note (pp. 254–5), which elaborates on the association of Cinderella with Vestal Virgins and once again stresses that ashes are a sign of purity as well as of mourning. For a brief and useful account of the many versions of 'Cinderella', see Iona and Peter Opie, *The Classic Fairy Tales* (1974; rpt. New York and Toronto, 1980), pp. 152–9. The Opies reprint the first English translation of Perrault's tale, published in London in 1729 (pp. 161–6).

28. Fustel de Coulanges, *The Ancient City*, pp. 34–9. 'This paternal fire is her [a daughter's] god. Let a young man of the neighbouring family ask her in marriage, and something more is at stake than to pass from one house to the other. She must abandon the paternal fire, and henceforth invoke that of the husband. ... Was it not quite necessary that the young girl should be initiated into the religion that she was henceforth to follow by some sacred ceremony? Was not a sort of ordination or adoption necessary for her to become a priestess of this sacred fire, to which she was not attached by birth?' (pp. 35–6).

29. In *Narrative and Its Discontents*, pp. 85–90, D.A. Miller offers a shrewd analysis of the 'closure practised' (p. 89) on Mary in this scene. Miller notes the partial detachment of the narrator from Edmund and Fanny here, and rightly observes that 'in the narrator's final wrap-up' of Mary's subsequent history, she is allowed to regain some of her earlier complexity (p. 87). That Jane Austen could imagine Edmund departing without even a word or an answering gesture is still something of a problem, however; the awkwardness, even the unimaginability, of the scene remains.

30. See Barbara Bail Collins, 'Jane Austen's Victorian Novel', *Nineteenth-Century Fiction*, 4 (1949), 175–85; and Julia Prewitt Brown, 'The Victorian Anxieties of *Mansfield Park*', in *Jane Austen's Novels*, pp. 80–100.

31. Sarah Stickney Ellis, *The Women of England, Their Social Duties, and Domestic Habits* (New York, 1839), pp. vi–vii. Mrs Ellis was already a poet and novelist when she wrote *The Women of England*. First published in 1839, the work was reprinted frequently during the following decade: the British Museum Catalogue lists a ninth edition, published in London and Paris, in 1850.

32. Ibid. Quotations are from pp. 32, 26, 33, 25.

33. Ibid. Quotations are from pp. 21, 37, 26, 32.

34. Letter to Cassandra Austen (11 Feb. 1801), *Letters*, p. 121.

35. Letter to Cassandra Austen (1 Oct. 1808), and Letter to Fanny Knight (23 March [1817]): *Letters*, pp. 210, 488.

36. Sarah Stickney Ellis, *The Women of England*. Quotations are from pp. 32, 48, 50.

# 5

# The True English Style

*MARY POOVEY*

Beside the charming, outspoken Elizabeth Bennet, Fanny Price holds little appeal for many readers, but as a response to the complex dangers threatening the values of traditional society, she promises a more convincing solution than Elizabeth Bennet could offer. For though Elizabeth's impertinence could be schooled into love, the individualistic energy she represented was ominously akin to one of the primary antagonists of social order. By contrast, Fanny Price is outwardly everything a textbook Proper Lady should be; she is dependent, self-effacing, and apparently free of impermissible desires. If so ideal an exemplar of femininity could be made both sympathetic and powerful, Austen would be able to demonstrate how traditional society could be regenerated from within its own values and institutions.

The necessity of moral regeneration is established by Austen's depicting the dangers threatening class society as more numerous and more potent than they had seemed in her earlier novels. In *Mansfield Park* the danger is not confined to a single avaricious male or to a female who indulges anarchic desire; instead, internal decay undermines the health of the landed gentry even as dangerous outsiders invade Mansfield's expansive grounds. In many ways, Mansfield Park seems a citadel in a turbulent world; compared to London or Portsmouth, Mansfield enjoys quiet and order, everyone has his or her own place and possessions, everyone is cared for, and the labour necessary to sustain this life goes on unseen, miraculously efficient and apparently part of the natural order of things. But in other ways the shadow of the outside world falls across

Mansfield Park more darkly than in Austen's earlier novels. Sir Thomas departs for Antigua and returns, a changed man, to a home strangely disrupted in his absence; Portsmouth, Fanny Price's birthplace, home of the twin spectres of poverty and selfishness, is an ever-present reminder of the past that was and the future that so easily might be; and London, with its casual morality and its confusion of rank, is always close by, always ready to disgorge more people like the Crawfords, hungry for whatever diversion the quaint country estate can yield.

The Crawfords epitomise the external challenge to Mansfield Park and the values it ideally superintends; for though Henry Crawford owns an estate in Norfolk, he does not fulfil his patriarchal responsibilities until love for Fanny inspires him to reform. He and his sister have been raised to practise London habits: they maintain that anything can be got with money and that morality is simply a matter of convenience or inclination, not of principle. 'Nothing ever fatigues me', Mary Crawford cavalierly remarks, 'but doing what I do not like' (p. 68). But the Crawfords are so openly welcomed to Mansfield that it is difficult to believe that this external threat is in any way decisive. Indeed, the secure, stable life at Mansfield has already begun to deteriorate before the Crawfords arrive. When the novel opens, the extravagance of Tom Bertram, heir to the estate, has already squandered his brother's patrimony (the Norwood living), and Tom's continuing thoughtlessness so undermines the family's wealth that his father must go to Antigua to shore up the family holdings there. Tom's general fecklessness also causes him to associate with decadent gentlemen like Yates, and it eventually leads to the overindulgence and fever that almost deprive Mansfield Park of its heir. The decay has not originated with Tom, however, for Sir Thomas has raised his children with an unhealthy combination of restraint and indulgence that has given them – especially his daughters – an idiosyncratic education instead of the principles of 'duty' they should have learned. 'They had never been properly taught to govern their inclinations and tempers, by that sense of duty which can alone suffice' (p. 463).

The threat to the traditional habits and values that had originally sprung from humanity's dependence on the land is posed most generally in *Mansfield Park* by an ethics based on convenience, ready cash, and individual pleasure. *Lover's Vows*, the play rehearsed at Mansfield in Sir Thomas's absence, brings together all the elements and agents of this threat and unleashes within the great house itself the anarchic energies that social conventions ideally restrain. The play itself, as numerous critics have pointed out, is an example of 'Continental political radicalism expressed in the conventions of sentimental comedy';[1] it denounces the entire upper class and substitutes for the values traditionally associated with the landed classes the morality based on individual desire that Hannah More so roundly berated. The rehearsals of this play at Mansfield liberate each character's repressed desires, preoccupations, or anxieties, and the fact that the anticipated performance necessitates physical alterations in the house, and the lesson that emotion, once indulged, will inevitably find an outlet, also point to the dangers this new ethic poses.

Austen's graphic depiction of the moral deterioration within the landed gentry suggests her growing awareness that she might need to create a family of readers with a common set of values instead of merely assuming that such readers already existed. To do so, she makes her heroine embody and enforce ideal principles and then humanises these principles so that they perfectly accommodate desire. Austen's goal is to make propriety and romantic desire absolutely congruent. By showing how self-effacement can yield self-fulfilment, she will imaginatively purge ideology of the inequities and self-interest that currently make the expression of individual desire dangerous to society as a whole.

One function of the novel's plot is to redeem propriety by distinguishing between conduct based on absolute, selfless principles and the superficial accomplishments that serve merely to display the self. In the contrasts she establishes between Fanny Price and Mrs Norris, Maria Bertram, or Mary Crawford, Austen is essentially exposing the fundamental paradox of propriety, separating its ideal substance from the surface that belies this substance. Fanny's grave self-effacement, for example – 'I can never be important to any one' (p. 26) – is followed immediately by the passive aggression that is its other face. 'What could I do with Fanny?' Mrs Norris whimpers. 'Me! A poor helpless, forlorn widow, unfit for any thing' (p. 28). Maria Bertram repeatedly proves that the 'duty' that Fanny so rigorously interprets is susceptible to a more 'liberated' reading. 'Being now in her twenty-first year', the narrator tells us, 'Maria Bertram was beginning to think matrimony a duty; and as a marriage with Mr Rushworth would give her the enjoyment of a larger income than her father's ... it became, by the same rule of moral obligation, her evident duty to marry Mr Rushworth if she could' (pp. 38–9). As skilful as Mrs Norris and Maria Bertram are at exploiting the paradoxes of propriety, their accomplishments are overshadowed by Mary Crawford's ability not only to use manners for flirting but to convince Edmund, the novel's sternest moralist, that her 'liveliness' and beauty merit their own ethical yardstick. Edmund reveals Mary's influence when he lectures Fanny that 'The right of a lively mind, ... seizing whatever may contribute to its own amusement or that of others, [is] perfectly allowable, when untinctured by ill humour or roughness' (p. 64).

When we see the hypocrisy that propriety allows so graphically demonstrated in these characters, and when we see its subversive potential explode in Maria's final revolt, we cannot help but contrast and prefer quiet Fanny's fidelity to a more rigid code of behaviour. But Austen does not propose so straightforward a reversal of 'accomplishments' into 'conduct', for neither the social implications of propriety nor its psychological function is so simple. Indeed, one of the most significant of Austen's achievements in *Mansfield Park* is the way that she uses psychological realism, briefly introduced in *Pride and Prejudice*, to explore the complex appeal and limitations of propriety.

Like *Sense and Sensibility*, *Mansfield Park* opens with a summary history that anchors the subsequent action. Here, however, the economic factors that affect the characters have much more extensively developed psychological implications, for the story of the ambitions and achievements of the three Ward sisters actively helps to explain the formation of Fanny Price's personality. In the background story, each of the sisters acts out one of the possible fates that romantic expectations can lead to in bourgeois society. One sister has 'the good luck' to succeed in the competitive business of getting a husband: she 'captivate[s] Sir Thomas Bertram, of Mansfield Park' (p. 3). A second sister, her expectations no doubt reinforced by her sister's success, 'had used to look forward to' a similar future of consequence and luxury, but her romantic expectations are frustrated by the cruel disproportion between promises and possibilities: 'there certainly are not so many men of large fortune in the world, as there are pretty women to deserve them', the narrator explains, and this Miss Ward is 'obliged to be attached to the Rev. Mr Norris', a man 'with scarcely any private fortune', but conveniently placed so as to benefit from Sir Thomas's patronage. The third sister – Fanny's mother – for reasons never extensively explored, completely rejects the romantic fantasies that have shaped her sisters' ambitions. 'To disoblige her family', she marries a man 'without education, fortune, or connections', a lieutenant of marines whose profession places him beyond the pale of Sir Thomas's generosity.

This brief history of the fate of romantic expectations provides the context in which we will eventually interpret Fanny's more modest desires. More immediately, it helps explain the origin of the defences that Fanny consolidates upon her arrival at Mansfield Park. Significantly, of the three sisters, neither Fanny's mother nor her patron aunt, Lady Bertram, proves as influential as Mrs Norris, the sister whose hopes have been thwarted by society's inability to satisfy the expectations romance has generated. 'Having married on a narrower income than she had been used to look forward to', the narrator explains,

> she had, from the first, fancied a very strict line of economy neces-
> sary; and what was begun as a matter of prudence, soon grew into a
> matter of choice, as an object of that needful solicitude, which there
> were no children to supply. Had there been a family to provide for,
> Mrs Norris might never have saved her money; but having no care of
> that kind, there was nothing to impede her frugality, or lessen the
> comfort of making a yearly addition to an income which they had
> never lived up to. Under this infatuating principle, counteracted by
> no real affection for her sister, it was impossible for her to aim at
> more than the credit of projecting and arranging so expensive a
> charity; though perhaps she might so little know herself, as to walk
> home to the Parsonage after this conversation, in the happy belief of
> being the most liberal-minded sister and aunt in the world.
>
> (pp. 8–9)

Needing to be needed, needing to express her 'spirit of activity', yet lacking any vehicle for expression more meaningful than accumulating capital or 'projecting' charity, Mrs Norris is a typical victim of the discrepancy between romantic expectations and social possibilities. Her irritating officiousness focuses this discrepancy, for it is really a woman's imaginative energy misdirected by her dependence and social uselessness. To the extent that Mrs Norris becomes an artist manquée, she does so because she has been deprived of an appropriate profession by the strictures society has placed on the very imagination it has aroused.

Mrs Norris arranges for Sir Thomas to adopt Fanny Price as a means of reinforcing what meagre power she has. For just as the office of patron flatters Sir Thomas (and thus indirectly enhances

Mrs Norris's value), so the activity of moral instructor reinforces Mrs Norris's tenuous sense of her own superiority – especially when the lessons she prescribes all project onto her little niece the worthlessness, inferiority, and indebtedness she is so anxious to deny in herself. Fanny's 'education' begins as soon as she enters her aunt's charge: 'Mrs Norris had been talking to her the whole way from Northampton of her wonderful good fortune, and the extraordinary degree of gratitude and good behaviour which it ought to produce' (p. 13).

The fact that Austen so fully details the origins of Fanny's timidity demonstrates how the behaviour associated with propriety can answer very pressing psychological needs. Young Fanny is effectively pushed and pulled into becoming a textbook Proper Lady. On the one hand, she is driven to self-effacement and passivity by Mrs Norris's admonitions about the 'evil' of ingratitude, by Sir Thomas's stern and wary disapproval, and by her female cousins' 'easy indifference'. On the other hand, she is drawn toward propriety by the only attention she receives – the indolent tolerance of Lady Bertram and the more discriminating approval Edmund seems to offer. What we later see of Fanny's first home in Portsmouth suggests that she has thus far received little attention or guidance. Thus, when Edmund begins to notice her and to initiate her education, Fanny is anxious to please – because pleasing Edmund accords her her only sense of personal value or success. Twice Austen informs us that, in every important respect, Edmund has 'formed [Fanny's] mind' (pp. 64, 470). While Austen only alludes to the actual process of this moral and intellectual education – we must understand it from the results it produces in Fanny's behaviour and from Edmund's discussion of the clergy at Sotherton – we can infer that its principles were strict and that Fanny has been carefully taught how to distinguish the 'conduct' that is the 'result of good principles' from mere 'refinement and courtesy ... the ceremonies of life' (p. 93).

Fanny's embrace of propriety is, therefore, intimately bound up with her defence against rejection, and it is likewise linked to her ideas about love. Even though she has never had the kind of romantic expectations that are her cousins' birthright, her greatest ambition still involves romance and love. For her, the ultimate reward of propriety would be simply to be loved by the man who has made her what she is. Yet, because she has taken her model of propriety not from other women or from books but from a man whose vocation incarnates absolute virtue, Fanny Price knows only one dimension of propriety. From her education by Edmund she acquires neither the superficial accomplishments her cousins perfect nor the knowledge of how to make propriety express the desire she feels. More specifically, in direct contrast to both Mary Crawford and her cousins, Fanny does not know how to make propriety express her sexuality and thus earn her the romance that is theoretically its reward. When Fanny's modesty and susceptibility finally do arouse a man's attention – and every moralist assured young women that these traits would produce this result – the poor girl does not know how to defend herself from Henry Crawford or how to make her real desires known.

In presenting the psychological and social origins of propriety and the costs that it can exact, Austen alerts her readers to complexities of the ethical code that the conservative moralists overlooked. But Austen does so in order to endorse this code; dramatising the emotional turmoil hidden behind Fanny's impassive face generates sympathy for the principles Fanny consistently struggles to defend. For, even more than Maria or Mary, Fanny is a character besieged by intense feelings; and, even more than Catherine Morland or Marianne Dashwood, she is a heroine of feeling. Numerous critics have commented on Fanny's sensitivity to nature and to art; throughout the novel her responses are a veritable barometer of the emotional undercurrents of the action, and her periodic outbursts of 'agitation' – whether induced by pain or by intense joy – mark the moral turning points of the plot. That for most of the novel only the reader recognises the extent and direction of Fanny's passion enhances our sense of her isolation and the complexity of what might look to her fellow characters like unyielding self-righteousness. Because we – and no one else – see Fanny's struggles to bring her strong feelings into line with propriety, we are asked to appreciate the difficulties of her task and thus to share in the triumph of her eventual accomplishment.

In order to give Fanny's feelings moral authority and power, Austen subjects her to two tests, each of which pits her hard-earned principles against what should be a bulwark of patriarchal values. In the first of these trials, Fanny must choose between the principles Edmund has inculcated in her and the love he has aroused. This test is particularly difficult for Fanny because, despite Edmund's initial severity, *his* principles have given way to love for Mary Crawford. The dilemma is brought to a crisis for Fanny by

Edmund's decision to act in *Lovers' Vows*. Fanny knows that she loves Edmund, and she knows that acting in this play, in Sir Thomas's absence, is wrong. Yet, so entangled are her 'disinterested' principles in all kinds of self-interested feelings and fears that, for a moment, we are allowed to glimpse the complexities involved in even the best of intentions. Realising that at least *she* will be spared the embarrassment of acting – but only because Mary Crawford has spoken in her defence – Fanny abandons herself to tumultuous emotions that border on self-pity:

> She was safe; but peace and safety were unconnected here. Her mind had been never farther from peace. She could not feel that she had done wrong herself, but she was disquieted in every other way. Her heart and her judgment were equally against Edmund's decision; she could not acquit his unsteadiness; and his happiness under it made her wretched. She was full of jealousy and agitation. ... Every body around her was gay and busy, prosperous and important. ... She alone was sad and insignificant; she had no share in any thing; she might go or stay.
>
> (pp. 159–60)

By this point in the novel, Fanny has become Edmund's conscience, a silent reminder of the principles he is now violating. But in scenes like this one Austen reminds us that, though conscience may be authoritative and even reliable, it does not take its stand without effort and pain.

In this case, and at the moment when her resolution is most hard-pressed, Fanny is spared, by Sir Thomas's return, from having to choose between love and principle. But in her second trial she *is* required to assert herself, and now against an even more intimidating authority figure. Just as Edmund allowed his passion to undermine his judgement, so Sir Thomas now lets his pride overwhelm his growing affection for Fanny. Henry Crawford's proposal is in itself easy for Fanny to reject, but disappointing Sir Thomas is extremely painful. For her fidelity to her feelings, Fanny is called 'self-willed, obstinate, selfish, and ungrateful' (p. 319) – all the qualities she has struggled to avoid – and she is exiled to Portsmouth, which has long since ceased to be her home. It is in Portsmouth, however, that Fanny finally begins to gain the same confidence in her feelings that Edmund taught her to have in principles. Empowered by her comparative wealth and stimulated by the 'potent' appeal of books, Fanny takes the initiative for the first time when she purchases a silver knife to resolve her sisters' quarrel. Feeling her love answered by Susan's gratitude, she is emboldened to undertake her sister's education: 'she [gives] advice' to Susan, as Edmund had once done for her, and she joins a circulating library to increase Susan's knowledge even more. 'Amazed at being any thing *in propria persona*, amazed at her own doings in every way' (p. 398), Fanny finally realises that she *is* important and that her deepest feelings really will point out her proper duty.

For Jane Austen, the 'heroism of principle' is the most important lesson of *Mansfield Park*. In the course of the novel Fanny must learn two things: to understand her feelings enough to be able to distinguish between selfishness and self-denying love, and to trust her feelings enough to be willing to act on them, even when they contradict more traditional, but less authentic, authority. Strengthened by the confederacy of principle and feeling, Fanny is ultimately able to superintend the moral regeneration of Mansfield Park; simply by the 'comfort' her quiet example provides, she is able to arrest the moral cancer that has spread from Sir Thomas's combined neglect and indulgence. Significantly, Fanny's prominence at the end of the novel is perfectly in keeping with what moralists described as woman's proper role: her actions are always indirect, and she finally engages Edmund's love, not by aggressively exposing Mary's treachery, but through the irresistible appeal of her constant love. Edmund is always allowed to sense his own superiority; his love for Fanny is founded on her 'most endearing claims of innocence and helplessness', and she soon grows necessary to him 'by all his own importance with her' (p. 470). Fanny also becomes a dutiful daughter to Sir Thomas – 'the daughter that he wanted' – a salve to his damaged ego and a 'rich repayment' for his initial generosity.

Through these two tests of Fanny's character, Austen effectively strips propriety of its potential for selfishness and its tempting offer of invisibility and crowns it with romantic love. As Fanny finally exemplifies it, 'the heroism of principle' is tough-minded and tender-hearted; its struggles and its victories are, in many ways, more difficult and more rewarding than those any contemporary moralist described. But it is important to recognise that Austen can engineer Fanny's triumph only by skilfully managing any trial that would actually pit Fanny's principles against feeling. To avoid such confrontations completely would be to undermine the authority that Fanny's arduous defence of principle has earned, but to dramatise them would be to risk losing the consensus about values that the action aspires to establish. Austen solves the dilemma by alluding to possibilities she never allows to enter her fictional world. For example, she informs the reader that, had Fanny's 'affection' not been engaged by Edmund, she would eventually have been 'persuaded into love' by Henry Crawford (p. 231); but Austen never lets the reader forget that Fanny's heart *is* prepossessed by Edmund, and Henry succumbs to Maria's wiles before Fanny's feelings square off against her principles. Similarly, Austen acknowledges Mary Crawford's powerful appeal; indeed, even Fanny feels 'a kind of fascination' for Mary's charms (p. 208). But Austen tries not to let our emotional response to Mary undermine the values that Fanny represents. Many of the narrator's overt comments underscore the contrast between Mary and Fanny precisely in order to reinforce these values: Mary 'had none of Fanny's delicacy of taste, of mind, of feeling; she saw nature, inanimate nature, with little observation' (p. 81). In order to ensure that the reader will censure this character who constantly threatens to escape narrative control, Austen awards the final, harsh assessment of Mary to the character who has most thoroughly succumbed to her charms: 'Hers is not a cruel nature,' Edmund explains, fumbling for a formula that will negate his love; 'The evil lies yet deeper; in her total ignorance, unsuspiciousness of there being such feelings, in a perversion of mind. ... Hers are faults of principle, Fanny, of blunted delicacy and a corrupted, vitiated mind' (p. 456).

A genuine contest between feelings and principles would finally challenge the power – and, implicitly, the moral authority – of Fanny's triumph. Austen therefore cannot admit into her fictional world any graphic dramatisation of the forces that made this triumph so contrived. Antigua and everything it represents – poverty, slavery, the challenge to authority that the slave uprising posed – all of these things remain distant, vague; Sir Thomas returns from Antigua chastened and changed, but we never know why or how the change occurred. Similarly, the 'guilt and misery' to which the narrator alludes in the final chapter are conveniently left offstage; Maria may suffer constant anguish, but her suffering is relegated to 'another country, remote and private', for Austen cannot acknowledge that the society she is so anxious to defend can either accommodate Maria's passion or punish it, remorselessly, forever. Finally, Austen alludes to but does not dramatise the complete disintegration of the family, the institution upon which her ideal society is based. The following narrative aside interrupts the description of the reunion between Fanny and William, for only their surprisingly resilient love can contradict the possibility that Austen's lament introduces. 'Even the conjugal tie is beneath the fraternal', the narrator tells us.

> Children of the same family, the same blood, with the same first associations and habits, have some means of enjoyment in their power, which no subsequent connections can supply; and it must be by a long and unnatural estrangement, by a divorce which no subsequent connection can justify, if such precious remains of the earliest attachments are ever entirely outlived. Too often, alas! it is so – Fraternal love, sometimes almost every thing, is at others worse than nothing.
>
> (p. 235)

If there were, finally, no family bonds, impervious to the effects of distance or time, there would be no basis for the society Austen wants to defend or for the consensus she counts on to anchor her moral and narrative authority. The notion that such bonds might disappear must be admitted in order to be emphatically dismissed by both the narrator and the novel's action; even the exiled Maria remains under Sir Thomas's protection, and, at the novel's conclusion, every character can be appropriately 'placed' for all time by the narrator. Indeed, in one sense or another, the whole world seems 'within the view and patronage of Mansfield Park'.

Ideally, the values epitomised by Fanny and centred in Mansfield Park will, by the end of the fiction, be shared by all of Austen's readers. To effect this consensus, Austen employs another version of the narrative strategy she used in *Pride and Prejudice*. Here, as there, most of the action is dramatic, and here, by manipulating sequences of perspectives on certain important events, Austen duplicates the interpretive freedom that she achieved there through irony. Thus, for example, when Edmund initially begins to love Mary, we are given the opinions of Edmund, Mary, and Fanny without authoritative narrative commentary. Similarly, the account of the ball that Sir Thomas organises after his return is narrated in turn by Mary, Fanny, Sir Thomas, and Edmund; and Henry Crawford's proposal is presented from the points of view of Henry, Fanny, and Sir Thomas.

In *Pride and Prejudice* ironic ambiguity is in the end dispelled by the narrative closure, and in *Mansfield Park* the relativity of multiple points of view is ultimately abolished by the prominence and authority Austen gives to Fanny's perspective. The episodes in which our correct judgement is most critical are all narrated from Fanny's point of view because, even before she has learned to trust her moral intuitions, hers are the standards by which we are asked to judge. For this reason, Fanny's perspective dominates the scene in Sotherton Park, the debate about the theatre, and the rehearsal between Amelia and Anhalt. Because Fanny participates in these episodes only reluctantly, if at all, the reader is protected from the dangerous emotional currents they introduce. Instead, because Fanny's emotional struggles are foregrounded, we are encouraged to exercise our imaginative sympathy in the cause of self-denying principles, not self-serving passions.

Austen also seeks to control the reader's judgement through her use of symbolism. Unlike Shelley's symbolism in *Frankenstein*, Austen's symbols do not multiply the diverse and sometimes contradictory interpretations an event or object may inspire. Instead, they multiply the contexts in which individual incidents or objects can repeat their single meaning. For example, the fact that William's cross will fit only the chain that Edmund gives her has the same implication for Fanny's life as it has for her choice of jewellery. Similarly, the key to the gate at Sotherton, the gambits in the game of Speculation, and the most elaborate symbol of all, the play-within-the-novel, extend their influence simply by virtue of the symbolic status Austen accords them.[2]

In spite of the strategies by which Austen tries to shore up her narrative authority and make Fanny's principles both imaginatively and morally appealing, many readers have found *Mansfield Park* Austen's most problematic novel. Part of the problem finally seems to stem from the inherent difficulty of distinguishing between Fanny's emotions, which are moral, and the emotions of the other characters, which often are not. Austen demonstrates that feeling is an extremely powerful force, but she cannot unequivocally grant or deny its inherent morality. We know that Maria's passion is uncontrollable and destructive, and we see Edmund's desire subvert his judgement; but when Mary Crawford is drawn to Edmund despite her coldest calculations, or when Henry begins to love Fanny in spite of himself, what value are we supposed to grant their affections?

The difficulty of determining the morality of feeling emanates, of course, from the fundamental ambivalence toward the individual that constitutes the heart of *Mansfield Park*. On the one hand, the moral regeneration Austen dramatises within the world of the novel is initiated by an individual. Indeed, Sir Thomas's climactic insight seems to ratify an ethic based on individual effort within an essentially competitive world: he realises 'the advantages of early hardship and discipline, and the consciousness of being born to struggle and endure' (p. 473). On the other hand, the materialism and ethical relativity that are the theoretical corollaries of individualism have consistently been shown by Austen to be dangerous – potentially subversive to the patriarchal authority and practical patronage that Mansfield Park ideally represents. The inherent contradiction of Austen's proposed 'solution' – individual reform, leading to individuals protecting society against individualism – is ultimately as disruptive to the ethical closure of the novel as it is inadequate to real behaviour in a real society.

A second factor that jeopardises the novel's didactic scheme is related to the nature of the authority that Fanny finally represents. In order to persuade the reader of the severity of the challenge to paternalism and its values, Austen must dramatise both the internal moral decay of the landed gentry and the powerful individualism of the Crawfords. But even though Fanny triumphs at the end of the novel, the qualities of passivity, reserve, and self-depreciation she embodies make it difficult to understand how she has overcome either the Bertrams' moral inertia or the Crawfords' anarchic power. Fanny emerges victorious simply because the others falter: Tom drinks himself into illness, Mary exposes her callousness, Maria seduces Henry, and Sir Thomas, in loneliness and despair, recalls Fanny to Mansfield Park. And Edmund finally falls in love with Fanny simply because she is faithfully, silently *there* when his feelings are in 'that favourable state which a recent disappointment gives' (p. 470).

These same qualities threaten to undermine our engagement with Fanny Price and therefore our acceptance of the moral authority she ideally represents. Only if we find Fanny's internal struggle more absorbing than Mary Crawford's energetic wit will we finally value self-denial over self-indulgence. The novel's point of view encourages us to identify with Fanny, but, because she is so passive, we are accorded no vicarious experience of the power her principles have to conquer anything but her own desires. In fact, our sense of triumph comes not from Fanny but from the tone and machinations of the narrator, whose vitality is far closer to Mary Crawford's energy than to Fanny's passivity. In other words, the imaginative energy that first encourages us and then enables us to enter into a fiction is defused by the passivity of the character with whom we are asked to identify. If our identification with Fanny *could* be rendered complete, we would – like Mansfield Park itself – be reformed by an internal agent (the principled imagination), not by an external and authoritarian teacher. But as long as her example contradicts the energy we seek and express in imaginative activity, it is difficult to imagine how Fanny might engage readers who do not already share her principles and priorities.

From Mary Poovey, *The Proper Lady and the Woman Writer: Ideology as Style in the Works of Mary Wollstonecraft, Mary Shelley and Jane Austen* (Chicago, 1984), pp. 212–24.

## NOTES

[Mary Poovey's feminist materialist analysis of *Mansfield Park* is extracted from her book-length study of Mary Wollstonecraft, Mary Shelley and Jane Austen, and these writers' complicated relationship with codes of female conduct which operated in late eighteenth- and early nineteenth-century English society. Poovey's focus on female propriety exposes the inherent contradictions of this concept: notably between the apparent status of the 'Proper Lady' and the simultaneous restriction of women's roles which denies them any real political power. The study is based on the model of classic Marxist critique which takes the view that all literature is implicated in the economic system that has produced it, and extends this to incorporate gender as a key item in that economy. Poovey's discussion of the three female authors identifies an ideological tension in their work, a tension between conformism and rebellion in a bourgeois system which establishes strict controls on women's behavioural codes. The essay concentrates on ways in which *Mansfield Park* negotiates these tensions so as to produce an acceptable resolution which will satisfy what Poovey sees as Austen's goal, the validation of a fundamentally conservative position. References to *Mansfield Park* are to the edition by R.W. Chapman, 3rd edn (London, 1934). Ed.]

[All references to the novel are given in parentheses in the text. Ed.]

1.  Avrom Fleishman, *A Reading of Mansfield Park: An Essay in Critical Synthesis* (Minneapolis, 1967), p. 27.

2.  See Lloyd W. Brown, *Little Bits of Ivory: Narrative Technique in Jane Austen's Fiction* (Baton Rouge, LA, 1973), pp. 81–96, and Alistair M. Duckworth, *The Improvement of the Estate: A Study of Jane Austen's Novels* (Baltimore, MD, 1971), pp. 59–60.

# 6

# Jane Austen and Empire

*EDWARD SAID*

In 1902 J.A. Hobson described imperialism as the expansion of nationality, implying that the process was understandable mainly by considering *expansion* as the more important of the two terms, since 'nationality' was a fully formed, fixed quantity,[1] whereas a century before it was still in the process of *being formed*, at home and abroad as well. In *Physics and Politics* (1887) Walter Bagehot speaks with extraordinary relevance of 'nation-making'. Between France and Britain in the late eighteenth century there were two contests: the battle for strategic gains abroad – in India, the Nile delta, the Western Hemisphere – and the battle for a triumphant nationality. Both battles contrast 'Englishness' with 'the French', and no matter how intimate and closeted the supposed English or French 'essence' appears to be, it was almost always thought of as being (as opposed to already) made, and being fought out with the other great competitor. Thackeray's Becky Sharp, for example, is as much an upstart as she is because of her half-French heritage. Earlier in the century, the upright abolitionist posture of Wilberforce and his allies developed partly out of a desire to make life harder for French hegemony in the Antilles.[2]

These considerations suddenly provide a fascinatingly expanded dimension to *Mansfield Park* (1814), the most explicit in its ideological and moral affirmations of Austen's novels. Raymond Williams once again is in general dead right: Austen's novels express an 'attainable quality of life', in money and property acquired, moral discriminations made, the right choices put in place, the correct 'improvements' implemented, the finely nuanced language affirmed and classified. Yet, Williams continues,

> What [Cobbett] names, riding past on the road, are classes. Jane Austen, from inside the houses, can never see that, for all the intricacy of her social description. All her discrimination is, understandably, internal and exclusive. She is concerned with the conduct of people who, in the complications of improvement, are repeatedly trying to make themselves into a class. But where only one class is seen, no classes are seen.[3]

As a general description of how Austen manages to elevate certain 'moral discriminations' into 'an independent value', this is excellent. Where *Mansfield Park* is concerned, however, a good deal more needs to be said, giving greater explicitness and width to Williams's survey. Perhaps then Austen, and indeed, pre-imperialist novels generally, will appear to be more implicated in the rationale for imperialist expansion than at first sight they have been.

After Lukács and Proust, we have become so accustomed to thinking of the novel's plot and structure as constituted mainly by temporality that we have overlooked the function of space, geography, and location. For it is not only the very young Stephen Dedalus, but every other young protagonist before him as well, who sees himself in a widening spiral at home, in Ireland, in the world. Like many other novels, *Mansfield Park* is very precisely about a series of both small and large dislocations and relocations in space that occur before, at the end of the novel, Fanny Price, the niece, becomes the spiritual mistress of Mansfield Park. And that place itself is located by Austen at the centre of an arc of interests and concerns spanning the hemisphere, two major seas, and four continents.

As in Austen's other novels, the central group that finally emerges with marriage and property 'ordained' is not based exclusively upon blood. Her novel enacts the disaffiliation (in the literal sense) of some members of a family, and the affiliation between others and one or two chosen and tested outsiders: in other words, blood relationships are not enough to assure continuity, hierarchy, authority, both domestic and international. Thus Fanny Price – the poor niece, the orphaned child from the outlying city of Portsmouth, the neglected, demure, and upright wallflower – gradually acquires a status commensurate with, even superior to, that of most of her more fortunate relatives. In this pattern of affiliation and in her assumption of authority, Fanny Price is relatively passive. She resists the misdemeanours and the importunings of others, and very occasionally she ventures actions on her own: all in all, though, one has the impression that Austen has designs for her that Fanny herself can scarcely comprehend, just as throughout the novel Fanny is thought of by everyone as 'comfort' and 'acquisition' despite herself. Like Kipling's Kim O'Hara, Fanny is both device and instrument in a larger pattern, as well as a fully fledged novelistic character.

Fanny, like Kim, requires direction, requires the patronage and outside authority that her own impoverished experience cannot provide. Her conscious connections are to some people and to some places, but the novel reveals other connections of which she has faint glimmerings that nevertheless demand her presence and service. She comes into a situation that opens with an intricate set of moves which, taken together, demand sorting out, adjustment, and rearrangement. Sir Thomas Bertram has been captivated by one Ward sister, the others have not done well, and 'an absolute breach' opens up; their 'circles were so distinct', the distances between them so great that they have been out of touch for eleven years; fallen on hard times, the Prices seek out the Bertrams. Gradually, and even though she is not the eldest, Fanny becomes the focus of attention as she is sent to Mansfield Park, there to begin her new life. Similarly, the Bertrams have given up London (the result of Lady Bertram's 'little ill health and a great deal of indolence') and come to reside entirely in the country.

What sustains this life materially is the Bertram estate in Antigua, which is not doing well. Austen takes pains to show us two apparently disparate but actually convergent processes: the growth of Fanny's importance to the Bertrams' economy, including Antigua, and Fanny's own steadfastness in the face of numerous challenges, threats, and surprises. In both, Austen's imagination works with a steel-like rigour through a mode that we might call geographical and spatial clarification. Fanny's ignorance when she arrives at Mansfield as a frightened ten-year-old is signified by her inability to 'put the map of Europe together', and for much of the first half of the novel the action is concerned with a whole range of issues whose common denominator, misused or misunderstood, is space: not only is Sir Thomas in Antigua to make things better there and at home, but at Mansfield Park, Fanny, Edmund, and her aunt Norris negotiate where she is to live, read, and work, where fires are to be lit; the friends and cousins concern themselves with the improvement of estates, and the importance of chapels (i.e. religious authority) to domesticity is envisioned and debated. When, as a device for stirring things up, the Crawfords suggest a play (the tinge of France that hangs a little suspiciously over their background is significant), Fanny's discomfiture is polarisingly acute. She cannot participate, cannot easily accept that rooms for living are turned into theatrical space, although, with all its confusion of roles and purposes, the play, Kotzebue's *Lovers' Vows*, is prepared for anyway.

We are to surmise, I think, that while Sir Thomas is away tending his colonial garden, a number of inevitable mismeasurements (explicitly associated with feminine 'lawlessness') will occur. These are apparent not only in innocent strolls by the three pairs of young friends through a park, in which people lose and catch sight of one another unexpectedly, but most clearly in the various flirtations and engagements between the young men and women left without true parental authority, Lady Bertram being indifferent, Mrs Norris unsuitable. There is sparring, innuendo, perilous taking on of roles: all of this of course crystallises in preparations for the play, in which something dangerously close to libertinage is about to be (but never is) enacted. Fanny, whose earlier sense of alienation, distance, and fear derives from her first uprooting, now becomes a sort of surrogate conscience about what is right and how far is too much. Yet she has no power to implement her uneasy awareness, and until Sir Thomas suddenly returns from 'abroad', the rudderless drift continues.

When he does appear, preparations for the play are immediately stopped, and in a passage remarkable for its executive dispatch, Austen narrates the re-establishment of Sir Thomas's local rule:

> It was a busy morning with him. Conversation with any of them occupied but a small part of it. He had to reinstate himself in all the wonted concerns of his Mansfield life, to see his steward and his bailiff – to examine and compute – and, in the intervals of business, to walk into his stables and his gardens, and nearest plantations; but active and methodical, he had not only done all this before he resumed his seat as master of the house at dinner, he had also set the carpenter to work in pulling down what had been so lately put up in the billiard room, and given the scene painter his dismissal, long enough to justify the pleasing belief of his being then at least as far off as Northampton. The scene painter was gone, having spoilt only

the floor of one room, ruined all the coachman's sponges, and made five of the under-servants idle and dissatisfied; and Sir Thomas was in hopes that another day or two would suffice to wipe away every outward memento of what had been, even to the destruction of every unbound copy of 'Lovers' Vows' in the house, for he was burning all that met his eye.

(p. 206)

The force of this paragraph is unmistakable. Not only is this a Crusoe setting things in order: it is also an early Protestant eliminating all traces of frivolous behaviour. There is nothing in *Mansfield Park* that would contradict us, however, were we to assume that Sir Thomas does exactly the same things – on a larger scale – in his Antigua 'plantations'. Whatever was wrong there – and the internal evidence garnered by Warren Roberts suggests that economic depression, slavery, and competition with France were at issue[4] – Sir Thomas was able to fix, thereby maintaining his control over his colonial domain. More clearly than anywhere else in her fiction, Austen here synchronises domestic with international authority, making it plain that the values associated with such higher things as ordination, law, and propriety must be grounded firmly in actual rule over and possession of territory. She sees clearly that to hold and rule Mansfield Park is to hold and rule an imperial estate in close, not to say inevitable association with it. What assures the domestic tranquillity and attractive harmony of one is the productivity and regulated discipline of the other.

Before both can be fully secured, however, Fanny must become more actively involved in the unfolding action. From frightened and often victimised poor relation she is gradually transformed into a directly participating member of the Bertram household at Mansfield Park. For this, I believe, Austen designed the second part of the book, which contains not only the failure of the Edmund–Mary Crawford romance as well as the disgraceful profligacy of Lydia and Henry Crawford, but Fanny Price's rediscovery and rejection of her Portsmouth home, the injury and incapacitation of Tom Bertram (the eldest son), the launching of William Price's naval career. This entire ensemble of relationships and events is finally capped with Edmund's marriage to Fanny, whose place in Lady Bertram's household is taken by Susan Price, her sister. It is no exaggeration to interpret the concluding sections of *Mansfield Park* as the coronation of an arguably unnatural (or at very least, illogical) principle at the heart of a desired English order. The audacity of Austen's vision is disguised a little by her voice, which despite its occasional archness is understated and notably modest. But we should not misconstrue the limited references to the outside world, her lightly stressed allusions to work, process, and class, her apparent ability to abstract (in Raymond Williams' phrase) 'an everyday uncompromising morality which is in the end separable from its social basis'. In fact Austen is far less diffident, far more severe.

The clues are to be found in Fanny, or rather in how rigorously we are able to consider her. True, her visit to her original Portsmouth home, where her immediate family still resides, upsets the aesthetic and emotional balance she has become accustomed to at Mansfield Park, and true she has begun to take its wonderful luxuries for granted, even as being essential. These are fairly routine and natural consequences of getting used to a new place. But Austen is talking about two other matters we must not mistake. One is Fanny's newly enlarged sense of what it means to be *at home*; when she takes stock of things after she gets to Portsmouth, this is not merely a matter of expanded space.

> Fanny was almost stunned. The smallness of the house, and thinness of the walls, brought every thing so close to her, that, added to the fatigue of her journey, and all her recent agitation, she hardly knew how to bear it. *Within* the room all was tranquil enough, for Susan having disappeared with the others, there were soon only her father and herself remaining; and he taking out a newspaper, the accustomary loan of a neighbour, applied himself to studying it, without seeming to recollect her existence. The solitary candle was held between himself and the paper, without any reference to her possible convenience; but she had nothing to do, and was glad to have the light screened from her aching head, as she sat in bewildered, broken, sorrowful contemplation.
>
> She was at home. But alas! it was not such a home, she had not such a welcome, as – she checked herself; she was unreasonable ... A day or two might shew the difference. *She* only was to blame. Yet she thought it would not have been so at Mansfield. No, in her uncle's house there would have been a consideration of times and seasons, a regulation of subject, a propriety, an attention towards every body which there was not here.
>
> (pp. 75–6)

In too small a space, you cannot see clearly, you cannot think clearly, you cannot have regulation or attention of the proper sort.

The fineness of Austen's detail ('the solitary candle was held between himself and the paper, without any reference to her possible convenience') renders very precisely the dangers of unsociability, of lonely insularity, of diminished awareness that are rectified in larger and better administered spaces.

That such spaces are not available to Fanny by direct inheritance, legal title, by propinquity, contiguity, or adjacence (Mansfield Park and Portsmouth are separated by many hours' journey) is precisely Austen's point. To earn the right to Mansfield Park you must first leave home as a kind of indentured servant or, to put the case in extreme terms, as a kind of transported commodity – this, clearly, is the fate of Fanny and her brother William – but then you have the promise of future wealth. I think Austen sees what Fanny does as a domestic or small-scale movement in space that corresponds to the larger, more openly colonial movements of Sir Thomas, her mentor, the man whose estate she inherits. The two movements depend on each other.

The second more complex matter about which Austen speaks, albeit indirectly, raises an interesting theoretical issue. Austen's awareness of empire is obviously very different, alluded to very much more casually, than Conrad's or Kipling's. In her time the British were extremely active in the Caribbean and in South America, notably Brazil and Argentina. Austen seems only vaguely aware of the details of these activities, although the sense that extensive West Indian plantations were important was fairly widespread in metropolitan England. Antigua and Sir Thomas's trip there have a definitive function in *Mansfield Park*, which, I have been saying, is both incidental, referred to only in passing, and absolutely crucial to the action. How are we to assess Austen's few references to Antigua, and what are we to make of them interpretatively?

My contention is that by that very odd combination of casualness and stress, Austen reveals herself to be *assuming* (just as Fanny assumes, in both senses of the word) the importance of an empire to the situation at home. Let me go further. Since Austen refers to and uses Antigua as she does in *Mansfield Park*, there needs to be a commensurate effort on the part of her readers to understand concretely the historical valences in the reference; to put it differently, we should try to understand *what* she referred to, why she gave it the importance she did, and why indeed she made the choice, for she might have done something different to establish Sir Thomas's wealth. Let us now calibrate the signifying power of the references to Antigua in *Mansfield Park*; how do they occupy the place they do, what are they doing there?

According to Austen we are to conclude that no matter how isolated and insulated the English place (e.g. Mansfield Park), it requires overseas sustenance. Sir Thomas's property in the Caribbean would have had to be a sugar plantation maintained by slave labour (not abolished until the 1830s): these are not dead historical facts but, as Austen certainly knew, evident historical realities. Before the Anglo-French competition the major distinguishing characteristic of Western empires (Roman, Spanish, and Portuguese) was that the earlier empires were bent on loot, as Conrad puts it, on the transport of treasure from the colonies to Europe, with very little attention to development, organisation, system within the colonies themselves; Britain and, to a lesser degree, France both wanted to make their empires long-term, profitable, ongoing concerns, and they competed in this enterprise, nowhere more so than in the colonies of the Caribbean, where the transport of slaves, the functioning of large sugar plantations, the development of sugar markets, which raised the issues of protectionism, monopolies, and price – all these were more or less constantly, competitively at issue.

Far from being nothing much 'out there', British colonial possessions in the Antilles and Leeward Islands were during Jane Austen's time a crucial setting for Anglo-French colonial competition. Revolutionary ideas from France were being exported there, and there was a steady decline in British profits: the French sugar plantations were producing more sugar at less cost. However, slave rebellions in and out of Haiti were incapacitating France and spurring British interests to intervene more directly and to gain greater local power. Still, compared with its earlier prominence for the home market, British Caribbean sugar production in the nineteenth century had to compete with alternative sugar-cane supplies in Brazil and Mauritius, the emergence of a European beet-sugar industry, and the gradual dominance of free-trade ideology and practice.

In *Mansfield Park* – both in its formal characteristics and in its contents – a number of these currents converge. The most important is the avowedly complete subordination of colony to metropolis. Sir Thomas, absent from Mansfield Park, is never seen as *present* in Antigua, which elicits at most a half-dozen references in the novel. There is a passage from John Stuart Mill's *Principles of*

*Political Economy* that catches the spirit of Austen's use of Antigua.
I quote it here in full:

> These are hardly to be looked upon as countries, carrying on an
> exchange of commodities with other countries, but more properly as
> outlying agricultural or manufacturing estates belonging to a larger
> community. Our West Indian colonies, for example, cannot be
> regarded as countries with a productive capital of their own ... [but
> are rather] the place where England finds it convenient to carry on
> the production of sugar, coffee and a few other tropical commodities.
> All the capital employed is English capital; almost all the industry is
> carried on for English uses; there is little production of anything
> except for staple commodities, and these are sent to England, not to
> be exchanged for things exported to the colony and consumed by its
> inhabitants, but to be sold in England for the benefit of the pro-
> prietors there. The trade with the West Indies is hardly to be consid-
> ered an external trade, but more resembles the traffic between town
> and country.[5]

To some extent Antigua is like London or Portsmouth, a less
desirable setting than a country estate like Mansfield Park, but producing goods to be consumed by everyone (by the early nineteenth
century every Britisher used sugar), although owned and maintained by a small group of aristocrats and gentry. The Bertrams and
the other characters in *Mansfield Park* are a subgroup within the
minority, and for them the island is wealth, which Austen regards
as being converted to propriety, order, and, at the end of the novel,
comfort, an added good. But why 'added'? Because, Austen tells us
pointedly in the final chapters, she wants to 'restore every body, not
greatly in fault themselves, to tolerable comfort, and to have done
with all the rest'.

This can be interpreted to mean first that the novel has done
enough in the way of destabilising the lives of 'every body' and
must now set them at rest: actually Austen says this explicitly, in a
bit of meta-fictional impatience, the novelist commenting on her
own work as having gone on long enough and now needing to be
brought to a close. Second, it can mean that everybody may now be
finally permitted to realise what it means to be properly at home,
and at rest, without the need to wander about or to come and go.
(This does not include young William, who, we assume, will
continue to roam the seas in the British navy on whatever commercial and political missions may still be required. Such matters draw
from Austen only a last brief gesture, a passing remark about

William's 'continuing good conduct and rising fame'.) As for those
finally resident in Mansfield Park itself, more in the way of domesti-
cated advantages is given to these now fully acclimatised souls, and
to none more than to Sir Thomas. He understands for the first time
what has been missing in his education of his children, and he
understands it in the terms paradoxically provided for him by
unnamed outside forces, so to speak, the wealth of Antigua and the
imported example of Fanny Price. Note here how the curious alter-
nation of outside and inside follows the pattern identified by Mill of
the outside *becoming* the inside by use and, to use Austen's word,
'disposition':

> Here [in his deficiency of training, of allowing Mrs Norris too great a
> role, of letting his children dissemble and repress feeling] had been
> grievous mismanagement; but, bad as it was, he gradually grew to
> feel that it had not been the most direful mistake in his plan of edu-
> cation. Some thing must have been wanting *within*, or time would
> have worn away much of its ill effect. He feared that principle, active
> principle, had been wanting, that they had never been properly
> taught to govern their inclinations and tempers, by that sense of duty
> which can alone suffice. They had been instructed theoretically in
> their religion, but never required to bring it into daily practice. To be
> distinguished for elegance and accomplishments – the authorised
> object of their youth – could have had no useful influence that way,
> no moral effect on the mind. He had meant them to be good, but his
> cares had been directed to the understanding and manners, not the
> disposition; and of the necessity of self-denial and humility, he feared
> they had never heard from any lips that could profit them.
>
> (p. 448)

What was wanting *within* was in fact supplied by the wealth
derived from a West Indian plantation and a poor provincial
relative, both brought in to Mansfield Park and set to work. Yet on
their own, neither the one nor the other could have sufficed; they
require each other and then, more important, they need executive
disposition, which in turn helps to reform the rest of the Bertram
circle. All this Austen leaves to her reader to supply in the way of
literal explication.

And that is what reading her entails. But all these things having
to do with the outside brought in seem unmistakably *there* in the
suggestiveness of her allusive and abstract language. A 'principle
wanting within' is, I believe, intended to evoke for us memories of
Sir Thomas's absences in Antigua, or the sentimental and near-

whimsical vagary on the part of the three variously deficient Ward
sisters by which a niece is displaced from one household to another.
But that the Bertrams did become better if not altogether good, that
some sense of duty was imparted to them, that they learned to
govern their inclinations and tempers and brought religion into
daily practice, that they 'directed disposition': all of this did occur
because outside (or rather outlying) factors were lodged properly
inward, became native to Mansfield Park, with Fanny the niece its
final spiritual mistress, and Edmund the second son its spiritual
master.

An additional benefit is that Mrs Norris is dislodged; this is
described as 'the great supplementary comfort of Sir Thomas's life'
(p. 450). Once the principles have been interiorised, the comforts
follow: Fanny is settled for the time being at Thornton Lacey 'with
every attention to her comfort'; her home later becomes 'the home
of affection and comfort'; Susan is brought in 'first as a comfort to
Fanny, then as an auxiliary, and at last as her substitute' (p. 456)
when the new import takes Fanny's place by Lady Bertram's side.
The pattern established at the outset of the novel clearly continues,
only now it has what Austen intended to give it all along, an
internalised and retrospectively guaranteed rationale. This is the
rationale that Raymond Williams describes as 'an everyday, uncompromising morality which is in the end separable from its social
basis and which, in other hands, can be turned against it'.

I have tried to show that the morality in fact is not separable
from its social basis: right up to the last sentence, Austen affirms
and repeats the geographical process of expansion involving trade,
production, and consumption that predates, underlies, and guaran-
tees the morality. And expansion, as Gallagher reminds us, whether
'through colonial rule was liked or disliked, [its] desirability
through one mode or another was generally accepted. So in the
event there were few domestic constraints upon expansion'.[6] Most
critics have tended to forget or overlook that process, which has
seemed less important to critics than Austen herself seemed to
think. But interpreting Jane Austen depends on *who* does the interpreting, *when* it is done, and no less important, from *where* it is
done. If with feminists, with great cultural critics sensitive to history
and class like Williams, with cultural and stylistic interpreters, we
have been sensitised to the issues their interests raise, we should
now proceed to regard the geographical division of the world –
after all significant to *Mansfield Park* – as not, neutral (any more

than class and gender are neutral) but as politically charged, beseeching the attention and elucidation its considerable proportions require. The question is thus not only how to understand and with what to connect Austen's morality and its social basis, but also *what* to read of it.

Take once again the casual references to Antigua, the ease with which Sir Thomas's needs in England are met by a Caribbean sojourn, the uninflected, unreflective citations of Antigua (or the Mediterranean, or India, which is where Lady Bertram, in a fit of distracted impatience, requires that William should go '"that I may have a shawl. I think I will have two shawls"'[p. 308]). They stand for a significance 'out there' that frames the genuinely important action *here*, but not for a great significance. Yet these signs of 'abroad' include, even as they repress, a rich and complex history, which has since achieved a status that the Bertrams, the Prices, and Austen herself would not, could not recognise. To call this 'the Third World' begins to deal with the realities but by no means exhausts the political or cultural history.

We must first take stock of *Mansfield Park's* prefigurations of a later English history as registered in fiction. The Bertrams' usable colony in *Mansfield Park* can be read as pointing forward to Charles Gould's San Tomé mine in *Nostromo*, or to the Wilcoxes' Anglo-Imperial Rubber Company in Forster's *Howards End*, or to any of these distant but convenient treasure spots in *Great Expectations*, Jean Rhys's *Wide Sargasso Sea, Heart of Darkness* – resources to be visited, talked about, described, or appreciated for domestic reasons, for local metropolitan benefit. If we think ahead to these other novels, Sir Thomas's Antigua readily acquires a slightly greater density than the discrete, reticent appearances it makes in the pages of *Mansfield Park*. And already our reading of the novel begins to open up at those points where ironically Austen was most economical and her critics most (dare one say it?) negligent. Her 'Antigua' is therefore not just a slight but a definite way of marking the outer limits of what Williams calls domestic improvements, or a quick allusion to the mercantile venturesomeness of acquiring overseas dominions as a source for local fortunes, or one reference among many attesting to a historical sensibility suffused not just with manners and courtesies but with contests of ideas, struggles with Napoleonic France, awareness of seismic economic and social change during a revolutionary period in world history.

Second, we must see 'Antigua' held in a precise place in Austen's moral geography, and in her prose, by historical changes that her novel rides like a vessel on a mighty sea. The Bertrams could not have been possible without the slave trade, sugar, and the colonial planter class; as a social type Sir Thomas would have been familiar to eighteenth- and early nineteenth-century readers who knew the powerful influence of the class through politics, plays (like Cumberland's *The West Indian*), and many other public activities (large houses, famous parties and social rituals, well-known commercial enterprises, celebrated marriages). As the old system of protected monopoly gradually disappeared and as a new class of settler-planters displaced the old absentee system, the West Indian interest lost dominance: cotton manufacture, an even more open system of trade, and abolition of the slave trade reduced the power and prestige of people like the Bertrams, whose frequency of sojourn in the Caribbean then decreased.

Thus Sir Thomas's infrequent trips to Antigua as an absentee plantation owner reflect the diminishment in his class's power, a reduction directly expressed in the title of Lowell Ragatz's classic *The Fall of the Planter Class in the British Caribbean, 1763–1833* (1928). But is what is hidden or allusive in Austen made sufficiently explicit more than one hundred years later in Ragatz? Does the aesthetic silence or discretion of a great novel in 1814 receive adequate explication in a major work of historical research a full century later? Can we assume that the process of interpretation is fulfilled, or will it continue as new material comes to light?

For all his learning Ragatz still finds it in himself to speak of 'the Negro race' as having the following characteristics: 'he stole, he lied, he was simple, suspicious, inefficient, irresponsible, lazy, superstitious, and loose in his sexual relations'.[7] Such 'history' as this therefore happily gave way to the revisionary work of such Caribbean historians as Eric Williams and C.L.R. James, and more recently Robin Blackburn, in *The Overthrow of Colonial Slavery, 1776–1848*; in these works slavery and empire are shown to have fostered the rise and consolidation of capitalism well beyond the old plantation monopolies, as well as to have been a powerful ideological system whose original connection to specific economic interests may have gone, but whose effects continued for decades.

> The political and moral ideas of the age are to be examined in the very closest relation to the economic development...

> An outworn interest, whose bankruptcy smells to heaven in historical perspective, can exercise an obstructionist and disruptive effect which can only be explained by the powerful services it had previously rendered and the entrenchment previously gained...
>
> The ideas built on these interests continue long after the interests have been destroyed and work their old mischief, which is all the more mischievous because the interests to which they corresponded no longer exist.[8]

Thus Eric Williams in *Capitalism and Slavery* (1961). The question of interpretation, indeed of writing itself, is tied to the question of interests, which we have seen are at work in aesthetic as well as historical writing, then and now. We must not say that since *Mansfield Park* is a novel, its affiliations with a sordid history are irrelevant or transcended, not only because it is irresponsible to do so but because we know too much to say so in good faith. Having read *Mansfield Park* as part of the structure of an expanding imperialist venture, one cannot simply restore it to the canon of 'great literary masterpieces' – to which it most certainly belongs – and leave it at that. Rather, I think, the novel steadily, if unobtrusively, opens up a broad expanse of domestic imperialist culture without which Britain's subsequent acquisition of territory would not have been possible.

I have spent time on *Mansfield Park* to illustrate a type of analysis infrequently encountered in mainstream interpretations, or for that matter in readings rigorously based in one or another of the advanced theoretical schools. Yet only in the global perspective implied by Jane Austen and her characters can the novel's quite astonishing general position be made clear. I think of such a reading as completing or complementing others, not discounting or displacing them. And it bears stressing that because *Mansfield Park* connects the actualities of British power overseas to the domestic imbroglio within the Bertram estate, there is no way of doing such readings as mine, no way of understanding the 'structure of attitude and reference' except by working through the novel. Without reading it in full, we would fail to understand the strength of that structure and the way it was activated and maintained in literature. But in reading it carefully, we can sense how ideas about dependent races and territories were held both by foreign-office executives, colonial bureaucrats, and military strategists and by intelligent novel-readers educating themselves in the fine points of moral evaluation, literary balance, and stylistic finish.

There is a paradox here in reading Jane Austen which I have been impressed by but can in no way resolve. All the evidence says that even the most routine aspects of holding slaves on a West Indian sugar plantation were cruel stuff. And everything we know about Austen and her values is at odds with the cruelty of slavery. Fanny Price reminds her cousin that after asking Sir Thomas about the slave trade, 'There was such a dead silence' (p. 213) as to suggest that one world could not be connected with the other since there simply is no common language for both. That is true. But what stimulates the extraordinary discrepancy into life is the rise, decline, and fall of the British empire itself and, in its aftermath, the emergence of a postcolonial consciousness. In order more accurately to read works like *Mansfield Park*, we have to see them in the main as resisting or avoiding that other setting, which their formal inclusiveness, historical honesty, and prophetic suggestiveness cannot completely hide. In time there would no longer be a dead silence when slavery was spoken of, and the subject became central to a new understanding of what Europe was.

It would be silly to expect Jane Austen to treat slavery with anything like the passion of an abolitionist or a newly liberated slave. Yet what I have called the rhetoric of blame, so often now employed by subaltern, minority, or disadvantaged voices, attacks her, and others like her, retrospectively, for being white, privileged, insensitive, complicit. Yes, Austen belonged to a slave-owning society, but do we therefore jettison her novels as so many trivial exercises in aesthetic frumpery? Not at all, I would argue, if we take seriously our intellectual and interpretative vocation to make connections, to deal with as much of the evidence as possible, fully and actually, to read what is there or not there, above all, to see complementarity and interdependence instead of isolated, venerated, or formalised experience that excludes and forbids the hybridising intrusions of human history.

*Mansfield Park* is a rich work in that its aesthetic intellectual complexity requires that longer and slower analysis that is also required by its geographical problematic, a novel based in England relying for the maintenance of its style on a Caribbean island. When Sir Thomas goes to and comes from Antigua, where he has property, that is not at all the same thing as coming to and going from Mansfield Park, where his presence, arrivals, and departures have very considerable consequences. But precisely because Austen is so summary in one context, so provocatively rich in the other, precisely because of that imbalance we are able to move in on the novel, reveal and accentuate the interdependence scarcely mentioned on its brilliant pages. A lesser work wears its historical affiliation more plainly; its worldliness is simple and direct, the way a jingoistic ditty during the Mahdist uprising or the 1857 Indian Rebellion connects directly to the situation and constituency that coined it. *Mansfield Park* encodes experiences and does not simply repeat them. From our later perspective we can interpret Sir Thomas's power to come and go in Antigua as stemming from the muted national experience of individual identity, behaviour, and 'ordination', enacted with such irony and taste at Mansfield Park. The task is to lose neither a true historical sense of the first, nor a full enjoyment or appreciation of the second, all the while seeing both together.

From Edward W. Said, *Culture and Imperialism* (London, 1993), pp. 99–116.

## NOTES

[Edward Said's postcolonial reading of *Mansfield Park* starts from the view that the world depicted in the novel is characterised by discourses of power, which reinforce internalised preconceptions about national, class and gender hierarchies. He argues moreover that the text draws attention to the sense of division which permeates it. Sir Thomas Bertram's position as a property owner both in England and in the Caribbean consequently becomes for Said a crucial signifier in determining the meaning of Mansfield Park and the question of its inheritance. Said argues that the book's concern with the condition of England, as exemplified by the internal debates about the status and role of Mansfield, can only operate in a climate which acknowledges the existence of a world elsewhere: in the novel this is underscored by the use of alternative, if not necessarily fully realised, locations, such as Portsmouth, London and the West Indies. This essay which, like Yeazell's, is concerned with the interpretation of spatial tropes, marks an important turning point in the critical history of *Mansfield Park*. It shows how a novel such as *Mansfield Park* can be transformed when distanced from conventional interpretative frameworks and reviewed from perspectives which themselves challenge Western ideological assumptions. References to *Mansfield Park* are to the edition by Tony Tanner (Harmondsworth, 1966). Ed.]

[All references to the novel are given in parentheses in the text. Ed.]

1. J.A. Hobson, *Imperialism: A Study* (London, 1938), p. 6.

2. This is most memorably discussed in C.L.R. James's *The Black Jacobins: Toussaint L'Ouverture and the San Domingo Revolution* (1938; rpt. New York, 1963), especially ch. 2, 'The Owners'. See also Robin Blackburn, *The Overthrow of Colonial Slavery, 1776–1848* (London, 1988), pp. 149–53.

3. Raymond Williams, *The Country and the City* (Harmondsworth, 1973), p. 117.

4. Warren Roberts, *Jane Austen and the French Revolution* (London, 1979), pp. 97–8. See also Avrom Fleishman, *A Reading of Mansfield Park: An Essay in Critical Synthesis* (Minneapolis, 1967), pp. 36–9 and *passim*.

5. John Stuart Mill, *Principles of Political Economy*, Vol. 3, ed. J.M. Robson (Toronto, 1965), p. 693. The passage is quoted in Sidney W. Mintz, *Sweetness and Power: The Place of Sugar in Modern History* (New York, 1985), p. 42.

6. John Gallagher, *The Decline, Revival and Fall of the British Empire* (Cambridge, 1982), p. 76.

7. Lowell Joseph Ragatz, *The Fall of the Planter Class in the British Caribbean, 1783–1833: A Study in Social and Economic History* (1928; rpt. New York, 1963), p. 27.

8. Eric Williams, *Capitalism and Slavery* (New York, 1961), p. 211. See also his *From Columbus to Castro: The History of the Caribbean, 1492–1969* (London, 1970), pp. 177–254.

# 7

# The Radical Pessimism of *Persuasion*

*JULIA PREWITT BROWN*

*Persuasion* is Jane Austen's most 'modern' work – perhaps the only novel that fully justifies F.R. Leavis's placing its author at the beginning of the modern tradition. In narrative mode, social view, and character conception, it marks a radical change from all that has gone before. Its debilitating ambiguities and hatreds, its conception of society, its surrender to disgust, take us through George Eliot and Henry James to, finally, the theories of Georg Lukács. For *Persuasion* is a novel as Lukács defined the novel: the epic of a failed world, or of the failure of the self to fulfil itself in the world.

*Persuasion* is the first novel by Jane Austen, for example, in which society is conceived of no longer as a meaningful whole, but as a series of disparate parts. Both *Mansfield Park* and *Emma* rely on an ethos of place for their sense of society; the organised propriety of Mansfield and the cooperative energy of Highbury provide each novel, and the characters in them, with a clear sense of context. But *Persuasion* is made up of a meaningless variety of places and the conflicting minor identities that attend them: Sir Walter's Kellynch Hall, Uppercross Cottage, Uppercross Great House, the Hayters' farm, the Crofts' Kellynch Hall, the various habitations of Lyme and Bath, and so on. It is perhaps for this reason that in *Persuasion* social structures are contemplated with almost systematic dissatisfaction. The society of *Mansfield Park* is an infected whole, but a whole nonetheless; its only virtue lies in its ability to provide some context for the individual. In *Persuasion* this last consolation has disappeared. The heroine moves from place to place, disoriented, isolated. Almost every community and form within which she functions is made meaningless by sheer disparity, or by the inevitable necessity of removal.

For this reason, Anne Elliot may be said to be 'alienated' – certainly the first heroine in Jane Austen to be so, and perhaps the first in English fiction. She passes beyond the mere loneliness of Fanny Price and the magisterial conceit of Emma, into an egocentric isolation very similar to that experienced by Dorothea Brooke or Isabel Archer. For Anne is genuinely estranged – overcome and enfeebled by her homeless condition. Her fate will never flow into the communities through which she passes, and her marriage signifies a movement out of the communities she has known. The navy represents the only adequate community in the novel, and Anne's final association with it provides the only antidote to what would otherwise be a completely private resolution or an exclusively lyrical finish. But the special status accorded to the navy is qualified by its precarious military destiny, as the last page of the novel suggests.

The robust security of *Emma*, written a few years before *Persuasion*, comes precisely from this safety from alienation, from its implicit confidence that a reconciliation between interiority and reality, between Emma and Highbury, is possible. The same may be said of *Mansfield Park*, whose reconciliation is actually enhanced by its joylessness. Its population purged and reshuffled, Mansfield finally opens itself to meaning, and the piteous integrity of Fanny Price is at last rewarded. Fanny had always struggled to maintain the connection between interiority and reality. (Compared to her, the Crawfords seem 'free', as indeed they are, because they have released themselves from the struggle.) Self-deceiving as she sometimes is, only Fanny probes continually: how much of what I feel or know to be true can I perform? For both Fanny Price and Emma Woodhouse the way is open to salvation, and through various comic and tragic struggles and sacrifices, salvation is attained: the embracing of an outside order that corresponds to interiority, and that therefore includes love. For the modern soul who seeks fulfilment in this correspondence with reality, as Lukács has said, irony must be the texture and form of his experience, but this irony does not compromise the ideal itself, which is the lived experience of meaning in the world. When the ideal is attained, as it is at the close of all Jane Austen's novels except the last, it is experienced to some degree by more than just the main characters; it is, or was, potentially accessible to all.

This belief in the possibility of common meaning and common destiny is greatly weakened in *Persuasion*. Unlike the conclusions of the earlier novels, that of *Persuasion* does not resound with other marriages, but rather with a series of failed unions. We do not feel that others will follow Anne into paradise. Even the marriage between hero and heroine has far less communal significance than those of earlier novels, for the navy is an accidental home for Anne, as Kellynch Hall is for the Crofts. The sense of impermanence felt in *Persuasion* anticipates the anxieties of many nineteenth-century novels.

The moral and aesthetic order sustained by Austen's earlier narrators, then, is no longer possible in the dislocated world of *Persuasion*. As a result, Anne Elliot – whose social circumstances make her a passive observer – almost becomes the central consciousness of the novel. Yet the transference of moral perception is never complete, because Anne is still too dependent on the various communities she visits. She can judge the Musgrove girls, for example, but not completely or absolutely (the way the authorial voice judges Mrs Bennet in the first chapter of *Pride and Prejudice*); Anne lives among the Musgroves and knows she lives among them. She is in a position to resist them in certain ways but not to decide against them. She is more isolated than the earlier heroines but still she must participate; she does not have the choices, say, of Jane Eyre, Dorothea Brooke, or Isabel Archer.

The opening portrait of Sir Walter is perhaps the best example of what Austen could do within the new mode of perception produced by the loss of a narrative frame. Sir Walter is inelastic, implacable, conceptualised. There is no air between him and the author's conception of him. He is a fixed image in the book, and Austen's genius makes him so. In *Emma* Austen explored questions of human nature in a Shakespearean way; in *Persuasion* her sense of the social world she wrote about had changed so as to make this approach impossible. The description of Sir Walter paging through the Baronetage in search of his own name and lineage, or contemplating his reflection in his mirror-filled room, is a psychological portrait of the dissociation of the self. Sir Walter is a man in search of an existence, in search of some exterior proof of his existence in the world. He derives his existence from the volume, and he bestows in it the existences of others. Birth, death, and 'heir presumptive' are recorded there. One of the novel's closing ironies is Wentworth's acquisition of an existence in Sir Walter's eyes: Sir Walter inscribes his name in the Baronetage.

The portrayal of Sir Walter is a social portrait of the dislocation of role. Role is the self's 'job', the self's direction, and Sir Walter fails in his role as the baronet of an estate. *Persuasion* deals with the crisis of separation between self and role in society. In an increasingly democratic society, such separations are inevitable as individuals assume roles they were not born to (the Crofts move into Kellynch) and lose roles they were born to (Sir Walter is forced to leave). The basic uncertainties in the novel separate it markedly from Austen's earlier works.

*Persuasion* is the only one of the novels that ends with a vague ignorance of where the hero and heroine are going to live, and even of what the years will bring for them. Wentworth does not have an estate, and the novel's close acknowledges the possibility of another separation to come (another war). The nature of society in *Persuasion* makes assurance about the future impossible, and there- fore causes a loss of personal assurance. (Uncertainty about the future is what leads Anne to reject Wentworth in the first place.) Unlike the earlier heroines and their lovers, Anne and Wentworth, or the love between them, lack the simplicity of will to overcome illusions and obstacles; they fail before the novel opens. Nowhere is Austen's irony more emphatic than in the beginning of her dénoue- ment: 'who can be in doubt of what follows? When any two young people take it into their heads to marry, they are pretty sure by perseverance to carry their point' (p. 248).

Let us now take a closer look at the social world of *Persuasion*. Actually the term 'social world' is slightly misleading. We can speak of the social world of *Pride and Prejudice*, of the Mansfield estate, of Highbury, but the world of *Persuasion* is made up of separate and divided communities of opinion and idea, of imagination and memory: 'Anne had not wanted this visit to Uppercross, to learn that a removal from one set of people to another, though at a distance of only three miles, will often include a total change of conversation, opinion and idea' (p. 42). From Uppercross she moves to Kellynch-Lodge, Lady Russell's house: 'When they came to converse, she was soon sensible of some mental change. The sub- jects of which her heart had been full on leaving Kellynch, and which she had felt slighted, and been compelled to smother among the Musgroves, were now become but of secondary interest. She had lately lost sight even of her father and sister and Bath. Their concerns had been sunk under those of Uppercross' (p. 124). And from Kellynch-Lodge she moves to her family's house at Bath: 'Uppercross excited no interest, Kellynch very little, it was all Bath' (p. 137). The only continuity among these worlds is Anne's consciousness: 'It was highly incumbent on her to clothe her imagination, her memory, and all her ideas in as much of Uppercross as possible' (p. 43). Only Anne is aware of the mental distance among the different locales she inhabits. This awareness above all sets Anne apart from the closed consciousnesses of other persons.

In the first part of *Persuasion*, until Anne's arrival at Bath, the separation of mind is primarily perceived as a separation of place. As Anne visits one house after another, she encounters different states of mind: Kellynch-Hall, Uppercross cottage and Uppercross Great House, Lyme, Kellynch-Lodge, and Kellynch-Hall again with the Crofts inhabiting it. At Bath all worlds seem to converge: the Crofts, Elliots, Musgroves, and Harvilles, and Lady Russell, Anne, and Wentworth all join there, and two figures out of the past, Mrs Smith and Mr Elliot, appear to make the convergence total. Yet the convergence is deceptive, and the geographical unity only serves to set off the actual disunity of the society. Distinctions of estate now become distinctions of street, as Sir Walter keeps reminding us. And the closer social milieu of Bath only seems to emphasise class distinctions in the minds of the people who live there. Elizabeth Elliot's unexpected invitation to Wentworth only confirms our consciousness of her conceit, for she is convinced that he will be flattered and grateful to receive it, just as she and her father are grateful to receive an invitation from the Dalrymples. Class snobbery is always criticised in Jane Austen, yet only in *Persuasion* is it presented with unrelieved seriousness and simplified disapproval. The Price family's relative poverty in *Mansfield Park* was clearly linked to their insensitivity. In *Persuasion*, Mrs Smith's poverty is more genteel than the Elliots' wealth; the snobbery that ostracises her is a destructive illusion. Similarly, Lady Dalrymple and her daughter, latter versions of Lady Catherine de Bourgh and her daughter, have an emptiness that is too offensive to Jane Austen to tempt her to treat them humorously, to allow them any eccentricity that could redeem their self-important mediocrity.

The sense of individuality gathers intensity throughout the novel, until at Bath all the characters are like so many autonomous beings, encountering one another with haphazard regularity, each expecting and seeing something unique to his or her self, each oblivious of the others. The reconciliation of Anne and Wentworth takes place gradually through a series of accidental encounters; that the proposal itself is spurred by an overheard conversation and realised in a note increases our sense of the tenuousness of human interchange. Even characters who pride themselves on their shrewd awareness, like Mr Elliot in his understanding of Mrs Clay, are always blind at some crucial point. Preoccupied with Mrs Clay's ambitions with Sir Walter, Mr Elliot overlooks her ambitions with himself. These disparities of view and personality are seen to originate in the disparities of age, experience, physical appearance, and family with which the novel is preoccupied. The narrative is saturated with allusions to differences between persons: Lady Russell's manners are old-fashioned and Elizabeth Elliot's are not; those who are in the navy see things differently from those who are not (even down to the painting of the ship that irritates Admiral Croft); those who are young and attractive are different from those who are not; Mrs Musgrove is fat and Anne, we are told several times, is slender. These details give *Persuasion* a dimension that is not felt in the other novels. *Pride and Prejudice*, for example, underplays all differences but those of mind; it opens with the disembodied voices of the Bennets. Physical differences, class differences, and so on are realised only in differences of state of mind. The same is true, though to a lesser degree, of *Emma*, in which communal interaction encompasses individual difference. In *Persuasion*, the individual is at once independent and estranged, looming and yet powerless.

The confidence of *Emma* in a stable, cooperative community is lost in the social and personal fragmentation of *Persuasion*. As a result, the heroine is far more uncertain. The ever changing egotism of the environment is too much for Anne to resist; hence her compliance with whatever environment or situation she is in. This compliance ranges from apathy (with Henrietta) to sympathy (with Benwick) to resignation (with her family) – all passive responses.

In discussing *Emma* I stressed the importance of the idea of cooperation in Jane Austen, and I pointed out that Austen saw a distinction between cooperation and compromise, restraint and repression, that we no longer see. This changes in *Persuasion*. Social cooperation assumes a stable community in which individual cooperation ultimately benefits the individual: Emma and Highbury go together. *Persuasion* does not have a Highbury at its base, a communal form with its own memory and imagination in which an

Emma could participate and thrive. Its heroine is the more uncertain Anne Elliot, who moves from community to community,
and who can only comply rather than cooperate. She is happy to be
'of use', which is to say that in the different environments she
enters, she is being used. The personal damage such a posture
incurs is fully realised later in the century by Henry James in the
character of Madame Merle. Madame Merle is another woman
whose life is a series of visits to other people's houses, and who by
necessity cultivates an ability to comply while preserving a secret
will. Anne Elliot's secret intelligence is far from the indomitable and
uncooperative will of Madame Merle, yet she too must live with
secret consolations: 'Anne always contemplated [the Musgrove
sisters] as some of the happiest creatures of her acquaintance; but
still, saved as we all are by some comfortable feeling of superiority
from wishing for the possibility of exchange, she would not have
given up her own more elegant and cultivated mind for all their
enjoyments' (p. 41). In statements like these Anne Elliot reminds us
of many nineteenth-century heroines. We think of her in these
instances almost as a 'case': an unmarried, unoccupied woman,
superior in mind and character to all about her, yet unrecognised,
unnoticed, and even shunned among them. In a reversal of the case
of Emma Woodhouse, Anne's situation defines her more than her
personality does. And that, of course, is her problem, and the
problem of so many other Victorian heroines.

Anne's consolation represents the Victorian (and modern) variation of stoicism. It is not the consolation we are asked to accept in
*King Lear*: that Cordelia's goodness is its own reward. Anne's protective conviction of her own rare 'cultivated mind' seems to state that
the burden of intelligence is its own reward: that the estranged
consciousness is better than the communal stupidity. This awareness
of the enforced isolation of the sensitive and thinking person appears
in the complaints of Victorian intellectuals. John Henry Newman,
who admired Jane Austen's novels, complained that the age was
becoming 'the paradise of little men, and the purgatory of great
ones', and Matthew Arnold complained in a letter to A.H. Clough
that the society was becoming 'more comfortable for the mass, and
more uncomfortable for those of any natural gift or distinction'.
Although both had in mind the decline in 'great careers' of men,
their sentiment is fundamentally analogous to Austen's intuition of
the burden that both the mediocrity and the discontinuity of social
life place on the intelligent and sensitive person.

This resentment of social life takes us back to the first half of *Sense and Sensibility*, to Marianne's Blakean exasperation with the insincerity of society. In the earlier novel, however, the burden is ultimately shown to have its source in the illiberal illusions of its sufferer, for several of the seemingly unfeeling supporters of society (from Mrs Jennings to Elinor) turn out to be sincere, while the romantic lover is actually shallow and worldly. In *Persuasion* suffering is also rooted in a particular weakness of the heroine, yet social life remains intolerable to the end. In its general structure, *Persuasion* registers a fundamental, almost Weberian crisis of belief in the legitimacy of social structures. Certainly one of the most radical statements in all of Jane Austen is Anne's subversive sentiment concerning her father's departure from Kellynch-Hall; that 'they were gone who deserved not to stay, and that Kellynch-Hall had passed into better hands than its owners' (p. 125). As Weber has said, established power is sustained only through a subjective belief in its legitimacy, through people believing it is legitimate and allowing themselves to be so dominated. Revolutions begin with a crisis of legitimacy. In *Persuasion* we see the beginning of a failure to support traditions, a failure that led to nineteenth-century reforms. The positive feeling toward the navy lies in its widespread invigoration of domestic life. In the words of Sir Walter, the navy was 'the means of bringing persons of obscure birth into undue distinction, and raising men to honours which their fathers and grandfathers never dreamt of' (p. 19). As the closing lines of the novel suggest, Austen rated the domestic advantages of this revitalisation as equal to the military achievements of the navy. 'Anne gloried in being a sailor's wife, but she must pay the tax of quick alarm for belonging to that profession which is, if possible, more distinguished in its domestic virtues than in its national importance' (p. 252).

These alterations in social life are perceived as transformations within and among families. As always in Jane Austen, the basic instrument of both division and unity is the family, of which marriage is the origin. Class feeling is an extension of family feeling, or pride of ancestry, as the opening of the novel makes clear. Jane Austen originally entitled her work *The Elliots*; her brother Henry changed it after her death to perhaps the more ingenious title. Yet the first title may hint at what Austen meant to explore: a family's mind and future. The culmination of Sir Walter's ancestral account is 'Heir presumptive, William Walter Elliot, Esq., great grandson of the second Sir Walter' (p. 4). The question of inheritance is central to many English novels and crucial to those of Jane Austen. Because she centred on the destinies of women, this question has been over-looked, together with her concern for establishing the difference between legal and rightful, between material and moral, in-heritance. In their concern with the passage of generations, all the Austen novels pose the question that Lionel Trilling perceives in Forster's *Howards End*: 'Who shall inherit England?'[1] In the opening pages we learn that William Elliot is the heir presumptive, but Mr Elliot's part in the plot is relatively insignificant; like all the novels, *Persuasion* focuses on the actual inheritors. Anne and Wentworth inherit the England of *Persuasion*, if only because they see it, and will experience it, as it really is: fragmented and un-certain. For the first time in Jane Austen, the future is not linked with the land, and the social order is completely dissociated from the moral order. William Elliot will inherit the improverished Kellynch, but that does not matter. The future is in the hands of Anne and Wentworth, as the present is in the hands of the Crofts, that almost comic national couple whose defence of England abroad makes them the rightful inhabiters of Kellynch. It is significant that to Anne the only temptation to marry Mr Elliot is that she would inherit her mother's position at Kellynch. Her rejection of him makes clear a distinction between familial and moral inheritance.

Anne's marriage to Wentworth represents an act of will to replace, through marriage, the old inadequate family with the new adequate family, an act that is at the core of the generational concept of every Jane Austen novel. The feminine conception of marriage, unlike the masculine one, traditionally assumes loss as well as gain, because until well into the nineteenth century only the woman left her family when she married; the woman also, of course, lost her name and assumed a new one. A basic movement in all Jane Austen's mature novels is the heroine's struggle to create a new 'family' for herself, to replace with a new relationship the unsatisfactory family in which she is unappreciated or unfulfilled. In *Persuasion* the sense of the pains of the original family is particu-larly keen. Sir Walter and Elizabeth's most serious failing is their lack of feeling for Anne. And Lady Russell's concern to see Anne married is analogous, in its awareness of the need for escape, to the concern felt for all the heroines after *Sense and Sensibility*. '[Lady Russell] would have rejoiced to see her at twenty-two, so respectably removed from the partialities and injustice of her father's house [through marriage to Charles Musgrove]' (p. 29).

In Jane Austen marriage represents a reorganisation of social life. Anne sees her marriage in part as the formation of a new social group, and regrets that in that respect she can offer so little: '[Anne] had no other alloy to the happiness of her prospects, than what arose from the consciousness of having no relations to bestow on him which a man of sense could value. – There she felt her own inferiority keenly' (p. 251). The marriage that ends *Persuasion* is viewed as part of the general revitalising of English society that took place upon the navy's return from the war.

The revitalising power of marriage is suggested in all the Austen novels, but most urgently, most despairingly, in *Persuasion*. In the earlier novels, marriage is linked to the general functioning of the society and to the land; marriage is a form of participation in society. In *Persuasion*, society no longer offers the couple a defined context for their adult identities; compared to Elizabeth and Darcy, Anne and Wentworth are directionless after their marriage. For this reason, the individuals themselves and the relationship they embark on carry a great burden. Marriage is no longer sustained by a larger framework; Anne Elliot will not receive the spontaneous social support and identity that Marianne Dashwood receives when, upon her marriage to Colonel Brandon, she finds herself 'placed in a new home, a wife, the mistress of a family, and the patroness of a village'.[2] Mary Musgrove 'would not change situations with Anne', for 'Anne had no Uppercross Hall before her, no landed estate, no headship of a family' (p. 250). Whatever social strength Anne and Wentworth's marriage possesses will be created and sustained by themselves. For this reason, the singular existence and quality of the marriage itself becomes vitally important.

It is the individual's lonely responsibility for his entire future that perhaps gives *Persuasion* its powerfully ambiguous mood. The closing marriages of the earlier novels seem to represent possibility more than necessity, a stage in the moral growth of the heroine, the nexus of generational change. In *Persuasion*, marriage between Anne and Wentworth is a matter of sheer need, the last hope for the individuals themselves and for the dissolving society around them. In the closing felicities of *Emma*, as I have said, we understand the different marriages through comparison. This statement holds true with a vengeance in *Persuasion*. Most of the major characters are literally or figuratively widowed; and among the complete pairs, only Admiral and Mrs Croft possess a moral existence. The only hope of the novel rests almost entirely upon two characters, Anne and Wentworth, who are alike in their superiority of mind and sensibility and yet are alienated from each other.

For this reason, the progress of Anne and Wentworth's reconciliation is fraught with tension and significance. All the novels are imbued with a tension between the pains of the present and the hopes of the future; and all implicitly contrast the lovers with the lesser world around them. The emotional intensity of *Persuasion* is heightened by the addition of another dimension: the past. Together with a sense of the isolation of the heroine, the use of the past is responsible for the intensity of feeling contained in the reconciliation of Anne and Wentworth.

Like *David Copperfield, Persuasion* poses the question: is the past a pain or a pleasure?[3] The pains of the present are rooted in Anne's past mistake, but so are the hopes for the future. The past seems to envelop the whole; we feel the hero and heroine are moving forward and backward in time simultaneously. This paradox lends the novel an urgency that is at once painful and hopeful. The exquisiteness of the novel's emotion, like that of Shelley's poem to the West Wind, lies in the consciousness that spring will come. Also as in the poem, this consciousness is held in check; it is realised only momentarily in Anne's feelings of fearful happiness. The dominant experience of the novel is one of loss; the movement, though urgent, is downward.

The mood and feelings imparted in the beginning of *Persuasion* – the sense of resignation and regret, the feeling of the inalterable circularity of time expressed in the seasonal imagery, and the inescapable redundancy of life expressed in allusions to the eventless years preceding the opening of the novel – gather intensity when Anne learns of Wentworth's return. Then very gradually Anne's despair is replaced by a desire to act; like the farmer ploughing the field, Anne finally 'means to have Spring again'. As this feeling grows, the sense of time lost and wasted becomes more intense. The hope for spring only makes the winter more acute.

Even though we know that Anne and Wentworth will be reconciled (either from previous reading or from romantic expectation) the novel seems to swirl downward to this conclusion. In the compression of events at Bath, there is a sense of rushing toward the reconciliation as though it were a last chance, as indeed it is. The grace of the language gives the novel an eerie quality because it contrasts so sharply with the separateness of events, the dislocation of characters. This grace may be why the novel is so frequently called 'elegiac'; it possesses the grace of despair, the grace of giving way to despair.

Perhaps because of this weight of despair, *Persuasion* is Jane Austen's finest expression of her view of time and personality as ambiguous movement, as continual reorganisation that has both progressive and regressive tendencies. There are no apocalyptic endings in Jane Austen; there is never a revolution, only a regeneration of attitudes. The heroine is never completely enlightened – that is to say, she is never as enlightened as the author or as the reader potentially is about her situation. Anne Elliot cannot take the final step in self-awareness by admitting that she was weak to take Lady Russell's advice, the step that would make the close of the novel a totally new beginning. Complete transcendence is not to be expected. That Anne and Wentworth are reconciled must satisfy us. In Jane Austen, social and personal changes are never absolute. That Austen could not conceive of a total revolution of consciousness is apparent in one of the most interesting minor incidents in all of her novels, Anne's response to Mr Elliot's insulting letter about her father. He calls Sir Walter a fool, which Anne and the reader and the narrator know him to be. The issue at hand is one of filial respect, but still Anne's response intrigues us: 'Anne could not immediately get over the shock and mortification of finding such words applied to her father' (p. 204). The significance of Anne's indignation is that it shows us she has some family feeling after all; and who among us has not experienced the same thing, the same surprise of feeling an involuntary allegiance toward those one has ceased to care for? Anne cannot be fully conscious of her past any more than she can transcend all ties to her family or to Lady Russell. Personal and social change in Jane Austen comes about through the ceaseless reorganisation of persons through marriage; in the words of her contemporary Erasmus Darwin, it consists of the power of 'delivering down those improvements by generation to its posterity, world without end!'[4] In her earlier novels, Jane Austen showed that right marriages are socially and morally vital to the worlds in which they are realised. In the environment of *Persuasion*, in which the individual's social identity is in a state of collapse, the marriage of 'intelligent love' becomes, for the well-being of the individuals involved, a stark necessity. And when we consider the peculiar, intense concern and suppressed hope with which later

novelists were to invest the marriages of their heroes and heroines –
the marriages, for example, of David Copperfield, Dorothea
Brooke, and Isabel Archer – we see that the ambiguous, autumnal
mood of *Persuasion* comes from neither sentimentality nor sickness
nor oncoming death, but from a full consciousness of the fate of
marriage in the century to come.

From Julia Prewitt Brown, *Jane Austen's Novels: Social Change and
Literary Form* (Cambridge, MA, 1979), pp. 128–9; 137–50.

## NOTES

[This essay is extracted from Julia Prewitt Brown's book-length study of
Jane Austen's work, which attempts to redress earlier criticism of Austen's
limitations as a writer. Brown argues against traditional historiography and
aesthetics which she suggests ignore the importance of the history of
domesticity, and instead reconceptualises a history in which Austen is a key
figure in a period of social transition. The study combines scrupulous
formal exegesis of the text with a close attention to socio-historical
perspectives in a discussion which for the most part avoids explicit theoretical engagement, although Brown's acknowledgement of the significance of
gender as an important element in Austen's social representation points in
the direction of later feminist scholarship.

In this excerpt, Brown focuses on varieties of textual fragmentation in
*Persuasion*, and argues that in its dramatisation of the dislocation of a
modern sensibility, the work is a forerunner of the mid-nineteenth-century
novel of alienation. Her emphasis on discontinuity and her dissection of the
disorientating function of the irony has much in common with D.A. Miller's
essay on the destabilising factors operating in *Mansfield Park*. Brown's
essay, however, preserves an implicit concept of aesthetic absolutism in its
view of the novel as an unresolved and transitional work in Austen's artistic
career. References to Jane Austen's work are to *The Works of Jane Austen*,
ed. R.W. Chapman, 3rd edn, 5 vols (London, 1932–34). Ed.]

[All references to the novel are given in parentheses in the text. Ed.]

1.   Lionel Trilling, *E.M. Forster* (Norfolk, CT, 1943), p. 118.

2.   Jane Austen, *Sense and Sensibility*, ed. R.W. Chapman, p. 379.

3.   Austen's language often turns on this paradox: 'She was deep in
     the happiness of such misery, or the misery of such happiness',
     *Persuasion*, p. 229.

4.   Quoted in Loren Eiseley, *Darwin's Century* (Garden City, NY, 1961),
     p. 48.

# 8

# Jane Austen's Cover Story

*SANDRA M. GILBERT and SUSAN GUBAR*

In all six of Austen's novels women who are refused the means of self-definition are shown to be fatally drawn to the dangerous delights of impersonation and pretence. But Austen's profession depends on just these disguises. What else, if not impersonation, is characterisation? What is plot, if not pretence? In all the novels, the narrator's voice is witty, assertive, spirited, independent, even (as D.W. Harding has shown) arrogant and nasty.[1] Poised between the subjectivity of lyric and the objectivity of drama, the novel furnishes Austen with a unique opportunity: she can create Mary Crawford's witty letters or Emma's brilliant retorts, even while rejecting them as improper; furthermore, she can reprove as indecent in a heroine what is necessary to an author. Authorship for Austen is an escape from the very restraints she imposes on her female characters. And in this respect she seems typical, for women may have contributed so significantly to narrative fiction precisely because it effectively objectifies, even as it sustains and hides, the subjectivity of the author. Put another way, in the novels Austen questions and criticises her own aesthetic and ironic sensibilities, noting the limits and asserting the dangers of an imagination undisciplined by the rigours of art.

Using her characters to castigate the imaginative invention that informs her own novels, Austen is involved in a contradiction that, as we have seen, she approves as the only solution available to her heroines. Just as they manage to survive only by seeming to submit, she succeeds in maintaining her double consciousness in fiction that proclaims its docility and restraint even as it uncovers the delights

*137*

of assertion and rebellion. Indeed the comedy of Austen's novels explores the tensions between the freedom of her art and the dependency of her characters: while they stutter and sputter and lapse into silence and even hasten to perfect felicity, she attains a woman's language that is magnificently duplicitous. In this respect, Austen serves as a paradigm of the literary ladies who would emerge so successfully and plentifully in the mid-nineteenth century, popular lady novelists like Rhoda Broughton, Charlotte Mary Yonge, Home Lee, and Mrs Craik who strenuously suppressed awareness of how their own professional work called into question traditional female roles. Deeply conservative as their content appears to be, however, it frequently retains traces of the original duplicity so manifest in its origin, even as it demonstrates their own exuberant evasion of the inescapable limits they prescribe for their model heroines.

Although Austen clearly escapes the House of Prose that confines her heroines by making her story out of their renunciation of story-telling, she also dwells in the freer prospects of Emily Dickinson's 'Possibility' by identifying not only with her model heroines, but also with less obvious, nastier, more resilient and energetic female characters who enact her rebellious dissent from her culture, a dissent, as we have seen, only partially obscured by the 'blotter' of her plot. Many critics have already noticed duplicity in the 'happy endings' of Austen's novels in which she brings her couples to the brink of bliss in such haste, or with such unlikely coincidences, or with such sarcasm that the entire message seems undercut:[2] the implication remains that a girl without the aid of a benevolent narrator would never find a way out of either her mortifications or her parents' house.

Perhaps less obvious instances of Austen's duplicity occur in her representation of a series of extremely powerful women each of whom acts out the rebellious anger so successfully repressed by the heroine and the author. Because they so rarely appear and so infrequently speak in their own voices, these furious females remain secret presences in the plots. Not only do they play a less prominent role in the novels than their function in the plot would seem to require; buried or killed or banished at the end of the story, they seem to warrant this punishment by their very unattractiveness. Like Lady Susan, they are mothers or surrogate mothers who seek to destroy their docile children. Widows who are no longer defined by men simply because they have survived the male authorities in their lives, these women can exercise power even if they can never legitimise it; thus they seem both pushy and dangerous. Yet if their energy appears destructive and disagreeable, that is because this is the mechanism by which Austen disguises the most assertive aspect of herself as the Other. We shall see that these bitchy women enact impulses of revolt that make them doubles not only for the heroines but for their author as well. ...

It is not only Austen's mad matriarchs who reflect her discomfort with the glass coffin of female submission. Her last completed novel, *Persuasion* (1818), focuses on an angelically quiet heroine who has given up her search for a story and has thereby effectively killed herself off. Almost as if she were reviewing the implications of her own plots, Austen explores in *Persuasion* the effects on women of submission to authority and the renunciation of one's life story. Eight years before the novel begins, Anne Elliot had been persuaded to renounce her romance with Captain Wentworth, but this decision sickened her by turning her into a nonentity. Forced into 'knowing [her] own nothingness' (I, ch. 6), Anne is a 'nobody with either father or sister' so her word has 'no weight' (I, ch. 1). An invisible observer who tends to fade into the background, she is frequently afraid to move lest she should be seen. Having lost the 'bloom' of her youth, she is but a pale vestige of what she had been and realises that her lover 'should not have known [her] again' (I, ch. 7), their relationship being 'now nothing!' Anne Elliot is the ghost of her own dead self; through her, Austen presents a personality haunted with a sense of menace.

At least one reason why Anne has deteriorated into a ghostly insubstantiality is that she is a dependent female in a world symbolised by her vain and selfish aristocratic father, who inhabits the mirrored dressing room of Kellynch Hall. It is significant that *Persuasion* begins with her father's book, the *Baronetage*, which is described as 'the book of books' (I, ch. 1) because it symbolises male authority, patriarchal history in general, and her father's family history in particular. Existing in it as a first name and birth date in a family line that concludes with the male heir presumptive, William Walter Elliot, Esq., Anne has no reality until a husband's name can be affixed to her own. But Anne's name is a new one in the *Baronetage*: the history of this ancient, respectable line of heirs records 'all the Marys and Elizabeths they had married' (I, ch. 1), as if calling our attention to the hopeful fact that, unlike her sisters

Mary and Elizabeth, Anne may not be forced to remain a character within this 'book of books'. And, in fact, Anne will reject the economic and social standards represented by the *Baronetage*, deciding, by the end of her process of personal development, that not she but the Dowager Viscountess Dalrymple and her daughter the Honourable Miss Carteret are 'nothing' (II, ch. 4). She will also discover that Captain Wentworth is 'no longer nobody' (II, ch. 12), and, even more significantly, she will insist on her ability to seek and find 'at least the comfort of telling the whole story her own way' (II, ch. 9).

But before Anne can become somebody, she must confront what being a nobody means: 'I'm Nobody!'[3] Emily Dickinson could occasionally avow, and certainly, by choosing not to have a story of her own, Anne seems to have decided to dwell in Dickinson's realm of 'Possibility', for what Austen demonstrates through her is that the person who has not become anybody is haunted by everybody. Living in a world of her father's mirrors, Anne confronts the several selves she might have become and discovers that they all reveal the same story of the female fall from authority and autonomy.

As a motherless girl, Anne is tempted to become her own mother, although she realises that her mother lived invisibly, unloved, within Sir Walter's house. Since Anne could marry Mr Elliot and become the future Lady Elliot, she has to confront her mother's unhappy marriage as a potential life story not very different from that of Catherine Morland's Mrs Tilney. At the same time, however, since serviceable Mrs Clay is an unattached female who aspires to her mother's place in the family as her father's companion and her sister Elizabeth's intimate, Anne realises that she could also become patient Penelope Clay, for she too understands 'the art of pleasing' (I, ch. 2), of making herself useful. When Anne goes to Uppercross, moreover, she functions something like Mrs Clay, 'being too much in the secret of the complaints' of each of the tenants of both households (I, ch. 6), and trying to flatter or placate each and all into good humour. The danger exists, then, that Anne's sensitivity and selflessness could degenerate into Mrs Clay's ingratiating, hypocritical service.

Of course, Mary Musgrove's situation is also a potential identity for Anne, since Charles had actually asked for Anne's hand in marriage before he settled on her younger sister, and since Mary resembles Anne in being one of Sir Walter's unfavoured daughters. Indeed, Mary's complaint that she is 'always the last of my family to be noticed' (II, ch. 6) could easily be voiced by Anne. Bitter about being nobody, Mary responds to domestic drudgery with 'feminine' invalidism that is an extension of Anne's sickening self-doubt, as well as the only means at Mary's disposal of using her imagination to add some drama and importance to her life. Mary's hypochondria reminds us that Louisa Musgrove provides a kind of paradigm for all these women when she literally falls from the Cobb and suffers from a head injury resulting in exceedingly weak nerves. Because incapacitated Louisa is first attracted to Captain Wentworth and finally marries Captain Benwick, whose first attentions had been given to Anne, she too is clearly an image of what Anne might have become.

Through both Mary and Louisa, then, Austen illustrates how growing up female constitutes a fall from freedom, autonomy, and strength into debilitating, degrading, ladylike dependency. In direct contradiction to Captain Wentworth's sermon in the hedgerow, Louisa discovers that even firmness cannot save her from such a fall. Indeed, it actually precipitates it, and she discovers that her fate is not to jump from the stiles down the steep flight of seaside stairs but to read love poetry quietly in the parlour with a suitor suitably solicitous for her sensitive nerves. While Louisa's physical fall and subsequent illness reinforce Anne's belief that female asser-tion and impetuosity must be fatal, they also return us to the elegiac autumnal landscape that reflects Anne's sense of her own diminish-ment, the loss she experiences since her story is 'now nothing'.

Anne lives in a world of mirrors both because she could have become most of the women in the novel and, as the title suggests, because all the characters present her with their personal pre-ferences rationalised into principles by which they attempt to per-suade her. She is surrounded by other people's versions of her story and offered coercive advice by Sir Walter, Captain Wentworth, Charles Musgrove, Mrs Musgrove, Lady Russell, and Mrs Smith. Eventually, indeed, the very presence of another person becomes oppressive for Anne, since everyone but she is convinced that his or her version of reality is the only valid one. Only Anne has a sense of the different, if equally valid, perspectives of the various families and individuals among which she moves. Like Catherine Morland, she struggles against other people's fictional use and image of her; and finally she penetrates to the secret of patriarchy through absolutely no skill of detection on her own part. Just as Catherine blunders on the secret of the ancestral mansion to understand the arbitrary power of General Tilney, who does not mean what he says, Anne stumbles fortuitously on the secret of the heir to Kellynch Hall, William Elliot, who had married for money and was very unkind to his first wife. Mr Elliot's 'manoeuvres of selfishness and duplicity must ever be revolting' (II, ch. 7) to Anne, who comes to believe that 'the evil' of this suitor could easily result in 'irremediable mischief' (II, ch. 10).

For all of Austen's heroines, as Mr Darcy explains, 'detection could not be in [their] power, and suspicion certainly not in [their] inclination' (II, ch. 3). Yet Anne does quietly and attentively watch and listen and judge the members of her world and, as Stuart Tave has shown, she increasingly exerts herself to speak out, only gradually to discover that she is being heard.[4] Furthermore, in her pilgrimage from Kellynch Hall to Upper Cross and Lyme to Bath, the landscapes she encounters function as a kind of psychic geography of her development so that, when the withered hedgerows and tawny autumnal meadows are replaced by the invigorating breezes and flowing tides of Lyme, we are hardly surprised that Anne's bloom is restored (I, ch. 12). Similarly, when Anne gets to Bath, this woman who has heard and overheard others has trouble listening because she is filled with her own feelings, and she decides that 'one half of her should not be always so much wiser than the other half, or always suspecting the other half of being worse than it was' (II, ch. 7). Therefore, in a room crowded with talking people, Anne manages to signal to Captain Wentworth her lack of interest in Mr Elliot through her assertion that she has no pleasure in parties at her father's house. 'She had spoken it', the narrator emphasises; if 'she trembled when it was done, conscious that her words were listened to' (II, ch. 10), this is because Anne has actually 'never since the loss of her dear mother, known the happiness of being listened to, or encouraged' (I, ch. 6).

The fact that her mother's loss initiated her invisibility and silence is important in a book that so closely associates the heroine's felicity with her ability to articulate her sense of herself as a woman. Like Elinor Tilney, who feels that 'A mother could have been always present. A mother would have been a constant friend; her influence would have been beyond all others' (*Northanger Abbey*, II, ch. 7), Anne misses the support of a loving female influence. It is then fitting that the powerful whispers of well-meaning Mrs Musgrove and Mrs Croft furnish Anne with the cover – the opportunity and the encouragement – to discuss with Captain

Harville her sense of exclusion from patriarchal culture: 'Men have had every advantage of us in telling their own story. ... The pen has been in their hands' (II, ch. 11). Anne Elliot will 'not allow books to prove anything' because they 'were all written by men' (II, ch. 11); her contention that women love longest because their feelings are more tender directly contradicts the authorities on women's 'fickleness' that Captain Harville cites. As we have already seen, her speech reminds us that the male charge of 'inconstancy' is an attack on the irrepressible interiority of women who cannot be contained within the images provided by patriarchal culture. Though Anne remains inalterably inhibited by these images since she cannot express her sense of herself by 'saying what should not be said' (II, ch. 11) and though she can only replace the *Baronetage* with the *Navy Lists* – a book in which women are conspicuously absent – still she is the best example of her own belief in female subjectivity. She has both deconstructed the dead selves created by all her friends to remain true to her own feelings, and she has continually re-examined and reassessed herself and her past.

Finally, Anne's fate seems to be a response to Austen's earlier stories in which girls are forced to renounce their romantic ambitions: Anne 'had been forced into prudence in her youth, she learned romance as she grew older – the natural sequel of an unnatural beginning' (I, ch. 4). It is she who teaches Captain Wentworth the limits of masculine assertiveness. Placed in Anne's usual situation of silently overhearing, he discovers her true, strong feelings. Significantly, his first response is to drop his pen. Then, quietly, under the cover of doing some business for Captain Harville, Captain Wentworth writes her his proposal, which he can only silently hand to her before leaving the room. At work in the common sitting-room of the White Hart Inn, alert for inauspicious interruptions, using his other letter as a kind of blotter to camouflage his designs, Captain Wentworth reminds us of Austen herself. While Anne's rebirth into 'a second spring of youth and beauty' (II, ch. 1) takes place within the same corrupt city that fails to fulfil its baptismal promise of purification in *Northanger Abbey*, we are led to believe that her life with this man will escape the empty elegance of Bath society.

That the sea breezes of Lyme and the watery cures of Bath have revived Anne from her ghostly passivity furnishes some evidence that naval life may be an alternative to and an escape from the corruption of the land so closely associated with patrilineal descent.

Sir Walter Elliot dismisses the navy because it raises 'men to honours which their fathers and grandfathers never dreamt of' (I, ch. 3). And certainly Captain Wentworth seems almost miraculously to evade the hypocrisies and inequities of a rigid class system by making money on the water. But it is also true that naval life seems to justify Sir Walter's second objection that 'it cuts up a man's youth and vigour most horribly'. While he is thinking in his vanity only about the rapidity with which sailors lose their looks, we are given an instance of the sea cutting up a man's youth, a singularly unprepossessing man at that: when worthless Dick Musgrove is created by Austen only to be destroyed at sea, we are further reminded of her trust in the beneficence of nature, for only her anger against the unjust adulation of sons (over daughters) can explain the otherwise gratuitous cruelty of her remarks about Mrs Musgrove's 'large fat sighings over the destiny of a son, whom alive nobody had cared for' (I, ch. 8). Significantly, this happily lost son was recognised as a fool by Captain Wentworth, whose naval success closely associates him with a vocation that does not as entirely exclude women as most landlocked vocations do: his sister, Mrs Croft, knows that the difference between 'a fine gentleman' and a navy man is that the former treats women as if they were 'all fine ladies, instead of rational creatures' (I, ch. 8). She herself believes that 'any reasonable woman may be perfectly happy' on board ship, as she was when she crossed the Atlantic four times and travelled to and from the East Indies, more comfortably (she admits) than when she settled at Kellynch Hall, although her husband *did* take down Sir Walter's mirrors.

Naval men like Captain Wentworth and Admiral Croft are also closely associated, as is Captain Harville, with the ability to create 'ingenious contrivances and nice arrangements ... to turn the actual space to the best possible account' (I, ch. 11), a skill not unrelated to a 'profession which is, if possible, more distinguished in its domestic virtue than in its national importance' (II, ch. 12). While Austen's dowagers try to gain power by exploiting traditionally male prerogatives, the heroine of the last novel discovers an egalitarian society in which men value and participate in domestic life, while women contribute to public events, a complementary ideal that presages the emergence of an egalitarian sexual ideology.[5] No longer confined to a female community of childbearing and childrearing, activities portrayed as dreary and dangerous in both Austen's novels and her letters,[6] Anne triumphs in a marriage that represents the union of traditionally male and female spheres. If such a consummation can only be envisioned in the future, on the water, amid imminent threats of war, Austen nonetheless celebrates friendship between the sexes as her lovers progress down Bath streets with 'smiles reined in and spirits dancing in private rapture' (II, ch. 11).

When Captain Wentworth accepts Anne's account of their story, he agrees with her highly ambivalent assessment of the woman who advised her to break off their engagement. Lady Russell is one of Austen's last pushy widows, but, in this novel which revises Austen's earlier endorsement of the necessity of taming the shrew, the cautionary monster is one of effacement rather than assertion. If the powerful origin of *Emma* is the psychologically coercive model of the woman as lady, in *Persuasion* Austen describes a heroine who refuses to become a lady. Anne Elliot listened to the persuasions of the powerful, wealthy, proper Lady Russell when she refrained from marrying the man she loved. But finally she rejects Lady Russell, who is shown to value rank and class over the dictates of the heart, in part because her own heart is perverted, capable of revelling 'in angry pleasure, in pleased contempt' (II, ch. 1) at events sure to hurt Anne. Anne replaces this cruel stepmother with a different kind of mother surrogate, another widow, Mrs Smith. Poor, confined, crippled by rheumatic fever, Mrs Smith serves as an emblem of the dispossession of women in a patriarchal society, and she is, as Paul Zietlow has shown, also the embodiment of what Anne's future could have been under less fortunate circumstances.[7]

While Lady Russell persuaded Anne not to marry a poor man, Mrs Smith explains why she should not marry a rich one. Robbed of all physical and economic liberty, with 'no child ... no relatives ... no health ... no possibility of moving' (II, ch. 5), Mrs Smith is paralysed, and, although she exerts herself to maintain good humour in her tight place, she is also maddened. She expresses her rage at the false forms of civility, specifically at the corrupt and selfish double-dealings of Mr Elliot, the heir apparent and the epitome of patriarchal society. With fierce delight in her revengeful revelations, Mrs Smith proclaims herself an 'injured, angry woman' (II, ch. 9) and she articulates Anne's – and Austen's – unacknowledged fury at her own unnecessary and unrecognised paralysis and suffering. But although this widow is a voice of angry female revolt against the injustices of patriarchy, she is as much a resident of Bath as Lady Russell. This fashionable place for cures reminds us that society *is* sick. And Mrs Smith participates in the moral degeneration of the place when she selfishly lies to Anne, placing her own advancement over Anne's potential marital happiness by withholding the truth about Mr Elliot until she is quite sure Anne does not mean to marry him. Like Lady Russell, then, this other voice within Anne's psyche can also potentially victimise her.

It is Mrs Smith's curious source of knowledge, her informant or her muse, who best reveals the corruption that has permeated and informs the social conventions of English society. A woman who nurses sick people back to health, wonderfully named nurse Rooke resembles in her absence from the novel many of Austen's most important avatars. Pictured perched on the side of a sickbed, nurse Rooke seems as much a vulture as a saviour of the afflicted. Her freedom of movement in society resembles the movement of a chess piece which moves parallel to the edge of the board, thereby defining the limits of the game. And she 'rooks' her patients, discovering their hidden hoards.

Providing ears and eyes for the confined Mrs Smith, this seemingly ubiquitous, omniscient nurse is privy to all the secrets of the sickbed. She has taught Mrs Smith how to knit, and she sells 'little thread-cases, pin-cushions and cardracks' not unlike Austen's 'little bit (two Inches wide) of Ivory'. What she brings as part of her services are volumes furnished from the sick chamber, stories of weakness and selfishness and impatience. A historian of private life, nurse Rooke communicates in typically female fashion as a gossip engaged in the seemingly trivial, charitable office of selling feminine handcrafts to the fashionable world. This and her gossip are, of course, a disguise for her subversive interest in uncovering the sordid realities behind the decorous appearances of high life. In this regard she is a wonderful portrait of Austen herself. While seemingly unreliable, dependent (as she is) for information upon many interactions which are subject to errors of misconception and ignorance, this uniquely female historian turns out to be accurate and revolutionary as she reveals 'the manoeuvres of selfishness and duplicity' (II, ch. 9) of one class to another. Finally, sensible nurse Rooke also resembles Austen in that, despite all her knowledge, she does not withdraw from society. Instead, acknowledging herself a member of the community she nurses, she is a 'favourer of matrimony' who has her own 'flying visions' of social success (II, ch. 9). Although many of Austen's female characters seem inalterably locked inside Mr Elton's riddle, nurse Rooke resembles the successful heroines of the author's works in making the best of this tight place.

That Austen was fascinated with the sickness of her social world, especially its effect on people excluded from a life of active exertion, is probably last illustrated through the Parker sisters in *Sanditon*, where officious Diana supervises the application of six leeches a day for ten days and the extraction of a number of teeth in order to cure her disabled sister Susan's poor health. One sister representing 'activity run mad' (ch. 9), the other languishing on the sofa, the two remind us of lethargic Lady Bertram, crippled Mrs Smith, ill Jane Fairfax, fever-stricken Marianne Dashwood, the infected Crawfords, hypochondriacal Mary Musgrove, ailing Louisa Musgrove, and pale, sickly Fanny Price. But, as nurse Rooke's healing arts imply, the diseased shrews and the dying fainters define the boundaries of the state in which Austen's most successful characters usually manage to settle. A few of her heroines do evade the culturally induced idiocy and impotence that domestic confinement and female socialisation seem to breed. Neither fainting into silence nor self-destructing into verbosity, Elizabeth Bennet, Emma Woodhouse, and Anne Elliot echo their creator in their duplicitous ability to speak with the tact that saves them from suicidal somnambulism on the one hand and contaminating vulgarity on the other, as they exploit the evasions and reservations of feminine gentility.

From Sandra M. Gilbert and Susan Gubar, *The Madwoman in the Attic: The Woman Writer and the Nineteenth-Century Literary Imagination* (New Haven, CT, 1979), pp. 174–83.


## NOTES

[This essay forms part of Sandra Gilbert and Susan Gubar's ambitious and influential study of female authorship, a study which has been subsequently criticised for what some would argue is its ultimately separatist and a-historical account of women's artistic practice. One view, for example (expressed by Julia Prewitt Brown among others), is that Gilbert and Gubar's valuation of the subtext as the key to real meaning in much women's literature has led to a marginalisation of writers such as Jane Austen, whose work contains a more classic and subtle formulation of social structures and female roles. Nonetheless, Gilbert and Gubar's work has been of great significance in opening up new perspectives on Austen in the light of feminist theory. Taking their lead from Harold Bloom's theory of the anxiety of authorship, Gilbert and Gubar identify distinctively female strategies of expression, which, they argue, emerge as a response to a dominantly masculine culture, and which disclose tensions in women's literature between overt and covert textual strands.

In their discussion of *Persuasion*, Gilbert and Gubar suggest that Anne Elliot's story is an untold story of loss and self-denial and that in order to gain autonomy in a society that is essentially hostile to her interests, Anne has to confront her own negation of identity through a series of antithetical female role models. In this way Austen's heroine acts as a surrogate for her creator. The reading offers a view of a society and a text which polarise gender relations, and which argues for a subversive Jane Austen who offers a sustained critique of an inimical patriarchal world. Ed.]

[All references to *Persuasion* are to volume and chapter of the text edited by R.W. Chapman, reprinted with an introduction by David Daiches (New York, 1958). Ed.]

1.  D.W. Harding, 'Regulated Hatred: An Aspect of the Work of Jane Austen', *Scrutiny*, 8 (March 1940), 340–62.

2.  The most sustained discussion of Austen's ironic undercutting of her own endings appears in Lloyd W. Brown, *Bits of Ivory: Narrative Technique in Jane Austen's Fiction* (Baton Rouge, LA, 1973), pp. 220–9.

3.  *The Poems of Emily Dickinson*, ed. Thomas Johnson, 3 vols (Cambridge, MA, 1955), p. 228.

4.  Stuart Tave, *Some Words of Jane Austen* (Chicago, 1973), pp. 256–87.

5.  Michelle Zimbalist Rosaldo suggests that the most egalitarian societies are those in which men participate in domestic life. See 'Women, Culture, and Society: A Theoretical Overview', in *Women, Culture, and Society*, ed. Michelle Zimbalist Rosaldo and Louise Lamphere (Princeton, NJ, 1974), p. 41.

6.  From Mrs Palmer's fear of red-gum in her newborn infant (*Sense and Sensibility*) to Mrs Musgrove's noisy and selfish household of siblings (*Persuasion*), Austen portrays the discomforts of motherhood.

7.  Paul Zietlow, 'Luck and Fortuitous Circumstance in *Persuasion*: Two Interpretations', *English Literary History*, 32 (1965), 179–95, argues that Mrs Smith is a 'goddess who descends on stage at a crucial moment to avert catastrophe' (p. 193).

# 9

## *Persuasion*: The 'Unfeudal' Tone of the Present Day

*CLAUDIA JOHNSON*

*Persuasion* has always signified more than what it singly comprises: its two slender volumes have been made to bear the imprint of Austen's entire career. Whereas *Pride and Prejudice* and *Emma* can be and most often are discussed without reference to Austen's other works, *Persuasion* is above all else the last novel, the apparent conclusion that determines the shape of everything that has come before. The critical tradition has designated *Persuasion* the 'autumnal' novel, and this adjective brings with it a parcel of value-laden and often quite pedestrian assumptions about both the course of Austen's career and the course of literary history in general. Wistful and romantically unfulfilled in the twilight of her life, so the argument goes, the author grows tenderer on romantic subjects she had disparaged in the confidence and severity of her youth; with her own opening out onto a new world of emotion, eighteenth-century 'objectivity' yields to nineteenth-century 'subjectivity'; the assured, not to say simple-minded, gives way to the ambiguous and complex.[1] The underlying assumption that Anne's autumn and Austen's are complementary – in other words, that *Persuasion*, like the other novels, indeed like all novels by women, is the author's own love story, composed with little or no aesthetic distance – is of course teeming with fallacies, not the least glaring of which in this particular case are those which result from the imposition of specious teleology. *Persuasion* will not look so unequivocally like Austen's last and most mature word about love and the changing world before death stopped her lips if we recollect that *Sanditon*, which recapitulates the raucous energy and renews the literary debates characteristic of Austen's earliest work, followed so closely on its heels. Austen, unlike her latter-day readers, did not have the benefit of knowing that her impending death would be imparting a gently resigned, autumnal melancholy to all her observations. Many prominent, yet seldom discussed, elements of *Persuasion* call the youthful *Sense and Sensibility* to mind – the apparently unfeeling allusion to Mrs Musgrove's 'fat sighings', the conventionalised villainy of William Elliot and the conspicuously artificial means of disclosing it, the overtness of its sarcasms at the expense of silly and uninformed people. To judge them in terms of the autumnal paradigm, with which they are at odds, these features can only be dismissed as unfortunate lapses in morbid foresight.

This of course is not to say that *Persuasion* gives us nothing new, but only that it should be considered without using the benefit of hindsight to beg so many important questions. Most readers note, for example, that *Persuasion* ridicules the ruling class. This fact appears distinctive, however, only when we assume that it is a departure from the practice of the earlier novels. But surely nothing said in *Persuasion* about the Musgroves or Elliots surpasses the satire to which the Middletons, Palmers, and John Dashwoods are treated in *Sense and Sensibility*. What is different about *Persuasion* is not that it shows how the improvident landowners, proving themselves unworthy of their station, have left England poised on the brink of a new world dominated by the best and the brightest, the Royal Navy. As one historian has observed, foolish and financially embarrassed landowners are nothing new to English social history or to Austen's fiction. Eventually, Sir Walter will reassume Kellynch, and yield it in the time-honoured way to his heir William Elliot, a man who, knowing how to serve 'his own interest and his own enjoyment' (p. 250), will doubtless not, as Sir Thomas had, lose his hold on 'the situation in which Providence has placed him' (p. 248).[2]

But if in *Persuasion* the landed classes have not lost their power, they have lost their prestige and their moral authority for the heroine. Whereas *Pride and Prejudice* could, with elaborately wrought qualifications and finely modulated discriminations, finally vindicate the highly controversial practice of 'prejudice', Lady Russell's 'prejudices on the side of ancestry' and 'value for rank and consequence' (p. 11) are never allowed to be anything more than amiable but groundless articulations of self-interest. Like her idea of what constitutes a 'little quiet cheerfulness' (pp. 134, 135) or, for that matter, Admiral Croft's idea of proper décor, Lady Russell's 'prejudices on the side of ancestry' are not favoured with any corroborative footing in 'objective' reality. As Admiral Croft puts it, 'Ay, so it always is, I believe. One man's ways may be as good as another's, but we all like our own best. And so you must judge for yourself ...' (p. 127). *Sense and Sensibility* makes it hard to believe that Austen ever shared Lady Russell's prejudices, yet even there she evinces a heartier tolerance for booby squires than what she somewhat wearily musters here. For all his absurdity, Sir John Middleton's bluff generosity commands some respect. But whether darting eagerly after weasels, defending the claims of eldest sons, or extolling the virtues of 'good, freehold property' (p. 76), Charles Musgrove has little to recommend himself. His ideas, like his activities, are tediously predictable, and his 'old country family of respectability and large fortune' (p. 6) has no charm: Anne never regrets her refusal to attach herself to this inoffensive, but unredeemably mediocre gentleman and the long-established kind of domestic life he represents.

*Persuasion*, then, distinctively minimises problems which had before been so momentous to the heroines. By centring her novel on a maturer heroine, of course, Austen is free to explore female independence without being obliged to explore the concomitant impertinence which always seems to accompany the self-assurance of younger heroines. The duty of filial piety, for example – Fanny Price's 'great rule to apply to' (*Mansfield Park*, p. 436) – is nowhere dignified with the status of being at issue here. Even though her 'word' has 'no weight' within her family circle (p. 5), Anne, like Emma, is an autonomous heroine. For this reason, to conceptualise *Persuasion*, as readers so often do, as a debate between individualism and propriety is not only to employ an opposition already curiously loaded in favour of conservative arguments, but it is also to underestimate the degree of Anne's independence from traditional, paternal authority and to misplace the emphasis of the plot.[3] Starting as early as the second chapter, for example, when we learn that she regards paying one's debts as an 'indispensable duty' (p. 12), Anne distances herself from an impropriety that is specifically paternal. General Tilney's wrath with Catherine is the catastrophe of *Northanger Abbey*. But the crisis in *Persuasion* – Anne's decision to break off her engagement – has little to do with

Sir Walter's paternal displeasure. On the contrary, it has everything to do with the advice, not the authority, of a trusted friend, Lady Russell, to whom Anne does not owe the comparable duty of obedience. Such is Anne's filial disposition at nineteen. At twenty-eight she pays Sir Walter even less mind. While Sir Walter pursues Lady Dalrymple, Anne visits a 'nobody' – Mrs Smith – without as much as informing him, let alone seeking his permission, and once his disapproval is expressed, it is ignored without fuss. For Anne, no hard conflict between duty and inclination is implied by defying or simply ignoring her father. Indeed, it is all too easy: 'Anne kept her appointment; the others kept theirs' (p. 158).

Although Anne's indifference to filial propriety can show us the distance Austen has come since *Northanger Abbey*, Austen's earlier novel is nevertheless tied up with *Persuasion*.[4] Published together posthumously in 1817, they seem unlikely companions, but in Austen's mind their partnership was deeper than the accident of their copublication. *Persuasion* itself speaks to problems that to all appearances pressed on Austen while she was reviewing, perhaps even revising, *Northanger Abbey* for publication. The 'hand of time' may have been 'lenient' (*Northanger Abbey*, p. 201) to Catherine Morland's feelings, but Austen considered it harsh to her novel. In the 'Advertisement' to *Northanger Abbey* she dwells on the 'thirteen years' during which 'places, manners, books, and opinions have undergone considerable changes', changes which render parts of her novel 'comparatively obsolete'. The 'thirteen years' marked here, of course, are the same thirteen years that cause such dislocation in *Persuasion*. This novel is constantly calling attention to a temporal gap, to the time unwritten, but everywhere felt, to the missing third volume, as it were. Austen's handling of time in her plots is famously exact, carefully coordinated with reference to almanacs. But for all her exactitude, once Austen forges the temporal schemata of her narratives, she generally proceeds to submerge them, and only the most determined of students would wish to note down references to years and dates and then arrange them sequentially. But *Persuasion* is a calculated tangle of years and dates, and the passage of time itself is foregrounded. Here, as in no other novel, we are constantly being pointed backwards – to the knell-like repetition of 'thirteen years' (pp. 6–7) that have left Elizabeth husbandless, to the heavy 'eight years' (p. 60) that have changed everything but Anne's feelings for Wentworth, to the tolled 'twelve years' that have transformed the smart young Miss Hamilton into the poor and crippled Mrs Smith (p. 153); in short, to the inconjurable difference time makes.

The years alluded to in the 'Advertisement' to *Northanger Abbey* and throughout *Persuasion* as the occasion of so much change are not just any years which would work changes at any time. With the benefit of hindsight, we look back upon those thirteen years as having sealed the reaction, but as they appear in *Persuasion* they do not present a repressive and politically monolithic aspect. Sir Walter himself seems firmly enough entrenched, to be sure, but he is not all there is. In his related capacities as general, pamphleteer, and stern paterfamilias, General Tilney is the obstacle in *Northanger Abbey* whose authority must be confronted and in some ways, however limited, overcome. But now, some two decades later, defenders of the nation appear under a different guise and are envisioned as alternatives to, rather than representatives of, the establishment. Admiral and Mrs Croft are not gentry. Far from presiding over a neighbourhood, they live most contentedly at sea, unconcerned with the production of heirs or the reproduction of ideologically correct values through the cultivation of local attachments. From some points of view, the differences between Admiral Croft and General Tilney may be minimal. The former, to be sure, nowhere expresses or implies progressive opinion. But to Anne, the difference is great. The years which bring the Admiral into prominence are those which mark off the disparity between the 'old English style' of the senior Musgroves, and the 'new' English style of their 'accomplished' daughters (p. 40), and which have brought changes with them accounting for what William Elliot calls the 'unfeudal tone of the *present* day' (p. 139, emphasis added). But the causes and the processes of such transformation are not themselves the subject of *Persuasion*. Instead they are the pervasive backdrop Austen establishes throughout *Persuasion* in order to consider the psychological impact that social arrangements have on women and the apparent possibilities which the 'unfeudal tone of the present day' may hold out for them.

In the Elliots' case, of course, self-importance is a birthright, a benefit conferred upon them by their social position. Sir Walter believes he is somebody to the 'nobody' of virtually everyone else. But though Sir Walter is convinced that, as a public figure, he carries his importance around with him irrespective of place, people only three miles away at Uppercross are contentedly oblivious to 'the affairs which at Kellynch-hall were treated as of such general publicity and pervading interest' (p. 42) by Sir Walter himself. Anne's mortification to discover that Sir Walter and Elizabeth 'see nothing to regret' in relinquishing 'the duties and dignity of the resident landholder' (p. 138) bespeaks her lingering sympathy with the life of the manor, but landholders less distinguished than her father are not spared either. As presented in *Persuasion*, at least, landed existence itself fosters an immobility that fixes delusions of self-consequence which cause so much conflict. Anne is an adept in 'the art of knowing our own nothingness beyond our own circle' (p. 42), and this is what makes her wise. But the otherwise unobjectionable Musgroves, whose views are bounded by the narrowness of their neighbourhood, cannot share such wisdom. Except in *Pride and Prejudice*, where a countrified Mrs Bennet takes umbrage at Darcy's cosmopolitan pretensions, only in *Persuasion* does Austen portray the provinciality of her characters as a disadvantage. Taken by himself, Charles Hayter, for example, could appear as an earnest and respectable gentleman. But placed alongside Frederick Wentworth and ineffectually pleading with a troublesome child, he fades into nonentity. And just as the Admiral's tendency to confuse Henrietta and Louisa suggests their indistinguishability, so the redundancy of Hayter's Christian name, doubling with that of Charles Musgrove, calls attention to what is undistinctive about eldest sons in general. And in no other novel is a gentry matron exposed to such painful comparisons with a woman with wider horizons. When Mrs Croft summarises her travels, adding 'We do not call Bermuda or Bahama, you know, the West Indies', poor Mrs Musgrove finds herself baffled: 'Mrs Musgrove had not a word to say in dissent; she could not accuse herself of having ever called them any thing in the whole course of her life' (p. 70).

Landed life is not taken to task simply because it promotes mediocrity or ignorance, but rather because its insularity is psychologically damaging, especially for women. Conservatives laud membership within a neighbourhood precisely on account of the strong and stabilising attachments, the changeless pace, and the unceasing familiarity that it carries with it. But for women it also carries with it a particularly narrow and unwholesome confinement, and discussion of this problem in *Persuasion* is specific, prolonged, and dramatically charged. Whatever baronetcy does for Sir Walter, it has not helped a daughter who has reached the age of twenty-nine without marrying. For Elizabeth the *Baronetage* cannot be the never-ending fund of solace unalloyed it is for her father. Every reading mercilessly reiterates an ever-receding birthdate and an un-changing status as spinster. Mr Bennet's sarcasm – 'a girl likes to be crossed in love a little now and then. ... It is something to think of' (*Pride and Prejudice*, pp. 137–8) – has a disturbing relevance to *Persuasion*, where such crosses are all that women have to think of. Being the mistress of Kellynch-hall – 'doing the honours, and laying down the domestic law at home' (pp. 6–7) – is not as engag-ing, as satisfying, and as adequate to Elizabeth's imagination as running Hartfield and its environs is to Emma's. Elizabeth is haunted by her disappointment in love, and the cares and duties of 'her scene of life' are not enough to keep her from revisiting and fixing her pain. Bitterness, mortification, regret, and worry are all she has 'to give interest to a long, uneventful residence in one country circle, to fill the vacancies which there were no habits of utility abroad, no talents or accomplishments for home, to occupy' (p. 9). Nor is Elizabeth's condition unique. Anne has more 're-sources', as they are termed in *Emma*, than her sister Elizabeth, yet she understands that her regret over Wentworth lingers because 'no aid had been given in change of place ... or in any novelty or en-largement of society' (p. 28) that could dislodge and eventually efface her painful impressions.

Whether it is because we typically exclude Austen in general from access to, capability for, or interest in arcana of any sort, or whether it is because we have a habit of regarding *Persuasion* in particular as a tender love story that is not conducive to such con-siderations, rather scant attention has been accorded to Austen's affiliation with the eighteenth-century tradition of liberal psycho-logy.[5] But readers of Johnson's essays, who recall his fears about the corrosiveness of hopes and disappointments, his recommenda-tion of 'change of place',[6] and his anxieties about the 'vacuities of recluse and domestick leisure',[7] will recognise the provenance of her concerns and the character of her diction, and will appreciate how, by linking women's confinement within their changeless neighbour-hoods to the strength and longevity of their feelings, she develops this tradition with particular emphasis on women's problems. Anne herself tells Harville that women do 'not forget you [men], so soon as you forget us' (p. 232). But far from presenting the constancy of woman's love in the light of a virtue, for example, loyalty, she pre-sents it as a burden – 'our fate rather than our merit' (p. 232). Men will love faithfully 'so long as [they] have an object', but woman's love can subsist indefinitely as fantasy alone: 'All the privilege I claim for my own sex ... is that of loving longest, when existence or when hope is gone' (p. 235). A dubious privilege indeed, this liability to hopeless fixation. Anne's rather technical explanation for the stubborn durability of women's love combines social criticism with psychological acuity:

> 'We live at home, quiet, confined, and our feelings prey upon us. You are forced on exertion. You have always a profession, pursuits, business of some sort or other, to take you back into the world immediately, and continual occupation and change soon weaken impressions.'
>
> (p. 232)

To Maria Edgeworth, whose access to moral psychology, unlike Austen's, is undisputed, Anne's analysis held special interest. The marginalia in her personal copy of *Persuasion* are very sparse until this episode, which prompts a flurry of scratches, underlinings, and comments. She, for example, reiterates Anne's socio-psychological argument here with 'our mind is continually fixt on one object'; to the claims that occupation and change weaken impressions, she writes a heartily concurring 'That it does'; and she brushes aside Harville's analogy between the strength of men's 'bodily frames' and the constancy of their feelings (p. 233) with an emphatic 'No'.[8] But whereas Edgeworth in conservative fashion upholds the traditional social arrangements that expose women to the problems she herself laments, on the grounds that defying such arrangements will not promote their happiness, *Persuasion* asks us to consider whether women's happiness may not be better served by cutting loose from those arrangements. Mrs Croft disapproves of long and uncertain engagements because they expose women to perilous anxieties and fantasies – and her brother, eavesdropping, appears to acknowledge that the application to his own case with Anne has a compelling legitimacy which he had never before considered. Mrs Croft's example as a wife suggests that life on the high seas, for all its dangers, is to be preferred to the 'safety' of helpless immobility she experienced when she lived conventionally, as most wives such as Mrs Musgrove do: 'The only time I ever really suffered in body or mind, the only time I ever fancied myself unwell, or had any ideas of danger, was the winter that I passed by myself at Deal, when the Admiral (*Captain* Croft then) was in the North Seas. I lived in perpetual fright at that time, and had all manner of imaginary complaints from not knowing what to do with myself' (p. 71).

The phenomena of change and relativity in *Persuasion* have long been considered symptoms of the dizzying modernity to come, a modernity usually described as either brave or degenerate, according to the axis of the critic. But to those characters who take notice at all, the deracination and relativity presented in *Persuasion* are not felt to be disturbing or disorienting. Except when she has pangs in tender remembrance of her dear mother, Anne cannot regret the Croft's tenancy at Kellynch-hall. She cannot say of her family seat what she knows social orthodoxy would have her say: 'These rooms ought to belong only to us. ... How unworthily unoccupied! An ancient family to be so driven away!' (p. 126). Rather than feel that their removal to the diminished accommodations at Camden-place constitutes a fall, Sir Walter and Elizabeth themselves find more than enough 'extent to be proud of between two walls, perhaps thirty feet asunder' (p. 138). Anne is not bewildered to learn that our somethingness is tenuous and relative, or sad to confront her nothingness beyond her family circle – she, after all, is rather less than something *in* her family circle as well. Only from within a mentality which organises people hierarchically from somebodies down to nobodies, and often according to whether or not they yield or are yielded to, does that status of nothingness feel so degrading. Anne does not possess such a mentality, and detached from a single neighbourhood and a fixed world of traditional institutions that make that mentality possible, she allows the alienation she experiences upon first coming to Uppercross to be a benefit. Anne finds it 'very fitting, that every little social commonwealth should dictate its own matters of discourse' (p. 43), and by learning different social discourses she is able to be a citizen of many commonwealths. Accordingly, she considers it 'highly incumbent on her to clothe her imagination, her memory, and all her ideas' (p. 43) in Uppercross. Though first undertaken as a duty, this reinvestiture is later experienced as a boon. After leaving, Anne discovers that subjects which she had felt obliged to 'smother among the Musgroves' assume only 'secondary interest' (p. 124). She is 'sensible of some mental change': her sorrow about Kellynch and even her tenacious loyalty to Wentworth loosens, and she now entertains thoughts of Benwick, and even of Walter Elliot.

If processes of inuring can be therapeutic – Anne, for example, 'was become hardened to such affronts' (p. 34) as she receives at home – some kinds of malleability can bring relief as well, even if it makes possible a certain erasure. Anne finally refuses to take sides in the debate about hardness and softness, and determination and submission, setting her sights instead on 'elasticity of mind, that disposition to be comforted, that power of turning readily from evil to good, and of finding employment' (p. 154). When Wentworth wittily explains how in marrying Anne he is not getting what he deserves, he elaborates on this quality: '"Like other great men under reverses", he added with a smile, "I must endeavour to subdue my mind to my fortune"' (p. 247). The ironic mode of his statement is oddly fitting, for the 'reverse' in question of course is the happiness of reconciliation, possible only after relinquishing the obduracy of his resentment and becoming susceptible to opposition. But the people in *Persuasion* who are pre-eminent for elasticity of mind are significantly far more remote than Wentworth, who after all by the end of the novel is acceptable even to Sir Walter. By the standards set in Austen's fiction, in fact, they are unusual, and by those set in conservative fiction, far too marginal to be the models they are here. They are mostly without the kinds of affiliations, idealised in such writing, that exact a high cost – confinement, unventuresomeness, fixity, boredom – for the stability they guarantee. Some Sir Walter regards as scarcely human: 'A Mrs Smith. A widow Mrs Smith. ... And what is her attraction? That she is old and sickly. – Upon my word, Miss Anne Elliot, you have the most extraordinary taste! Every thing that revolts other people, low company, paltry rooms, foul air, disgusting associations are inviting to you' (p. 157). Yet Mrs Smith above all others typifies the 'elasticity of mind' Anne values, and this is not only despite the reverses that have marginalised her, but also in some ways because she has undergone them.

In so far as salvos like these would console the unfortunate by contending that it is better to suffer after all, they condone the processes and conditions which cause such suffering to begin with, and so may be considered implicitly conservative. *Persuasion* is sometimes deeply tinged with such quietism. And yet Anne's preference of 'low company, paltry rooms, foul air' to the companionship of her father and those he would choose for her is nevertheless a pretty piece of social criticism. Fortune, Providence, luck, chance – these are extremely prominent entities in the novel, and are emblemised here by the sea itself. And the person with 'elasticity of mind' – the 'choicest gift of Heaven' (p. 154) – takes and resigns what they give with equal cheer, and makes her- or himself malleable to their impressions, much as the Crofts have let the sea air write itself on to their complexions without bothering with applications of Gowland's Lotion. On Mrs Smith, who lives beyond the margins of 'good' society, their marks have been the deepest: 'She had been very fond of her husband, – she had buried him. She had been used to affluence, – it was gone. She had no child to connect her with life and happiness again, no relations to assist in the arrangement of perplexed affairs, no health to make all the rest supportable' (p. 154). But though she is the least sheltered from fortune's blows – and as Mrs Croft says, 'We none of us expect to be in smooth water all our days' (p. 70) – she is also the most resilient for having 'weathered it' (p. 154), the least inclined to feel 'ill-used'. Her bodily immobility – roughly similar in kind, if not in degree, to the confinement undergone by proper ladies in their provincial homes – serves only to highlight her resources more brilliantly. In a similar way Harville lives just beyond society, bordering out onto the sea itself, which has not served him a fraction so generously as it has Wentworth. If his case is not so dire as Mrs Smith's – he is less crippled, less cramped, less destitute, and with a loving family, less disattached – by Sir Walter's standards he still ranks as a 'disgusting association'. But though even Anne herself suffers a 'moment's astonishment' at the meanness of his lodgings, she later regards them as the seat of 'great happiness' (p. 99).

While the people Anne casts her lot with are well-travelled citizens of many different commonwealths, to recall Anne's metaphor, they are proprietors of none. Always ready to determine orders of precedence and to feel 'ill-used' if opposed or neglected, Mary Musgrove decides after only a little consideration that even though Anne's accession to marriage restores her 'to the rights of seniority', her own situation is still superior: 'Anne had no Uppercross-hall before her, no landed estate, no headship of a family; and if they could but keep Captain Wentworth from being made a baronet, she would not change situations with Anne' (p. 250). To Anne, however, these lacks are a virtue. Religious intimations are more frequent in *Persuasion* than in any of Austen's other novels and more enmeshed into its outlook. But whereas in other novels the world of wealthy gentry in which Mary takes such pride is either genuinely or at the very least nominally in the service of such intimations, in *Persuasion* it is not. Characters here who are most like the glossy but impermeable and therefore irredeemable hazelnut in Wentworth's parable are not Wentworth himself, who finally yields after all, but members of the privileged class, such as Sir Walter, who is devoted to avoiding crow's-feet, and the 'polished' William Elliot, who is suspect precisely because he 'endured too well' (p. 161) and gives no evidence of friction or wear.

From the very beginning of the novel, Anne has valued 'cheerful confidence in futurity' and scorned to 'distrust Providence!' (p. 30). Peopled more with friends than family, and accepting the 'dread of war' that sometimes dims the 'sunshine' (p. 252) of domestic felicity, the society Anne finally selects – the 'best' company (p. 150) – removes itself from the institutions of the country manor to front more directly and hospitably onto Providence. But while the break Anne accomplishes with those institutions is more complete than what we find in any other novel, and while her efforts at accommodation are the most perfunctory, she and the alternative society she joins are also the least prone to overt indictment, and this constitutes a departure from Austen's early fiction especially. Whereas *Sense and Sensibility* and *Northanger Abbey* derive much of their dramatic tension from the defiance of tyrannical parents, *Persuasion* eludes, even frowns upon, overt rebellion. Social forms may be neglected – Anne dislikes 'give-and-take invitations, and dinners of formality and display' (p. 98) – but not outright opposed. Accordingly, Anne herself is capable of betraying some shame about her association with Lady Dalrymple and Miss Carteret, but she politely keeps it under wraps: '"Yes," sighed Anne, "we shall, indeed, be known to be related to them!" – then recollecting herself ... not wishing to be answered' (pp. 150–1). But William Elliot's history of expressed disrespect for rank itself is not acceptable. The narrator makes no bones about averring that 'Sir Walter was not very wise' (p. 24), but Anne shudders 'with shock and mortification' to learn that his heir applies words as irreverent as 'fool' (p. 204) to him. But before we conclude that Austen's willingness to cover for Sir Walter betrays deplorable bad faith, or perhaps less damningly, loyalties too deep and residual to permit penetrating social criticism, we would do well to ponder the typically confounding twist in her characterisation of William Elliot. Surely to identify the person who mouths social disrespect with the person who then panders to the very people of 'credit and dignity' (p. 151) whom he admits are 'nothing in themselves' (p. 150) is to underscore the particularly sterile conventionality of the entire system of 'blood and connexion' (p. 206) and the cynicism on which it subsists.

Of none of Austen's works, but of *Persuasion* perhaps least of all, can it be said, as Trilling has, 'Nothing in the novels questions the ideal of the archaic "noble" life which is appropriate to the great beautiful houses with the ever-remembered names – Northanger Abbey, Donwell Abbey, Pemberly, Hartfield, Kellynch Hall, Norland Park, Mansfield Park. In them "existence is sweet and dear", at least if one is rightly disposed. ... With what the great houses represent the heroines of the novels are, or become, completely in accord.'[9] Northanger Abbey is far from a haven to Catherine Morland, and this is not because *she* fails to be 'rightly disposed'; Norland Park provides no values with which the Dashwood sisters can accord; and Kellynch Hall, not even 'ever-remembered' by its own proprietors, is bidden a rather wistful good riddance by a daughter far superior to what it now 'represents'. Works of fiction written on the conservative model tirelessly exhort us to accept infelicity as the condition of life and urge us instead to seek our modest satisfactions in the consciousness of prescribed attachments well honoured, and duties well done. But Austen's novels are pervasively concerned, not with according ourselves to an existence 'sweet and dear', but with achieving a more active, expansive, and personally fulfilling happiness, and they persistently suggest that this is well worth the striving. Sometimes, as in *Pride and Prejudice*, Austen contrives to locate such happiness within conservative institutions themselves, but as we have seen, it takes some work before Pemberly will accommodate Elizabeth. And once Pemberly does make a place for her, one suspects that it is the 'great beautiful house' itself, rather than Elizabeth, that will be essentially improved for her presence there, because whatever its previous dignity, it never seemed a place of pleasure. The word 'happy' rings as frequently across the pages of *Persuasion* as it does those of *Pride and Prejudice*, and it should tell us something that in *Persuasion* it is the nefarious Walter Elliot who wishes to dissuade Anne from pursuing the highest happiness she can conceive of. When he discovers that she prefers the 'best' company to merely 'good' company, he warns, 'You have a better right to be fastidious than almost any other woman I know; but will it answer? Will it make you happy? Will it not be wiser to accept the society of these good ladies in Laura-place, and enjoy all the advantages of the connexion as far as possible?' (p. 150). Fortunately, Anne's fastidiousness, like Elizabeth's, finally does 'answer'. But unlike Elizabeth's, it is achieved not at a great beautiful house with an ever-remembered name, but rather in a disposition only discernible in people who do not belong to such houses, people such as the Crofts, who walk 'along in happy independence' (p. 168), or like Harville, whose weather-beaten lodgings are a 'picture of repose and domestic happiness' (p. 98).

The interests of happiness, piety, and well-being demand removal from Kellynch Hall, its proprieties and priorities. But whether moving beyond Kellynch or any equivalent bespeaks a victory of autonomy from what a great house represents, or a despair of its ever improving enough to be desirable, is hard to say. Not surprisingly, since they belong exclusively to the years which assured the reaction, Austen's last three novels reflect a strong sense of the increasing immovability of established authority. While *Sense and Sensibility* concludes with an opposition and a withdrawal that are angry, permanent, and committed, in *Northanger Abbey* General Tilney finally does yield, if minimally, and in *Pride and Prejudice* Darcy is improved by confrontation, and eventually even Lady Catherine comes around. But even though Sir Thomas's judgement in *Mansfield Park* is thoroughly impeached, his authority is fixed. In *Emma*, when his kind of authority is transformed and feminised, and joined with Knightley's, it assumes a benign aspect. But in *Persuasion*, stately houses and their proprietors are no longer formidable, and their intransigence is matched only by their vapidity. Good characters depart from them without a breach, differ from them without defiance. Thus the overarching structure of *Persuasion* as a whole reproduces and asks us to accept the same sorts of unresolved tensions found in so many of its shorter, characteristically oxymoronic formulations – such as 'fat sighings', or 'she was deep in the happiness of such misery, or the misery of such happiness' (p. 229). *Persuasion* settles little: it resumes a debate interrupted eight years in the past without reaching an agreement, and without requiring one. Wentworth does not concede that Lady Russell had been right, Anne refuses to concede that yielding was wrong: 'cheerful confidence in futurity' precludes such regret, and Providence has been equally served by delay.

The 'elasticity of mind' celebrated in *Persuasion* accepts and surpasses both of these, as well as the broader social conflicts the book details. It is tempting to see this effort to define and endorse extensive difference from established institutions, without effecting an overt or impassible breach from them, as the perfection of the strategies and the positions that have marked Austen's fiction from the start. Austen, no less than Blake, wrote for an audience with what one critic has called 'war-manacled minds', and her works, no less than Blake's, attempt – inevitably with only limited success – to shed those manacles which she perforce wore too.[10] Among the least doctrinaire of all her contemporaries, Austen from the outset took on the materials which political controversy endowed with such importance, without inviting or aggravating partisan impulses. During a time when all social criticism, particularly that which aimed at the institution of the family in general and the place of women in particular, came to be associated with the radical cause, Austen defended and enlarged a progressive middle ground that had been eaten away by the polarising polemics born of the 1790s. If she very early opted definitely not to ratify the anarchism of the radical opposition, despite an allegiance to the liberal tradition which underlay much of it, she also avoided its irritability, its confusion, and its very early defeat. Conservative fiction was Austen's medium because it very quickly became the only fiction there was, other voices being quelled, and Austen persistently subjected its most cherished mythologies to interrogations from which it could not recover. The highly parodic style developed in the juvenilia, when applied to the stuff of conservative fiction, constituted a kind of piracy which commandeered conservative novelistic discourse and forced it to hoist flags of different colours, so to speak, to say things it was not fashioned to say – as when Catherine Morland, for example, assures herself with perfect trust that the good General Tilney 'could not propose any thing improper for her' (*Northanger Abbey*, p. 156); or when Marianne's 'sensibility' and Elinor's 'sense' turn out not to be antithetically opposed; or most optimistically, when Darcy himself absorbs the values of his antagonist in order to make her as well as himself happy. In none of the novels can conservative ideology be entirely overcome, but in all, as most forcibly in *Mansfield Park*, its basic imperatives – benevolence, gratitude, family attachment, female modesty, paternal authority – are wrested from their privileged claims and made, like Edmund Bertram, to relinquish their 'moral elevation' (*Mansfield Park*, p. 158).

From Claudia Johnson, *Jane Austen: Women, Politics and the Novel* (Chicago, 1988), pp. 144–8; 158–66.

## NOTES

[In this extract, taken from her book on Jane Austen's novels, Claudia Johnson argues convincingly for Austen as a progressive, rather than as either the conservative or radical writer she has been variously termed. Johnson thus takes issue directly with the views put forward by critics such as Marilyn Butler and Sandra Gilbert and Susan Gubar. This lucid and scholarly essay locates *Persuasion* in a precisely documented context of contemporary discussions of gender, with an emphasis on sexually differentiated manners. Johnson draws attention to Austen's debt to eighteenth-century traditions of liberal psychology and points to the political middle ground Austen treads in a novel which explores the inadequacies at either extreme of the arguments about principle. She argues that in its analysis of female rationalism, contextualised by the novel's record of social transformations, *Persuasion* is a work focused on the idea of the present. Consequently Anne Elliot becomes the prototype of the modern woman, her modernity in part reflecting contemporary debates about gender and sexual politics. Johnson's cultural critique of the text, while heavily influenced by feminist readings of Austen, also has much in common with John Wiltshire's and other commentaries which read the literary work in tandem with its non-literary sources. References to *Persuasion* are to the edition of *The Works of Jane Austen* by R. W. Chapman (London, rpt. 1982). Ed.]

[All references to the novel are given in parentheses in the text. Ed.]

1.  For some of the many formulations of this view, see Virginia Woolf, *The Common Reader*, First Series (New York, 1953), pp. 147–8; Nina Auerbach, *Romantic Imprisonment: Women and Other Glorified Outcasts* (New York, 1986), pp. 38–54; the chapter devoted to *Persuasion* in David M. Monaghan, *Jane Austen: Structure and Social Vision* (Totowa, NJ, 1980).

2.  For a historian's sceptical outlook on the way literary scholars have misused historical arguments about social change as reflected in *Persuasion* see David Spring, 'Interpreters of Jane Austen's Social World', in Janet Todd, *Jane Austen: New Perspectives* (New York, 1983), p. 65.

3.  See, for example, Marilyn Butler, *Jane Austen and the War of Ideas* (Oxford, 1975), pp. 274–86; and Mary Poovey, *The Proper Lady and the Woman Writer* (Chicago, 1984), pp. 224–40.

4.  See B.C. Southam, '*Sanditon*: the Seventh Novel', in *Jane Austen's Achievement*, ed. Juliet McMaster (London, 1976), pp. 1–26. See also Joel L. Gold, 'The Return to Bath: Catherine Morland and Anne Elliot', *Genre*, 9 (1976), 215–29.

5. For some notable and welcome exceptions, see Frederick Keener, *The Chain of Becoming – The Philosophical Tale, the Novel, and a Neglected Realism of the Enlightenment* (New York, 1983), pp. 241–307; Lloyd W. Brown, *Bits of Ivory: Narrative Technique in Jane Austen's Fiction* (Baton Rouge, LA, 1973).

6. Samuel Johnson, *The Rambler*, 5, 47, *Yale Edition of the Works of Samuel Johnson*, ed. Jean Hagstrum and James Gray (New Haven, CT, 1978).

7. *Rambler*, 85.

8. Edgeworth's copy of *Persuasion* is located in the Edgeworth Collection in the Special Collections Division of the University Research Library at The University of California, Los Angeles.

9. Lionel Trilling, *Sincerity and Authenticity* (Cambridge, MA, 1972), pp. 73–4.

10. This phrase derives from David Erdman, *Blake, Prophet Against Empire* (Princeton, NJ, 1954).

# 10

# Loss and the Language of Restitution in *Persuasion*

*LAURA G. MOONEYHAM*

Most of Austen's novels educate their heroines away from error. Emma and Elizabeth, Catherine and Marianne, are taught by circumstances to see the nature of their egotism and folly and are led by repentance into a more mature understanding of the world and of themselves. Anne Elliot's error, however, occurs over seven years before the beginning of the novel. Her falling into chastened silence and suffering has constituted the whole of that intervening period. Anne's education is not one of seeing and avoiding the errors of imagination and wit; it is an education in how to overcome the suffering that follows the awareness of error. Though Anne was right to follow Lady Russell's advice, that advice was wrong. Anne's recognition of Lady Russell's misjudgement and of her own rectitude, however, does not bring into being a happy ending. How easily happiness can be missed! Being right, as Anne sorrowfully discovers, does not bring happiness. *Persuasion* offers one model after another of how the human personality copes with adversity, disappointment and lost opportunities. Anne and Wentworth are the only characters who learn that happiness cannot be regained until they seek it. And in their restricted society, the only means of regaining happiness is through language. Thus the barrier between Anne and Wentworth is appropriately linguistic. Words keep them apart; only words can bring them together. Anne's search for happiness, her transition from passive suffering into a more roused struggle

against fate, must lie in her breaking through the barrier of silence
or the equally deadly barrier of common speech, the 'nothingness'
of polite talk.

As the novel begins, Anne is trapped in a world of suppressed
speech. She can speak to no one of her presiding concern, her lost
opportunity with Wentworth. Her father and Elizabeth assume a
'general air of oblivion' (p. 30) in their scorn for Anne's past attachment. Even Lady Russell, Anne's only confidante, shares in this
assumed unconsciousness, though her motives in doing so are more
praiseworthy than those of Anne's immediate family. That Anne and
Lady Russell never discuss the past nonetheless renders the rest of
their communications awkward. Since 'they knew not each other's
opinion, either its constancy or its change, on the one leading point
of Anne's conduct' (p. 29), honest communication is impossible.

Honest communication of any variety is a rare commodity in
*Persuasion*. The first extended dialogue in the novel can hardly be
termed 'communication': Sir Walter announces his prejudices
against the navy, and the two sycophants, Mr Shepherd and Mrs
Clay, listen and approve. Though no sycophant, Anne too is forced
repeatedly to listen to the self-absorbed proclamations of those
around her. Even on those few occasions in which Anne speaks
more or less openly to others – with Captain Benwick at Lyme, for
example, or with Lady Russell after leaving Uppercross – there is
constraint, a suppression of information about Anne's deepest feelings. It is telling that the idea of Anne's speaking out is most often
expressed hypothetically or conditionally:[1]

> How eloquent could Anne Elliot have been, – how eloquent at least,
> were her wishes on the side of early warm attachment...
>
> (p. 30)

> Anne longed for the power of representing to them all what they
> were about, and of pointing out some of the evils they were exposing
> themselves to.
>
> (p. 82)

> ...when listening ... to Mary's reproach of 'Charles spoils the chil-
> dren', ... she never had the smallest temptation to say 'Very true.'
>
> (p. 44)

> Anne could have said much and did long to say a little, in defence of
> her friend ... but ... she made no reply.
>
> (p. 158)

We see one instance of Anne speaking out from a sense of duty: her warning to Elizabeth about Mrs Clay. Anne voices her misgivings even though she has 'little hope of success' and, in so doing, 'seemed only to offend' (p. 34). Elizabeth tells Anne: 'I think it rather unnecessary in you to be advising me' (p. 35). Here Anne's sense of moral responsibility forces her into an exercise of cautious speech, but she is ignored.

Anne's role throughout the novel is more often that of the listener and confidante. At Uppercross, she must listen to everybody's complaints and cross-complaints, though she is restrained by propriety from acting on her unwanted knowledge. It is important to see that Austen is as opposed to profuse communication as she is to the restraints of silence. Anne knows that the unrestricted flow of visits and chat between Uppercross Cottage and the Great House is 'highly imprudent', though she no longer attempts to interfere, 'believing that, though there were on each side continual subjects of offence, neither family could now do without it' (p. 40). Thus when the Miss Musgroves invite Mary for a walk but are displeased when she accepts, Anne must mitigate the friction by coming along herself. Again, an unconstrained social commerce is dangerous: 'Anne ... admired again the sort of necessity which the family-habits seemed to produce, of every thing to be communicated, and every thing being done together, however undesired and inconvenient' (p. 83). Thus the easy converse of the Musgroves is not to be envied. Anne is trapped in silence, but the solution to her problem is not a sudden rush to volubility. Anne's mission in *Persuasion* is to find a middle ground between mute constraint and undisciplined loquacity.

In a sense, Anne's silence after her broken engagement with Wentworth is parallel to the responses of Austen's other heroines after the recognition of error. Those heroines whose errors are chiefly imaginative, like Catherine Morland or Emma Woodhouse, fall into a period of chastened silence after their moment of crisis. Anne's early error was not one of imagination, but the reverse – a repudiation of imagination in favour of perceived duty. But her error nonetheless reaps the same harvest of chastened silence. Further, the period of time between the heroine's perception of error and the 'moment of assent' which allows her to be reunited with the hero in *Persuasion* is far longer than that of any other Austen novel: eight-and-half-years. Now beginning to be debilitated by the illness which would kill her, Austen no longer accepts the idea that clear perception in and of itself can furnish happiness.

When one considers Austen's work as a whole, the ratio of error to consequences in *Persuasion* seems lopsided; error causes far greater suffering in this novel than in the others. The restitution of past mistakes requires more than clear vision. In *Persuasion*, suffering must be combated.

Thus Anne is mistaken in her early self-effacement and resignation to her lot. Her early silence is an expression of this resignation. But Austen demands more of Anne than passive capitulation to loss. Anne must learn to speak out, not brazenly, but quietly, effectively, *fluently*. Happiness will no longer conveniently announce itself to the virtuous heroine, as it does in the form of Henry Tilney on the Morlands' doorstep in *Northanger Abbey*. Happiness is now the object of a quest, a quest whose perilous obstacles are the almost impossible conditions Anne's society presents for open communication.

The world of *Persuasion* is one of oblique, elusive and complex communication. Conversations are overheard; letters are reread; stories are retold by a second- or third-hand narrator.[2] Thus Anne is the unseen auditor of Charles's and Mary's negotiations about who will attend the first dinner with Captain Wentworth; of Wentworth's discourse on the nut to Louisa; of Elizabeth's extended invitation to Mrs Clay at Anne's expense; and, with Wentworth at the White Hart, of Mrs Croft's and Mrs Musgrove's adjudications on the subject of early and unwise marriages. Then in the climactic scene which precedes the romantic resolution, the roles of speaker and listener are reversed as Wentworth overhears Anne's conversation with Captain Harville. The motif of overheard conversations is extended in the excised chapter when Anne is forced to hear the Admiral and Wentworth discussing her presumed engagement to Elliot through the door of the Crofts' parlour. Letters too are less than perfect vehicles for communication. Not one of the letters in *Persuasion* is an uncomplicated transmission of information. Anne's correspondence with Elizabeth is 'slow and unsatisfactory'. Mary's letter to Anne in Bath is both self-contradictory and schizophrenic. The first part of her letter conveys many complaints but little information; the second revokes the earlier complaints while giving the astounding news of Louisa's engagement to Benwick. The theme of imperfect epistles is also strengthened by the lapsed condolence notes between Kellynch and Ireland, as well as by Sir Walter's servile letter of explanation and the 'three lines of scrawl' (p. 149) it garners in response from the Dowager Viscountess. There is moreover Elliot's letter of ten years back to

Mrs Smith's late husband, which provides Anne with unshakeable evidence of Elliot's perfidy. Anne is well aware of the morally dubious position of the unauthorised reader; she tempers her anger against Elliot by remembering that 'her seeing the letter was a violation of the laws of honour, that no one ought to be judged or be known by such testimonies [and] that no private correspondence would bear the eye of others' (p. 214). Last in the chain of less-than-straightforward letters is Wentworth's epistolary proposal to Anne. The content is from the heart, but he writes under the cover of another letter to Captain Benwick and under an impulse generated by Anne's equally indirect communications through Captain Harville to himself. Nothing is more difficult in Anne's world than to express what one means simply and directly; the very structure of her society works against honesty and sincerity.

Direct communication is hampered not only by social rules and proprieties but by the fact that social contact itself is a fleeting and transient proposition. If honest speech is rare, it is so to a large degree because opportunities for such speech are equally rare. An important theme of *Persuasion* is the tenuous nature of social encounters. Austen demonstrates this tenuousness by having Anne repeatedly prepare for crucial meetings which never materialise.[3] Thus Anne dreads the first visit of the Crofts to Kellynch but manages to be away, at Lady Russell's, on the day assigned. Again, Anne avoids her first meeting with Wentworth through the fortuitous happenstance of her nephew's fall. Later, she wastes a good deal of anxiety on the question of Lady Russell's and Wentworth's imminent encounter at Kellynch, but such a meeting never takes place. Thus too Anne plans for Benwick's visit to Lady Russell's home; he is expected for a week but never comes. Foresight is thus rendered useless. Further, this lesson that caution may be wasted strengthens Anne's – and the reader's – conviction that Anne's early refusal to marry Wentworth for caution's sake was in error. Equally unprofitable is Anne's great care to observe Lady Russell's reactions when she herself sees Wentworth on the street at Bath. But Lady Russell's intense stare is directed at some window curtains, not at Wentworth. And Anne worries herself into a frenzy of agitation over whether or not Captain Wentworth will attend Elizabeth's party. Wentworth does attend, but Anne's preparation and anxiety are rendered futile because the two lovers have proclaimed their mutual attachment and have undone every doubt several hours before the party takes place. Lastly, Anne's plans to tell Lady

Russell the secret of Elliot's true nature are purposely delayed three times by the narrator. As Anne herself notes, 'Mr Elliot's character, like the Sultaness Scheherazade's head, must live another day' (p. 229).[4] The missed communications with Lady Russell are part of Austen's design to make clear the limited nature of social intercourse.

Anne's attempts to reach Wentworth, however, are hampered by more than the restrictive conditions placed on communication by her society as a whole. They are impeded primarily by Wentworth himself, who erects one obstacle of language after another between himself and Anne. The primary barrier between Wentworth and Anne is linguistic. For though Wentworth is highly skilful with language, this skill diminishes markedly in those areas which apply to his own inner drama about Anne.[5] Our first insight into Wentworth's feelings occurs in chapter seven; the narrator here gives a third person but unadorned explication of Wentworth's position regarding Anne:

> He had not forgiven Anne Elliot. She had used him ill; deserted and disappointed him; and worse, she had shewn a feebleness of character in doing so, which his own decided, confident temper could not endure. She had given him up to oblige others. It had been the effect of over-persuasion. It had been weakness and timidity.
>
> (p. 61)

Wentworth's rhetoric betrays him, for this simplistic explanation of Anne's behaviour reveals his inability to distinguish the complex causes which led Anne to reject him.[6] He now admits only to curiosity regarding Anne, and asserts emotional independence from her influence: 'her power with him was gone for ever'. And when he shares his ideas on marriage with his sister – 'any body between fifteen and thirty may have me for asking' – he secretly excludes Anne. Even so, he knows he is speaking foolishly and that his standards are higher than he admits. Anne is at least unconsciously in his mind when he describes the woman he would like to marry: 'a strong mind, with sweetness of manner' (p. 62).

From the start of Wentworth's re-emergence into Anne's life, their relationship is dominated by flawed and indirect communication. Wentworth compounds those restrictions which society places on social contact with his own self-restrictions on speech with Anne. Even before he and Anne meet, he signals his wish to pretend that they have no romantic history. His inquiry after her at the Musgroves' dinner-party is such 'as might suit a former slight acquaintance' (p. 59). He contrives moreover to change the meeting-place for the next morning's hunt with Charles Musgrove from the Cottage to the Great House. Anne has no difficulty in decoding Wentworth's message; she understands that he wishes to avoid her.

In the early stages of their reacquaintance, Anne is as silent and reserved as Wentworth. But she is following his lead. He is thus responsible for their new verbal estrangement, and it is Anne's role to mend this emotional – and linguistic – rift. Their first meeting bears out the linguistic dimension of their alienation. Austen's treatment of the scene emphasises the noise in the room and Wentworth's voice:

> ... it was soon over. ... Her eyes half met Captain Wentworth's; a bow, a curtsey passed; she heard his voice – he talked to Mary, said all that was right; said something to the Miss Musgroves, enough to mark an easy footing; the room seemed full, full of persons and voices – but a few minutes ended it.
>
> (p. 59)

Anne hears Wentworth's voice distinctly, but the noise and confusion and her own emotional turmoil prevent her from knowing the particulars of his speeches. He 'said all that was right', but this phrase can only refer to Wentworth's easy adherence to social niceties. He is not able to '[say] all that [is] right' in a deeper sense until the end of the novel.

Until the structural centre of the novel, Louisa's fall at Lyme, the linguistic barrier between Anne and Wentworth remains unbroken. They say little to each other, and what is said is the stuff of civility and no more. What Anne hears of substance from Wentworth she either overhears or hears at second-hand. For instance, soon after Wentworth's and Anne's first meeting, Mary thoughtlessly informs Anne that Wentworth has described her as 'so altered he should not have known you again' (p. 60). Anne's response to this shattering information is noteworthy. She not only submits to his appraisal, but sees in it reason to 'rejoice' – not because it raises, but because it dashes, hope: '[His words] were of sobering tendency; they allayed agitation; they composed, and consequently must make her happier' (p. 61). Anne's stoicism speaks here, but she knows at heart that resignation does not bring happiness. Before Lyme, Anne is submissive and resigned. Though grieved by Wentworth's coldness and silence, she makes no attempt to change the status of their relationship. During this period, Anne's musings take the form of a debate between the emotional and irrationally hopeful self and the self which urges calm and circumspection. This inner debate between caution and hope is settled in caution's favour, but Anne's hopes refuse to die in spite of all the rational arguments against them. Thus Anne terms her excitement over the news of Wentworth's arrival 'folly' but nonetheless requires 'many a stroll and many a sigh ... to dispel the agitation of the idea' (p. 30). When the Musgroves discover that Wentworth may have been 'poor Richard's' commander, Anne finds a new trial in their constant repetition of Wentworth's name. She tells herself that 'she must teach herself to be insensible on such points' (p. 52). And as she nurses her injured nephew while the Musgroves' dinner-party proceeds with Wentworth as a guest, she tries to find comfort in her usefulness to the boy but cannot help thinking of her old love: 'what was it to her, if Frederick Wentworth were only a half a mile distant, making himself agreeable to others!' (p. 58). When the two finally meet, Anne is incapable of reasoning away her emotions: 'she began to ... try to be feeling less ... How absurd to be resuming the agitation which such an interval had banished into distance! ... What might not eight years do? ... Alas! with all her reasonings, she found, that to retentive feelings eight years may be little more than nothing' (p. 60).

Until Wentworth himself provides a reason for hope, Anne must be resigned and must scold herself for her unreasonable and unwise longings. She can only listen and observe at the many social functions they attend together, while Wentworth demonstrates to the Miss Musgroves his wit and charm. Anne must witness his careless courtship of these girls, and must remember too his more serious courtship of her. Louisa and Henrietta, as it happens, ask the same naïve questions about naval life which Anne herself had asked. And when Wentworth lightheartedly tells of his near miss with death on the *Asp*, the parallel between the sisters' position and Anne's is made explicit: 'Anne's shudderings were to herself, alone: but the Miss Musgroves could be as open as they were sincere, in their exclamations of pity and horror' (p. 66). Wentworth demonstrates verbal facility at these encounters, though he will not speak to Anne. Thus he refers to the year '06 as he relates his adventures to general acclaim, and Anne must listen and assume their shared consciousness of that date's significance, 'though she was very far from conceiving it to be of equal pain' (p. 65). Wentworth's wit is buoyed up in part by the admiration and flattery he finds at Uppercross; he has 'everything to elevate him, which general attention and deference, and especially the attention of all the young women could do' (p. 71). Wentworth is displaying his triumph in front of Anne, which explains his exuberant exhibition of charm. In any case, their linguistic division is most complete at these Uppercross gatherings; he speaks to everyone but Anne; she speaks as little as possible, and never to him:

> They had no conversation together, no intercourse but what the commonest civility required. Once so much to each other! Now nothing! ... Now they were as strangers; nay, worse than strangers, for they could never become acquainted. It was a perpetual estrangement.
>
> (p. 63)

Wentworth at this point is cold and courteous to Anne. She finds that his forced gestures and speeches are far worse than an absence of communication. As she plays alone at the piano,[7] a solitary observer of the company's gaiety, Wentworth determines from his partner, within Anne's range of hearing, that Anne has given up dancing – has, that is, absented herself from the arena of courtship. He speaks once to her, but addresses her with brief and formal civility. Anne assumes that Wentworth's studied speech betokens his closed heart: '[she] did not wish for more of such looks and speeches. His cold politeness, his ceremonious grace, were worse than any thing' (p. 72).

Since Wentworth does not speak to Anne except to discharge common civilities, Anne must rely on his more indirect modes of communication if she is to understand his mind. Unlike the reader, who has a limited access to Wentworth's consciousness, Anne must read his behaviour alone.[8] His first attempt at an accord with Anne is enacted physically, not verbally: he relieves her from her young tormenter, her nephew, who has attached himself tenaciously to her back. Both the rescue and its aftermath are entirely wordless:

> [Anne's] sensations on the discovery [of Wentworth's action] made her perfectly speechless. She could not even thank him. ... His kindness in stepping forward to her relief – the manner – the silence in which it had passed ... with the conviction soon forced on her by the noise he was studiously making with the child, that he meant to avoid hearing her thanks, and rather sought to testify that her con-

versation was the last of his wants, produced ... a confusion of
varying, but very painful agitation.

(p. 80)

The scene's pathos arises from the conjunction of the rightness of
Wentworth's small action and the more material wrongness of his
refusal to speak.[9]

Wentworth again acts to aid Anne without speaking when he
arranges with the Crofts for Anne to ride home in their gig. Again
what is stressed is silent action. Wentworth clears a hedge to speak
with Mrs Croft; he then hands Anne into the carriage 'without
saying a word' (p. 91). Anne is all the more affected by his compas-
sionate gesture because she has just overheard his conversation with
Louisa from behind a hedgerow.[10] Anne now believes that she understands Wentworth's feelings, that he has not forgiven her but
that he still feels compassion for her. The overheard conversation
provides Anne with an even more salient piece of information, for
Wentworth's startled reaction to Louisa's news about Anne's rejection of Charles Musgrove is proof that he has some interest in
Anne's love life. Not until Lyme, however, does romantic interest
reflower, and again jealousy plays a role. At Lyme, Anne is monop-
olised by Captain Benwick; here also Anne meets the then-unknown
Elliot, who regards her with frank sexual approval. Again, Anne
must rely on her knowledge of Wentworth to determine his reaction
to the unidentified gentleman's interest, and, significantly, Anne's
newly emergent self-confidence[11] allows her to recreate Wentworth's
response for herself with authority: '[Wentworth] gave her a
momentary glance, – a glance of brightness, which seemed to say,
"That man is struck with you, – and even I, at this moment, see
something like Anne Elliot again"' (p. 104).

Lyme is the structural centre of the novel because it marks the
point at which Anne's and Wentworth's roles begin to reverse.
Anne becomes more active, Wentworth more passive. Anne grows
into a new confidence; Wentworth loses much of his bravado. Anne
speaks up; Wentworth's speeches diminish in fluency and quantity.
Where Anne had feared that Wentworth would display too much
self-possession, and herself too little, in front of Lady Russell, we
find that from Lyme onward, it is Anne who controls the relationship and who has a clearer sense of how each feels for the other.
This reversal is first indicated when Lousia falls. Wentworth is
momentarily paralysed; both he and Charles Musgrove look

instinctively towards Anne for aid and advice. Throughout the disaster, Anne is cool-headed and effective. It is she who prods the stunned party – including Wentworth – into action. How significant it is then that what Anne overhears Wentworth saying at Lyme after the accident is a tribute to her activity: 'if Anne will stay, [there is] no one so proper, so capable as Anne!' (p. 114). And when he implores her in person to stay, he does so with a 'glow, and yet a gentleness, which seemed almost restoring the past' (p. 114).

After having arranged that both Louisa's old nurse and her parents should join Louisa at Lyme, Anne returns to Lady Russell. Here she has a new sense of possibilities, for despite her fear that Wentworth is bound to Louisa, she nonetheless has felt his renewed warmth towards herself, 'some breathings of friendship and reconciliation' (p. 123). She is amused to find that Lady Russell sees in her the same physical improvement which had prompted Elliot's look of admiration; she hopes that she is 'to be blessed with a second spring of youth and beauty' (p. 124). These promising developments are but buds, however. Wentworth still will not communicate with Anne directly. On a short visit to Kellynch, he praises Anne's 'exertions' at Lyme to the Crofts, but does not visit her. Instead he delivers anonymously the latest bulletin from Lyme.

Once Wentworth is in Bath, Anne, not he, directs the course of their relationship. In their first meeting there, for instance, Anne sees Wentworth before he sees her and thus has several moments in which to steady herself for the encounter. That Wentworth has lost his sense of control where Anne is concerned is demonstrated by his lack of self-possession:

> He was more obviously struck and confused by the sight of her, than she had ever observed before; he looked quite red. For the first time, since their renewed acquaintance, she felt that she was betraying the least sensibility of the two. She had the advantage of him, in the preparation of the last few moments. ... Mutual enquiries on common subjects passed; neither of them, probably, much the wiser for what they heard, and Anne continuing fully sensible of his being less at ease than formerly. They had, by dint of being so very much together, got to speak to each other with a considerable portion of apparent indifference and calmness; but he could not do it now ... it was Captain Wentworth not comfortable, not easy, not able to feign that he was.
>
> (pp. 175–6)

Unconcerned speech is no longer a possibility for Wentworth; he feels too deeply. Even so, the same pattern of action over speech prevails at this meeting: Wentworth offers to help Anne to her carriage, but 'by manner, rather than words' (p. 176).

At the concert, Anne arranges her actions and speech to give Wentworth the greatest possible encouragement. When he arrives and seems to be passing on with only a bow, Anne steps forward with a 'gentle "How do you do?"' Wentworth too is signalling to Anne; in the conversation which follows he dwells on his joy at Benwick's engagement, his belief that Benwick is superior to Louisa, and his conviction that Fanny has been too quickly forgotten. Furthermore, he makes a comment on romantic fidelity which offers a close parallel to Anne's own later speech at the White Hart on women's devotion. Says Wentworth, 'A man does not recover from such a devotion of the heart to such a woman! – He ought not – he does not' (p. 183). Wentworth's speech foreshadows Anne's professions to Captain Harville in that it too takes place in a public setting. The noise of other people, however, cannot drown out words such as these; as in the later scene at the inn, one lover hears the other distinctly despite the surrounding drone of common talk: 'Anne ... in spite of the agitated voice in which the latter [of Wentworth's speech] had been uttered, and in spite of all the various noises of the room, the almost ceaseless slam of the door, and ceaseless buzz of persons walking through, had distinguished every word' (p. 183).

Anne now knows that Wentworth loves her. But the barrier between them remains a difficulty of language, for Anne is aware that there is a gap between love and a declaration of love.[12] At the concert, Anne does her best to send Wentworth the message of her own love; she searches the crowd for his face and sits on the end of the bench so that she will be available for conversation. But even as Wentworth rejoins her, her efforts are counteracted by Elliot and his call for Anne to translate Italian for the Dalrymples: '[she] could not refuse; but never had she sacrificed to politeness with a more suffering spirit' (p. 190). That Anne is called upon to translate an Italian love song for her aristocratic cousins is an ironic touch; an aristocratic verbal exercise momentarily separates Anne from Wentworth. The division effected by social duty, however, is widened by Wentworth with his jealousy of Elliot; he compounds the difficulties imposed by the world around him with his own self-created impediments of misjudgement. Again the problem posed for

Anne is one of communication: 'How was the truth to reach him?' (p. 190).

In Anne's society, a direct declaration of love is impossible. But Anne is not rendered mute by social restrictions; society merely dictates that messages be transmitted by the code of social converse. Thus Anne must control and manipulate those opportunities which arise in public when she and Wentworth are in a crowd. Though Anne feels confident that her maturity – and Wentworth's – will enable them to come at the truth eventually, she knows that in their world of flawed and restricted communication, truth is never self-evident. At the inn among their large party, Anne muses on her situation:

> 'Surely, if there be constant attachment on each side, our hearts must understand each other ere long. We are not boy and girl, to be captiously irritable, misled by every moment's inadvertence and wantonly playing with our own happiness.' And yet, a few minutes afterward, she felt as if their being in company with each other, under their present circumstances, could only be exposing them to inadvertencies and misconstructions of the most mischievous kind.
>
> (pp. 221–2)

This 'inadvertency' presents itself in the form of Mary's sighting of Elliot and Mrs Clay. Mary invokes Anne to see the pair for herself, but Anne, wishing to convey her indifference to Elliot, refuses, using as calm and simple a speech as possible. When she is forced by Mary's warm importunings to come to the window, Anne is careful to display her unconcern for Elliot's presence. She is acting out her feelings for Wentworth's benefit. With the same concern for Wentworth's interpretation, Anne tells the Uppercross party that she would rather go to the play than to Elizabeth's evening affair with Elliot: 'She had spoken it; but she trembled when it was done, conscious that her words were listened to and daring not even to try to observe their effect' (p. 225). And when Charles Musgrove, wishing for the play over the party, proclaims 'What is Mr Elliot to me?', Anne finds 'life' in his 'careless expression'; 'Captain Wentworth was all attention, looking and listening with his whole soul; ... the last words brought his enquiring eyes from Charles to herself' (p. 224).

The romantic climax of the novel is reached when Anne, under the cover of bustle in the lobby of the White Hart, manages to tell Wentworth of her constancy and devotion while on a surface level discussing the relative fidelity of women and men with Captain Harville. Anne is made aware of Wentworth's eavesdropping halfway through her tête-à-tête with Harville when Wentworth drops his pen. And though her speeches to Harville are in a subdued voice for most of their conversation, Anne's overwrought emotions lead her to cry out her last few statements. Her summation, that women love 'longest when existence, or when hope is gone!' (p. 235), is delivered in a tone of voice which she must know Wentworth can hear. Austen's revisions of this scene demonstrate that she wished to give Anne the active verbal role in bringing the lovers together. In the excised chapter, Wentworth discovers Anne's love for him only when she is forced through his questions to acknowledge that she is not engaged to Elliot. *Persuasion* thus offers a model of the 'moment of assent' in which the heroine is fully responsible for propelling the romantic resolution into being. When Wentworth, understanding Anne's meaning, drops his pen in his desire to hear Anne's words more fully, his act symbolises his submission to Anne's dominant linguistic role. He writes his proposal in a letter under the influence of her words, responding on paper to her every nuance of speech: 'I am every instant hearing something which overpowers me' (p. 237). Their positions are reversed from their earlier roles in the noisy scenes at Uppercross in which Anne hears Wentworth but cannot respond. Wentworth acknowledges that although Anne sinks her voice, he can 'distinguish the tones of that voice when they would be lost on others'. The two lovers have achieved true communication, for neither can any longer 'listen in silence' (p. 240). Anne's proficiency and linguistic power enable her to communicate to her love without overstepping the boundaries of society's limits.[13] Since only indirect communication is allowed in the world of *Persuasion*, Anne must learn to use language's potential for communicating hidden meanings, and her mastery of this skill is her primary achievement.

Though it is important that Wentworth be receptive to Anne's indirect signals, and that he respond when the opportunity presents itself, nonetheless Anne plays the central role in the indirect communications which lead to their reunion. Wentworth himself acknowledges Anne's activity when he learns from her at the party that evening that had he tried to renew the engagement in the year '08, after he had achieved a certain measure of professional success and financial security, she would have been his. He contrasts his two achievements, naval and romantic, and concludes that only in the naval sphere has his success been the result of his own merit and activity: 'I have been used to the gratification of believing myself to earn every blessing that I enjoyed. I have valued myself on honourable toils and just rewards. Like other great men under reverses. ... I must endeavour to subdue my mind to my fortune. I must learn to brook being happier than I deserve' (p. 247). The credit for the restitution of their lost love must go to Anne alone.

*Persuasion* proves that loss can be undone, turned to gain by a proper use of language. For Anne and Wentworth, the gain is all the greater because loss and suffering have been endured: 'They returned again into the past, more exquisitely happy, perhaps, in their re-union, than when it had been first projected; more tender, more tried, more fixed in a knowledge of each other's character, truth and attachment; more equal to act, more justified in acting' (p. 241). Anne's courage in circumventing the barriers against speech erected both by society and by Wentworth's own blindness and stubbornness finally bears fruit. Anne has overcome more than error; she has overcome suffering and loss. Nonetheless, Anne's victory at the end is qualified, not by any failing on her part but by the universal conditions of human enmity: war and its potential for loss:

> [Wentworth's] profession was all that could ever make her friends wish [Anne's] tenderness less; the dread of a future war all that could dim her sunshine. She gloried in being a sailor's wife, but she must pay the tax of quick alarm for belonging to that profession which is, if possible, more distinguished in its domestic virtues than in its national importance.
>
> (p. 252)

But Anne's victory, qualified as it is, remains a triumph.

From Laura G. Mooneyham, *Romance, Language and Education in Jane Austen's Novels* (London, 1988), pp. 146; 162–75.

## NOTES

[This linguistically oriented discussion of *Persuasion* comes from Laura Mooneyham's book on Jane Austen, which examines the codes of communication operating in Austen's novels and their interaction with the traditional Austen narratives of romantic, social and moral education. This excerpt reads *Persuasion* as a study of a heroine trapped by suppressed speech in a society which erects barriers in the way of meaning.

In this context, the interplay between language and silence becomes central to understanding the means whereby romance can be expressed and realised. Like other formalist critics, Mooneyham is interested in the structural patterning of the text and in particular the narrative movement from loss to recovery. In associating this movement closely with the manipulation of spoken and unspoken signals, she grants Anne Elliot a degree of autonomy that is sometimes overlooked in analyses of what has frequently been assumed to be a passive heroine. References to *Persuasion* are to the edition by R.W. Chapman, 3rd edn (London, 1934). Ed.]

[All references to the novel are given in parentheses in the text. Ed.]

1. Sylvia Sieferman, '*Persuasion*: the Motive for Metaphor', *Studies in the Novel*, 11 (1979), 290. Elizabeth Bowen in '*Persuasion*', *London Magazine*, 4 (1967), 50, notes that 'all through *Persuasion*, ... we react to the tension of speechless feeling'.

2. D.W. Harding in his introduction to the Penguin edition of the novel discusses this device of overhead conversations and concludes that it 'conveys [Anne's] characteristic sense of the compressed social milieu, the criss-cross of unspoken awareness that ... makes privacy, especially within the family, a precarious luxury' (New York, 1968), p. 12.

3. There are other missed or almost-missed meetings in *Persuasion* which do not directly concern Anne and Wentworth but which add to the novel's atmosphere of tenuous social contact. Thus Henrietta almost abandons her chance of a reconciliation with Charles Hayter as she stands on the hill overlooking Winthrop; she lacks the courage to force the moment of romantic *rapprochement* into being. So too the party at Lyme just miss an introduction to Elliot, though Anne and he brush together in the hall. One crucial missed 'meeting' occurs when Louisa falls not into Wentworth's arms at the Cobb but onto the stones below.

4. It is interesting to note that Austen's allusion to *A Thousand and One Arabian Nights* works in reverse; that is, Scheherazade kept her head each night by telling a tale while Elliot's is protected by a tale *not* being told.

5. Sieferman, '*Persuasion*: the Motive for Metaphor', p. 285.

6. Ibid., p. 285.

7. Stuart Tave, *Some Words of Jane Austen* (Chicago, 1973), p. 258, notes that Anne plays the piano because, as the narrator tells us, she '[has] no voice'.

8. Norman Page gives examples of Wentworth's 'expressive behaviour' in his 'Orders of Merit', in *Jane Austen Today*, ed. Joel Weinsheimer (Athens, GA, 1975), pp. 105–6.

9.  Tave, *Some Words of Jane Austen*, p. 264.

10. Like Fanny Price at Sotherton, at Winthrop Anne becomes the one stationary figure in the midst of general movement. The heroines are left alone as the other characters disperse in various romantic pairings. Austen originally planned to use the device of the hedgerow for Fanny's scene, but discarded the idea when she learned from a correspondent that there were no hedgerows in Northamptonshire.

11. This self-confidence is demonstrated further by Anne's readiness later to believe that Benwick had, at least for a time, considered her a romantic object: 'she boldly acknowledged herself flattered' (p. 131).

12. Valerie Shaw, 'Jane Austen's Subdued Heroines', *Nineteenth Century Literature*, 30 (1975), 300.

13. D.W. Harding, p. 14, shows further that romantic love enables the sensitive and perceptive individual in part 'to escape from ... dependence on social support': 'Lovers assuage their loneliness without paying the price of full conformity.'

# 11

# *Persuasion*: The Pathology of Everyday Life

*JOHN WILTSHIRE*

The view that *Persuasion* is a novel diagnosing radical shifts in social power, and that this vision corresponds to a radical recension in Austen's techniques and values seems to be motivated by the still-lingering embarrassment that a novel should be, to use the ironic phrase she used in defence of her art in *Northanger Abbey*, 'only a novel'. It is as if to vindicate or explain Jane Austen's status as a canonical or classic author it was necessary to make her into a social theorist, to make Austen prophesy the downfall of the class to which she belonged, or attribute to her, if not a radical politics, at least a 'radical' rethinking of her techniques. It is the easier, perhaps, to think of Sir Walter Elliot as a representative figure (rather than as a patent eccentric) because Bath, a real place, seems to function in this novel as the symbol – the structural embodiment and institutionalisation – of his own vanity and snobbery. One could easily suppose that Bath is presented in *Persuasion* as a specific micro-culture, a place in which traditional values have been replaced by commodity values, a built environment which seems to give concrete expression to a culture of narcissistic self-involvement. One could point, for instance, to the antithesis set up between Anne's thoughts of the autumn months in the country 'so sweet and so sad' and her dread of 'the possible heats of September in all the white glare of Bath' (p. 33), and suggest that this is a hint at the false surface, the exclusion of the natural world and the inward turning that could be said to be characteristic of Bath's architecture.

Eighteenth-century Bath is a city of enclosure, Squares and Circuses of geometric design explicitly sequestering the gentry who were to inhabit them from any natural wildness or irregularity. Describing John Wood's early eighteenth-century proposals for Queen's Square, the social historian R.S. Neale writes that 'Nature, except in the shape of a green turf and formal shrubs, was expressly excluded. There were to be no forest trees in the square, only low stone walls and espaliers of elm and lime'.[1] Later in the century the lease of the Royal Crescent (1767–74) prevented the adjacent landowner from growing any tree more than eight feet high. The typical architecture of eighteenth-century Bath followed Wood's liking for 'enclosed spaces, designed to provide some isolation from the economic bustle of civil society and free from the intrusion of the labouring population who built and serviced the city'.[2] Separation of the gentry sections of the city both from the natural world and from the lower classes who were necessary to its existence was designed into its structure.

In Bath itself, in the novel, this social distribution of space is conveyed in the fact that addresses have a precisely calibrated economic and hence social value. Laura Place, for example, leased by the Elliots' cousin, Lady Dalrymple, a member of the (Irish, and therefore fringe) aristocracy, was an especially prestigious address, with one house built by John Eveleigh in 1792 advertised for letting at £120 per annum, with 'the special attraction of two water closets'.[3] The addresses are disposed in the novel as signifiers of social status – Camden-place, Gay Street, Lansdown Crescent, Marlborough Buildings – to be quickly, immediately, read as locating the addressee in a precise position on the social scale.[4] 'Westgate-buildings!' exclaims Sir Walter Elliot, 'and who is Miss Anne Elliot to be visiting in Westgate-buildings? – A Mrs Smith ... And what is her attraction? That she is old and sickly' (p. 157). Addresses are thus related to surnames and, as well, to fit and comely bodies, as markers of social rank.

Bath's *raison d'être* and subsequent prosperity was based upon its hot springs and medicinal waters. By Jane Austen's time it had become a resort which combined facilities for the renovation of health, and venues for the pursuit of social and sexual liaisons, a place in which the medicinal and the erotic were intertwined – an eighteenth-century Magic Fountain. 'Where the waters do agree, it is quite wonderful the relief they give', Mrs Elton tells Emma, and compounds the impertinence by adding 'And as to its recommendations to *you*, I fancy I need not take much pains to dwell on them. The advantages of Bath to the young are pretty generally understood' (*Emma*, p. 275). Mrs Smith is one of those among its visitors who is lodging there for the purpose of health; she has come on the – arguably rational – grounds that the hot baths will relieve, if not cure, her rheumatism. But Bath had been for many years, as Defoe declared, 'the resort of the sound rather than the sick',[5] and its culture as an elegant watering place treats the body in another mode. The body is perceived as an object; it's to be prized or appraised, like handsome furniture, as a commodity. Thus when Elizabeth Elliot bestows a card upon Wentworth, her gesture is not a sign of forgiveness or reconciliation, a prompting of the inner moral life: 'The truth was, that Elizabeth had been long enough in Bath, to understand the importance of a man of such an air and appearance as his. The past was nothing. The present was that Captain Wentworth would move about well in her drawing-room' (p. 226). The male body becomes an item of social circulation here as much as the female has always been, as for example at Netherfield. It is thus easy to elide Sir Walter Elliot's narcissism and vanity into representative status, as he stands 'in a shop in Bond-street' counting handsome faces as they go by (pp. 141–2). In its drawing rooms and evening parties the values he articulates can be seen to be reified, and he commodifies people on the streets as Lady Russell appraises handsome curtains.

Like all of Austen's novels, *Persuasion* is a study in the moral atmosphere of place. Obviously the novel contrasts, as does Anne Elliot herself, the warmth and hospitality of the Harvilles at Lyme, generous with their limited accommodation, with the cold formality of her father and sister in their two drawing rooms at Bath. The 'elegant stupidity' of their evening parties is evidently intended as typical of Bath society: on the other hand, as a resort, the city is atypical of the life of the gentry, and many aspects of the novel confirm this. *Persuasion* is certainly constructed in a more polarised mode than any other of Jane Austen's novels (even *Sense and Sensibility*): warmth, hospitality, enterprise, initiative, exertion and the future belonging – by and large – to the sailors, chill formality, snobbish self-regard, inertia and the past belonging – by and large – to the Elliots, their cronies and relations. But this simple polarity is actually greatly complicated by a number of features, not least of them the overlap, as I have already suggested, between the Musgroves and the Harvilles. The Musgroves are as hospitable as the Harvilles (one of the novel's subtle touches is the way the two families form an unobtrusive alliance as soon as events introduce them). Lady Russell is misguided and imperceptive, shares many of the dubious priorities of Sir Walter Elliot, but her value for rank does not prevent her from taking Anne to visit in Westgate Buildings, 'on the contrary, she approves it' (p. 157). Bath is as hospitable to the Crofts and their naval acquaintances as it is to the Elliots and their circle. Moreover it is a condition of the novel's plot that Anne Elliot's life be unusually confined and restricted so that opportunities for the depiction of representatives of the gentry other than the Elliots are necessarily curtailed.

Nevertheless, Bath and the Elliots are linked in a metonymic relationship, and the rest of the novel has a contrastive and interrogative function towards the corpus of values they represent. Bath excludes nature, excludes the labouring and serving classes, and attempts to repress the knowledge of growth and change, of decay and death. Sir Walter lives out an infantile fantasy of narcissistic omnipotence.[6] Bath society represses that knowledge of the body as an unstable and imperfect subjective condition upon which its economy initially wholly, and still in part, depends, just as the labouring classes and wilderness are expunged from its spaces. But the novel discloses a 'real world' both inside and outside Bath in which the reader's attention is constantly being drawn to these necessary conditions of human life, to what Lady Russell calls 'the uncertainty of all human events and calculations' (p. 159) and especially to thoughts about the human body very different from his simple equation of handsomeness and value.

Not being a great reader, Sir Walter Elliot is unlikely to have come across the quarto volumes of John Caspar Lavater's *Essays on Physiognomy*, widely as these circulated in the last decade of the eighteenth and the first of the nineteenth centuries, but if he had, he would have found there a notion of human nature not entirely at odds with his own. These heavy, profusely illustrated volumes outlined a theory of correspondence between features and moral character, between physical appearance and inner life. The many engravings of the faces of famous and unknown men and women with supplementary and elucidatory commentaries attempted to enforce the proposition that character can be read off from appearance, that, in Lavater's own words, 'virtue and vice, with all their shades, and in their most remote consequences, are beauty and deformity'.[7] Deviations from an ideal model of beauty were interpreted as 'symptomatic of analogous anomalies in the hidden psyche'.[8] 'Physiognomy', he wrote, 'is the science or knowledge of the correspondence between the external and the internal man, the visible superficial and the invisible contents.'[9]

But of course Sir Walter has no theory, and for him there is no correspondence: the 'invisible contents' might as well not exist: value exists only in appearance, and his moral world consists only of a hierarchy of assessments based exclusively on physical harmony and comeliness. Lavater is relevant to the novel he inhabits, none the less, because of the germ of truth, or of plausibility his new 'science' drew upon: the instinct, at its basis erotic or libidinal, to read health and vigour as virtue, to see handsomeness as integrity, an instinct in whose trap, for instance, Elizabeth Bennet is caught when she takes Wickham's presentation of himself as the injured but generous victim of Darcy's undeserved enmity on trust: 'Till I can forget his father, I never can defy or expose *him*', he asserts, piously enough. 'Elizabeth honoured him for such feelings', says the narrator, adding, 'and thought him handsomer than ever as he expressed them' (*Pride and Prejudice*, p. 80). It is an unconscious assumption often made in these novels, and *Persuasion*, which opens so decisively with a figure who equates value only with handsomeness, and who has, to all intents and purposes, no inner life or moral sense, carries the exploration of the problem of the relation between the face, the body, and the inner self further and into new, more disturbing areas. *Persuasion* is disturbed, too, by the collision between the enshrinement of that libidinal fantasy in the conventions of the romantic plot, and the promptings of a strenuous and critical realism.

Sir Walter thinks he and his like are immune from time: the narcissistic fantasy of his vanity expresses itself most powerfully in this delusion, which the novel subsequently underscores by emphasising the changes and vicissitudes wrought by time, and of the human body as an object besieged by its onslaughts. For time and vicissitude, the actions of nature, are more explicitly foregrounded in this novel than in any other of Jane Austen – with that much of the traditional critical readings one can wholeheartedly agree – and it is their action upon the body which makes the most salient contrast with the culture of Bath.

A. Walton Litz once claimed that *Persuasion* represents Jane Austen's most successful effort 'to build this sense of physical life into the language and structure of a novel'.[10] For Litz the 'deeply *physical* impact of *Persuasion*' is to be attributed to the novelist's 'poetic use of nature as a structure of feeling, which not only offers metaphors for our emotions but controls them with its unchanging rhythms and changing moods' and in the novel's development of 'a rapid and nervous syntax designed to imitate the bombardment of impressions upon the mind'.[11] Perceptive though these suggestions are, they fail to detect (perhaps because in one sense it is obvious) the series of occasions or events which refer explicitly to physical life and that are distributed through the novel as if to remind us (*pace* Sir Walter) that physical life is necessarily also physical vulnerability. After the opening Kellynch chapters in which he has been amply seen preening himself on his preservation from the ravages of time, Anne is claimed by Mary and goes to stay at Uppercross. Hardly has Wentworth been heard of in the neighbourhood, than her nephew falls and dislocates his collar-bone, and Anne, faced with Mary's hysterics and the general confusion, takes charge of the household, eventually becoming the little boy's nurse, a situation which effectively delays her encounter with her former lover. Several of the scenes which follow depict her, specifically, in the role of nurse, attending to the child. The pretext for the shift of the novel's scene to Lyme is Wentworth's desire to see his old friend Harville, who 'had never been in good health since a severe wound which he received two years before' (p. 94). Harville's lameness has curtailed his career and prospects in the navy, forced him into restricted accommodation, and makes it necessary for him to return home from their ramble in Lyme early, thus leaving only Anne and Wentworth to cope with subsequent events on the Cobb. Fatal injuries occur in civilian life too, and the scene of Louisa's jump, which climaxes events in the first volume of the novel, proves a turning point since it alters her personality and future and, in turn, the futures of Benwick, Wentworth and Anne Elliot. When, early in the second volume, Anne finally arrives in Bath, one of her first acts is to renew the friendship she had formed at school with a woman whom she had previously known 'in all the glow of health and confidence of superiority' and who is now poor and almost friendless, and, among her other misfortunes, is 'afflicted with a severe rheumatic fever, which finally settling in her legs, had made her for the present a cripple' (p. 152). In each of the novel's main locales is found someone who is disabled as a result of injury or disease, or occurs an incident that serves to remind us of the vulnerability or fragility of the body. Pervading it all is Anne Elliot's unspoken sense of her own loss and deprivation, the result of the 'rupture' (p. 28) with Wentworth. *Persuasion* is a novel of trauma: of broken bones, broken heads and broken hearts.

This reading of the novel then centres about the notion of injury, and for the most part, *Persuasion* depicts spiritual or mental pain and physical pain in the same terms, as when Wentworth speaks of Benwick's 'pierced, wounded, almost broken' heart. It's concerned with the ways people adjust to loss, or curtailment of life, and live through, or cope with, its deprivations. Mrs Smith appears now as an important figure, a significant commentary on the position of Anne. *Persuasion* is a short book, scarcely more than half the length of *Emma*. Even within this small compass, Mrs Smith is often considered a puzzlingly predominant flaw or intrusion, for conversations with her and discussions of her friend Nurse Rooke's ingenious ways of procuring advantages occupy two chapters in the second volume of the novel, the fullest just before its climax. The extended treatment the figure is given may be seen, in this light, as a crucial elaboration of the thought of the novel (though it cannot rescue the melodrama of her unmasking of Mr Elliot's 'hollow and black' heart) for the story of Mrs Smith, like the story of Anne Elliot, displays Jane Austen's intense interest in the resources of the human spirit in the face of affliction.[12] Austen's concern is not so much with accidents or misfortune as such, as with the positive human responses to suffering. In particular, she depicts (and critically examines) the isolated individual's attempt to gather the emotional resources to cope with chronic pain of a psychological nature, and the modes of support and nursing that enable others to endure and overcome their suffering and deprivation. And because pain and injury make so much of the material, it is inevitable that coping and nursing will also occupy the novel's attention.

Nurse Rooke's profession is a necessary element in the hidden economy of Bath: and, though essential to the plot of *Persuasion*, she is even more of an obscured figure in the novel she inhabits than Mr Perry is in his. Anne does not even notice her when she opens the door. Like Mr Perry in *Emma*, though, Nurse Rooke opens the door to one of *Persuasion*'s most important thematics. She is only one of a number of professional nursing figures who are momentarily noticed in the text, and who associate in the reader's mind nursing and femaleness, the nurse as the guardian of the small child with the nurse as attendant on the ailing adult. After Louisa

Musgrove's fall, for example, Henrietta, her sister, wants to nurse her but 'Charles conveyed back a far more useful person in the old nursery-maid of the family, one who having brought up all the children, and seen the last, the very last, the lingering and long-petted master Harry, sent to school after his brothers, was now living in her deserted nursery to mend stockings, and dress all the blains and bruises she could get near her' (p. 122). Nursing is thus linked not only with femaleness, but with social marginality. Sarah joins Mrs Harville, 'a very experienced nurse; and her nursery-maid, who had lived with her long and gone about with her every where, was just such another' (p. 113). Mary has her favoured nursery maid too, Jemima. Nurse Rooke, besides her other professional duties, is a mid-wife. She attends the fashionable lady Mrs Wallis in her confinement, and as Mrs Smith with characteristic impudence says to Anne, 'She must be allowed to be a favourer of matrimony you know, and (since self will intrude) who can say that she may not have some flying visions of attending the next Lady Elliot, through Mrs Wallis's recommendation?' (p. 208). Finally, as Anne and Wentworth take their reconciliatory stroll round Bath together they pass, unnoticed, 'nursery maids and children'. These glimpsed figures on the peripheries of the novel associate nursing with both mothering, and with social powerlessness: the nurse is a metaphor for both.[13] It is as if there were a necessary relationship between femaleness and nursing, as if true womanliness were expressed in devotion to the well-being of others, whether children or ailing adults.

Such was the view of moralists of this, as of later, periods. Thomas Gisborne's *Duties of the Female Sex* of 1796 proposes that the 'unassuming and virtuous activity' of the female character is especially developed 'in contributing daily and hourly to the comfort of husbands, of parents, of brothers and sisters, and of other relations, connections and friends, in the intercourse of domestic life, under every vicissitude of sickness and health, of joy and affliction'.[14] Alistair Duckworth explains that the incident at Uppercross in which Anne attends her nephew emphasises the 'utility' of her response: 'It suggests that the self, even when deprived of its social inheritance, may still respond affirmatively and in traditionally sanctioned ways, that deprivation need not lead to despair or to disaffection.'[15] This is certainly the view of Charles Musgrove, who announces that his son's dislocated collar-bone is 'quite a female case' and need not prevent him dining out to meet Captain Wentworth, and underlined by Anne Elliot herself, who declares more mildly to Mary, put out that she is left at home, 'Nursing does not belong to a man, it is not his province. A sick child is always the mother's property, her own feelings generally make it so' (p. 56). This conservative generalisation is immediately contradicted by Mary's alacrity at being released from the duty to her child by Anne's offer to stay at home. But the nobility of Anne's sacrifice is also qualified in this instance because of the ulterior motive behind her offer: her apparent dutifulness to the child is a means of protecting herself from the pain of an encounter with Wentworth. The social role, however 'traditionally sanctioned' here, as elsewhere, does not quite fit the emotions and motives of she who adopts it. Later, Anne's care of the child is to serve as a pretext for her not engaging in conversation with her former lover.

Femaleness and nursing are thus ideologically linked, but it is a curiously restricted femaleness. The nurse is a functional substitute for the nurturing and nurturant, supportive, mother – in Alexander Pope's phrase, 'the tender Second to a Mother's care': whilst being quintessentially female, her femaleness is thought of as maternal, not sexual. A true woman will necessarily be a good nurse, but her womanliness will be one in which her own purposes and sexual desires will be subordinated to, and sublimated in, her ministrations to the child or to the patient. Her hands are intimate with the body, and she has therefore a quasi-sexual relation to the subjects whom she attends, but her own sexuality is necessarily screened or suspended. Anne Elliot is assigned, or assigns herself, to a range of ancillary roles in the households at Uppercross and Lyme – listener, confidante, 'umpire' between husband and wife, accompanist on the piano – but her role as nurse subsumes these others, and it is precisely as a nurse that she values herself most and is most valued by those around her. In positioning herself thus as mother-substitute, as she does, for instance, by taking over the care of the injured child from Mary, she expunges herself as a desiring subject. In effect, she is representing to herself, and allowing her circle to assume, that her romantic story is closed, is in the past, that she does not entertain ambitions or desires on her own behalf, but only on behalf of those to whose well-being she attends. The role of nurse is eminently female, not without initiative, and not without strength, but without desire. It is a role in which Anne comes to be valued, but her value is predicated upon the obliteration (or suspension) of her own bodily needs. Whilst she plays, her hands mechanically at work, 'equally without error and without consciousness' (p. 72), others engage in the courtship dance; whilst she attends to Mrs Musgrove or her injured nephew, Wentworth narrates the history of how he was 'made', regales the admiring Musgroves with his exploits: he re-creates himself as an active, desiring principle, whilst she salvages what identity she can as listener and as confidante of others.

Anne's laborious and demanding attentions to the child (she has Mary to worry about, too, of course) are amusingly juxtaposed with the merely verbal solicitude of the Musgrove sisters for 'dear, good Dr Shirley's being relieved from the duty which he could no longer get through without most injurious fatigue', Dr Shirley being the elderly rector of Uppercross, whose curacy they have their eyes on for Charles Hayter. On the beach at Lyme, Anne listens and en-courages once again, amused to detect the motivation of Henrietta's enthusiasm for Dr Shirley's settling by the sea; 'The sea air always does good', that artless young lady exclaims, 'There can be no doubt of its having been of the greatest service to Dr Shirley, after his illness, last spring twelvemonth' (p. 102). Once again, like Mr Perry setting up his carriage, talk about health serves to disguise the economic and, in this case, sexual motives which are actually in operation. That caring for others may afford substitute gratifications is not, I think, a point the novel dwells on, but it is clear that nursing gives Anne a pretext for a semi-permanent adop-tion of that role of bystander to which she has consigned herself, and in which she takes both comfort and pride.

Yet because *Persuasion* depicts the body as fragile and vulnera-ble, nursing does emerge as an important value, despite its associa-tion with the sexually and socially subordinate. The companionate marriage of the Crofts is a good example. Mrs Croft herself remarks that the only time she has ever been ill was when she was left on shore, separated from her husband. 'I lived in perpetual fright at that time, and had all manner of imaginary complaints from not knowing what to do with myself ...' she tells Mrs Musgrove (p. 71). When they come to Bath, the Admiral is 'ordered to walk, to keep off the gout, and Mrs Croft seemed to go shares with him in every thing, and to walk for her life, to do him good. Anne saw them wherever she went' (p. 168). But this turns into genial parody as altruistic female attendance becomes self-injury. A week or so afterwards Anne sees Admiral Croft walking alone. Croft, asking her to take his arm, makes a remark that matches his wife's earlier ones. 'I do not feel comfortable if I have not a woman there', and explains why he is out without her. He may have kept down the gout, but she has become the invalid: 'She, poor soul, is tied by the leg. She has a blister on one of her heels, as large as a three shilling piece' (p. 170).

More importantly, the novel puts nursing in a new light by assigning nursing functions, or something equivalent to them, to the heroic male, Wentworth. The scene where he is first displayed (and displays himself) for example, is intercepted by a passage in which he exchanges places with the listening, attendant, Anne. His bragging of his achievements and prizes, his careless boasts of nonchalance in the face of danger are rendered indirectly, through her listening consciousness. Then when Anne's attention is claimed by Mrs Musgrove, he recedes into silence. In the foreground is Mrs Musgrove and her thoughts about her lost, apparently 'worthless' son, Dick.

> 'Ah! Miss Anne, if it had pleased Heaven to spare my poor son, I dare say he would have been just such another by this time.'
> Anne suppressed a smile, and listened kindly, while Mrs Musgrove relieved her heart a little more; and for a few minutes, therefore, could not keep pace with the conversation of the others.
>
> (p. 64)

When Wentworth is in turn appealed to by the grieving mother, his attitude replicates Anne's, and is relayed by her. She detects 'an indulgence of self-amusement' in his face at first, but 'in another moment he was perfectly collected and serious; and almost instantly afterwards coming up to the sofa, on which she and Mrs Musgrove were sitting, took a place by the latter, and entered into conversation with her, in a low voice, about her son, doing it with so much sympathy and natural grace, as shewed the kindest consideration for all that was real and unabsurd in the parent's feelings' (pp. 67-8). This is not that showy gallantry towards women which his sister shortly criticises him for, but a quick and intuitive solicitude that precisely matches Anne's. This passage is an example of the flexibility of the point of view in this novel: though the listening consciousness still remains Anne's, the narrative moves seamlessly away from her to inform us of the speech of Wentworth (which she could hardly hear) and even penetrates to the quality of Mrs Musgrove's feelings.

'No summons mocked by chill delay': Wentworth's responses to appeals for help and sympathy are always ready 'instantly'. The word is habitually tagged to his gestures, movements, and actions, an index of that bodily ease and confident physical efficiency which support his enterprise and daring. The most signal example of his humanity is recounted by Captain Harville just prior to the fall on the Cobb. Anne and Harville are talking of Benwick's recent bereavement. Fanny Harville died in June, but the news was not known to him until August, when he came home from the Cape. 'I was at Plymouth', says Harville, but Benwick's ship was due to dock at Portsmouth. 'There the news must follow him, but who was to tell it?':

> 'Nobody could do it, but that good fellow (pointing to Captain Wentworth). The Laconia had come into Plymouth the week before; no danger of her being sent to sea again. He stood his chance for the rest – wrote up for leave of absence, but without waiting the return, travelled night and day till he got to Portsmouth, rowed off to the Grappler that instant, and never left the poor fellow for a week; that's what he did, and nobody else could have saved poor James. You may think, Miss Elliot, whether he is dear to us!'
> Anne did think on the question with perfect decision, and said as much in reply as her own feelings could accomplish, or as his seemed able to bear.
>
> (p. 108)

Wentworth, in effect, nurses Benwick through the worst of his grief. (On the other hand, Mr Elliot, we are told, refused to help the widow of his friend, and by refusing to act as his executor, greatly increased her distress [p. 209].) Harville's tribute has the narrative function of displaying Wentworth as a courageous and enterprising as well as sympathetic man just before the incident which is to present him as very nearly inadequate or impotent, as he faces a crisis of a more complicated sort.

Wentworth's capacity for sympathetic attentiveness (what I have called nursing) is displayed, of course, most fully in his attentions to Anne Elliot herself. If we are to explain 'the deeply *physical* impact' of *Persuasion* we look first, I think, at the intensity of Anne Elliot's responses to her former fiancé's physical presence, and to the indirect, mediated evidence of his awareness of her. Anne and Wentworth are kept apart in the first scenes at Uppercross partly because (as David Monaghan suggests) Anne relegates herself to a peripheral position which the Musgroves do not have the perception or intelligence to see is less than she deserves. Wentworth's lingering resentment and Anne's modesty keep the two former lovers apart, since there is no one with any appreciation of Anne's value to give her the more prominent role that might have brought her to Wentworth's notice. Their intercourse is a minimal one of polite manners and careful avoidance. Wentworth arranges to avoid even the perfunctory physical contact of shaking hands that a formal introduction would require (p. 59). In the subsequent scenes at Uppercross, good manners and politeness, 'the exchange of the common civilities', acts as a barrier to closer intercourse, as the two ex-lovers manoeuvre to keep out of each other's way, even when they are in the same room.

But a child of two has no manners, none of these polite inhibitions, and therefore can be the agency through which the two people whom politeness would have kept 'perpetually estranged' (p. 64) can be brought together. Anne is forced to stay in the room with Wentworth because the sick boy demands her, and imprisoned by the younger child, who 'began to fasten himself upon her, as she knelt, in such a way that, busy as she was about Charles, she could not shake him off', she is rescued by Wentworth's resourceful action: 'In another moment, however, she found herself in the state of being released from him; some one was taking him from her, though he had bent down her head so much, that his little sturdy hands were unfastened from around her neck, and he was resolutely borne away, before she knew that Captain Wentworth had done it' (p. 80). The child is a 'transitional object' to borrow Winnicott's term: Wentworth relieves Anne's body through the agency of his physical contact with the body of the child. The breach of strict decorum is admissible because it appears in the guise of solicitude, and the incident is kept below the level of socially embarrassed consciousness by the silence in which it is transacted. The rescue leaves Anne quite speechless, overwhelmed with confused emotions. They are not due merely to being the recipient of an act of courtesy.

A similar act of solicitude, but this time wholly volunteered by Wentworth and thus showing a fuller attention to Anne, comes in the next chapter where on the return from Winthrop the party meets the Crofts in their gig, who offer a ride to any lady who might be tired. Anne's tiredness has not been dwelt on, though Charles Musgrove's inattention to her has, so that when Wentworth 'cleared the hedge in a moment to say something to his sister' and then, the Crofts having offered a place to Anne, 'without saying a word' turns to her and 'quietly obliged her to be assisted into the carriage' (p. 91) the reader perceives it as a strikingly solicitous action. These deeds may be read as Anne reads them, fully persuaded as she is from the conversation she has just overheard between Wentworth and Louisa, that Wentworth is now indifferent about her: but his detection of Anne's fatigue (the topic has not come up – she has made no complaint) suggests that for a man supposedly courting another woman, his mind is unusually occupied with her. In Highbury misplaced attention to bodily well-being reflects ignorance about or obliviousness to the subject's inner life. In these two instances, in a wonderful twist to the Highbury mode, nursing concern for the body becomes the permissible vehicle in which awakening (or latent) desire can find a plausible and socially sanctioned, because apparently sexually neutral, expression. Anne misreads Wentworth's behaviour in just this way, as chivalry or solicitude without sexual motivation: 'though becoming attached to another, still he could not see her suffer, without the desire of giving her relief'. The irony is far more muted than the irony that attaches to Emma Woodhouse's misconstruings, but Anne's supposition is not unqualified by the narrational circumstances.

In a parallel way, Wentworth's awakened or awakening love for Anne is expressed in his regard for her in that woman's exemplary role as a nurse. It is clear that everyone in the novel values Anne as a nurse, or rather that her value, unrecognised until then, is made visible when she emerges as a nurse, or needs to be used as one, but there is something more to that moment after the accident on the Cobb when Anne, coming downstairs, overhears Wentworth praising her competence:

> '... If Anne will stay, no one so proper, so capable as Anne!'
> She paused a moment to recover from the emotion of hearing herself so spoken of. The other two warmly agreed to what he said, and she then appeared.
> 'You will stay, I am sure; you will stay and nurse her'; cried he, turning to her and speaking with a glow, and yet a gentleness, which seemed almost restoring the past. – She coloured deeply; and he recollected himself, and moved away.
>
> (p. 114)

To speak publicly in praise of Anne in the role of nurse is permissible, because of that separation of nursing from sexuality I have described. Whilst the relation is actually one of desire, it is conducted here, once more, according to the canons of solicitude. Wentworth's feeling for Anne can thus be masked by its ideological vehicle. In fact, though, as Anne intuits, he is expressing love for her, and the mutual embarrassment of this passing moment circles round this unspoken, almost unthought, disclosure.

'*Persuasion*', as Judy van Sickle Johnson writes, 'is Jane Austen's most unreservedly physical novel.' Its power, as she describes it, 'resides in Austen's success in sustaining the credibility of a renewed emotional attachment through physical signs. Although they are seemingly distant, Anne and Wentworth become increasingly more intimate through seductive half-glances, conscious gazes and slight bodily contact'.[16] But the problem is, both for the figures and the narration, that these bodily signs are not enough in themselves to achieve the final rapprochement. Wentworth's 'manner and look ... sentences begun which he could not finish – his half averted eyes and more than half expressive glance' (p. 185) may give warrant to Anne Elliot's belief in his returned or returning affection, but by themselves they do not inevitably convey the meaning she divines, nor overcome the obstacles that their life in the social world, as well as the inhibitions generated by their past history, present to the articulation or fulfilment of the lovers' desires. In the original climactic chapter, the embarrassment and the self-consciousness that are the recurrent motif of their meetings, he 'looking not exactly forward', her emotion 'reddening [her] cheeks, and fixing her eyes on the ground' (p. 182) become intensified, and the final reconciliation is achieved, in fact, by a scene in which body language is made to seem an effective substitute for the spoken word, and to communicate that full and precise meaning of which the previous manifestations of feeling were scarcely decipherable tokens:

> He was a moment silent. She turned her eyes towards him for the first time since his re-entering the room. His colour was varying, and he was looking at her with all the power and keenness which she believed no other eyes than his possessed.
> 'No truth in any such report?' he repeated. 'No truth in any *part* of it?' 'None.'
> He had been standing by a chair, enjoying the relief of leaning on it, or of playing with it. He now sat down, drew it a little nearer to her, and looked with an expression which had something more than penetration in it – something softer. Her countenance did not

> discourage. It was a silent but a very powerful dialogue; on his side
> supplication, on hers acceptance. Still a little nearer, and a hand
> taken and pressed; and 'Anne, my own dear Anne!' bursting forth in
> the fulness of exquisite feeling, – and all suspense and indecision
> were over.
>
> (p. 258)

The power of the 'dialogue', by its own admission, can only be rendered in language, in words, and therefore this moment, however
appropriate a climax to the series of physical signs which have communicated the lovers' feelings to the reader, and however skilfully
tumescent emotion is conveyed in the continuous tenses, is bound
to seem perfunctory.

Added to this, the machinery creaks by which the two figures are
brought together in a room without a third person. The two chapters which replace the original volume II, chapter X are, in their
fulness and richness – re-presenting the whole cast of characters in
the novel – much superior. By having her speak, and speak eloquently and fully, if indirectly, of her own experience and love, the
famous climactic scene at the White Hart Inn grants Anne Elliot a
central position for the first time in the novel. At the same moment
it keeps to the narrative logic whereby what finally brings the pair
together is also an accident, or providential, since Anne speaks from
her heart, without being sure whether Wentworth, who is seated in
the same room writing a letter, can in fact, with the preternatural
alertness of the lover, overhear her.

The length and eloquence of Captain Harville's and Anne
Elliot's speeches form a consummate duet, almost operatic in its
final affirmative intensity, on the theme of constancy. That their
dialogue fulfils the desire, repressed or suppressed throughout
the novel, for Anne to speak, to be eloquent, that Anne and
Wentworth change their typical narrative positions – she speaking, he hanging on her words, she narrating (if indirectly) her
deepest experience of life, actively speaking her passive experience, he the dependent listener, at that moment performing a
service for a colleague, whose pen drops whilst she (and Austen
through her) affirms the experience of women: these aspects of the
scene have been in their turn eloquently commented upon. Anne
holds the floor at this point, and finds, in terms of the narrative,
her fulfilment. She speaks, he writes. In a reversal of the original
intention, the role of bodily communication is minimised; only

lips and fingers move, and it is through language, not nervous gesture or looks, that the truth is revealed. Anne's speeches combine the authorising procedures of rational debate with the authenticity of (indirect) confession. The presence of the body is in fact reduced to a metaphor, in this disputatious discourse, but one which brings apparently casually to the surface a theme, or a problematic that can be seen, in retrospect, to be deeply embedded in the novel.

Captain Harville believes in 'a true analogy between our bodily frames and our mental; and that as our bodies are the strongest, so are our feelings; capable of bearing most rough usage, and riding out the heaviest weather'. Anne takes up the analogy, to argue her own position: man is more robust than woman, but he is not longer lived, and if women live longer than men, they also love longer (p. 233). And this relation between bodily frailty and strength of attachment is given a precise enactment in Anne's final contribution to the dialogue:

> 'All the privilege I claim for my own sex (it is not a very enviable one, you need not covet it) is that of loving longest, when existence or when hope is gone.'
> She could not immediately have uttered another sentence; her heart was too full, her breath too much oppressed.
> 'You are a good soul,' cried Captain Harville, putting his hand on her arm quite affectionately. 'There is no quarrelling with you. – And when I think of Benwick, my tongue is tied.'
>
> (pp. 235–6)

Is there an analogy, in fact, between the body and the spirit? How is the body to be read, and just how does the body disclose or communicate the secrets of the self? These are questions about which *Persuasion* has circled on a series of occasions. To read from the face and the body to the soul, Lavater claimed, was infallibly possible, but depended upon hermeneutic skills which he did not trouble to impart. How the body feels, still less how the body looks, may be far from a reliable guide to its own condition, and say still less about the inner life. But it is common to assume a parallel or analogy between the two, or to take one for the other, – to read, as Highbury reads, body as access to total self. For Sir Walter and Elizabeth Elliot nothing could be simpler: there is no question of an analogy between the body and the mind or spirit, since questions of spirit or value are resolved merely into questions of the comeliness or otherwise of the body and face. Mrs Smith's name, her address, and her infirmity sit together on a continuum read according to a primitive scale of 'objective' value. Of course, the novel deconstructs this summarily as soon as Sir Walter's disposition to overlook Mrs Clay's freckles and awkward wrist is demonstrated. But the desire to see a correspondence between bodily condition and inner nature, to read one as a sure transcription of the secrets of the other, is strong enough for critics, in their turn, to suggest that Mrs Clay's freckles, for which Sir Walter has recommended Gowland's lotion, are the outward sign of her inner corruption – since Gowland's lotion can be linked to venereal disease.[17]

Enough to say that this novel is sometimes troubled and sometimes amused by the mismatchings that occur between inner being and outer appearance. Simple contrastive irony about body and spirit abounds, for wounded and disabled bodies are pictured as emblems of healthy living and spiritual resource. Wentworth is reported as saying that Anne is 'so altered he should not have known her again', speaking of her appearance after seven years, but she is in fact, unaltered, unchanged in spirit, and this very constancy is not unrelated to her decline in looks. In the first draft of the conclusion, after the *rapprochement*, as the lovers retrace the past, and Wentworth goes over his feelings, Anne is said to have 'the felicity of being assured that in the first place (so far from being altered for the worse), she had gained inexpressibly in personal loveliness'. In the revised version this is amplified to form a little moment of muted comedy: Wentworth tells her that he fled to his brother's after the accident at Lyme:

> 'He enquired after you very particularly; asked even if you were personally altered, little suspecting that to my eye you could never alter.'
> Anne smiled, and let it pass. It was too pleasing a blunder for a reproach. It is something for a woman to be assured in her eight-and-twentieth year, that she has not lost one charm of earlier youth: but the value of such homage was inexpressibly increased to Anne, by comparing it with former words, and feeling it to be the result, not the cause of a revival of his warm attachment.
>
> (p. 243)

Anne smiles at the blundering offence against chivalry and it is her feelings rather than Wentworth's that now become 'inexpressible'. In smiling she demonstrates her own maturity and cultivation, her own self-irony, but also acknowledges the erosions of time and the inexact correspondence between human emotions or desire and the physical objects that are their focus and motivation. The first incident was a gratifying narrative of dream fulfilment: in its reworking and rephrasing Austen incorporates within the same moment two themes deeply relevant to her novel – acknowledging both time's depredations and the contingencies of human subjectivity – and thereby authenticates the romance she is simultaneously qualifying.

But the problematic is exposed most thoroughly in Austen's representation of Mrs Musgrove's grief in chapter VIII of the first volume. To quote only part of the notorious passage: 'while the agitations of Anne's slender form, and pensive face, may be considered as very completely screened, Captain Wentworth should be allowed some credit for the self-command with which he attended to her large fat sighings over the destiny of a son, whom alive nobody had cared for' (p. 68). If there were a true harmony between body and spirit, then the dismissal of the body as grotesque could stand for dismissal of the feelings: the problem is that each demands a different, but concurrent, simultaneous, response. Austen cannot resolve the problem of her attitude here. Partly the writing insists there is an analogy, at the very least, between our bodily frames and our emotions, otherwise why describe Mrs Musgrove's sighings as 'fat'? But another part of the intention is to mark the disjunction, the separation between 'deep affliction' and 'a large bulky figure': the fact that appraisal of the body, whether approving or otherwise, can make no claim to knowledge or valuation, none whatsoever, of the inner life. Is Mrs Musgrove's sorrow, then, to be framed comically or tragically? The text is at this point riven between the tone adopted for its introspective, subjective narration of Anne's sufferings, a tone inflected towards the nuanced presentation of internal processes – 'all that was real and unabsurd in the parent's feelings' and which it here extends towards this minor character – and its wish to instantiate, once again, the irony that body and spirit may tell off in different directions. But here the narrative capitulates to that crude reading of the body as a decipherable text which the novel examines and repudiates almost everywhere else. The result is a paragraph of defensive floundering.[18]

The puzzle of relations between body and spirit is brought up once again in the little comic aftermath to the proposal scene. Even after reading Wentworth's passionately penned declaration – which shows him as agitated and nervous as ever Anne has been – her troubles are not finished. Overwhelmed, this time with happiness, her body takes over. What she is feeling is joy, what it displays is illness, and her chance to meet Wentworth on the way home is threatened, momentarily, when the Musgroves notice how she looks:

> She began not to understand a word they said, and was obliged to plead indisposition and excuse herself. They could then see that she looked very ill – were shocked and concerned – and would not stir without her for the world. This was dreadful! Would they only have gone away, and left her in the quiet possession of that room, it would have been her cure; but to have them all standing or waiting around her was distracting, and, in desperation, she said she would go home.
>
> 'By all means, my dear,' cried Mrs Musgrove, 'go home directly and take care of yourself, that you may be fit for the evening. I wish Sarah was here to doctor you, but I am no doctor myself. Charles, ring and order a chair. She must not walk.'
>
> (p. 238)

In this coda to the emotional heights of the declaration scene, the kindly, uncomprehending Musgroves enact a brief farcical replay of Highbury's misplaced solicitude about Jane Fairfax. But for the most part in *Persuasion*, as I have been suggesting, nursing and solicitude, if not 'doctoring', are central and serious matters. Because *Persuasion* is so much more than *Emma* about the miscarriages of life, about suffering and vulnerability, it has also necessarily brought to a finer focus the role, as well as the profession, of the nurse, and advocated more urgently the need, the seriousness of care, coping and support. The novel is shot through with recognitions of the body's fragility and mutability, and of the tenuousness of the emotions and valuations that are forever seeking an anchor in its immanent truths. This is a novel about 'the art of losing', to quote Elizabeth Bishop's very apposite poem, 'One Art': the art of existing without bitterness, despite multiple deprivations, of care of the self, the art of composure that is, for the writer, simultaneously the art of composition. If I have argued, too, that *Persuasion* was no radical revisioning of Jane Austen's social world, and that the historicist dimension of the novel may well be exaggerated, it is impossible to deny that the next work she undertook, to which the thematics of ill health are even more germane, was certainly to focus on contemporary social developments.

From John Wiltshire, *Jane Austen and the body* (Cambridge, 1992), pp. 159–74; 190–6.

## NOTES

[John Wiltshire's study of Jane Austen's novels illustrates the impact of cultural and New Historicist theory on recent criticism of Jane Austen's work. The discussion of *Persuasion* draws on a range of disciplines, including psychoanalysis, gender studies and economic history, in its theorising of the body as cultural sign. The approach contrasts with Laura Mooneyham's analysis of sign systems and with earlier studies of *Persuasion* which consider the novel's emphasis on physicality in relation to a more conventional metaphoric structure. Wiltshire's concern with the discourses of sickness and health and the power structures they encode shows his indebtedness to Foucauldian theory. He does not purport to resolve the contradictions or ambiguities of the novel, but is intent rather on exploring how contemporary ideas about the body permeate the text with significant implications. This results in an analysis of the relation between physical and psychic health, and a revised view of the choice of Bath as a key location for the narrative. References to *Persuasion* are to the *Oxford Illustrated Jane Austen*, ed. R.W. Chapman, 5 vols, 1923, revised editions 1965, 1967. Ed.]

[All references to the novel are included in parentheses in the text. Ed.]

1.  R.S. Neale, *Bath, 1680–1850: A Social History* (1981), pp. 193–6.

2.  Neale, *Bath*, pp. 207, 205.

3.  Neale, *Bath*, p. 246.

4.  Patricia Bruckman, 'Sir Walter Elliot's Bath address', *Modern Philology*, 80: 1 (1982), 56–60, notes the precision of the novel's assignment of lodgings to its various characters and especially the location of Sir Walter in Camden Place, a never completed, architecturally flawed Crescent. See also Sir Nikolaus Pevsner, 'The architectural setting of Jane Austen's novels', *Journal of the Warburg and Courtauld Institutes*, 31 (1968), 404–22.

5.  Quoted in Roy Porter, *English Society in the Eighteenth Century* (Harmondsworth, 1982), p. 245.

6.  Freud described the primary narcissism parents project upon their infant child: 'Illness, death, renunciation of enjoyment, restrictions on his own will, shall not touch him; the laws of nature and society shall be abrogated in his favour'. Sigmund Freud, 'On Narcissism' (1912), in the *Standard Edition of the Works*, ed. J. Strachey et al. (1957, reprinted 1986), XIV, p. 91.

7.  John Caspar Lavater, *Essays on Physiognomy for the promotion of knowledge and the love of mankind*, trans. Thomas Holcroft, second edition, 4 vols (1804), I, p. 175. For Lavater's influence see Graeme Tytler, *Physiognomy in the European Novel: Faces and Fortunes* (New Jersey, 1982).

8.  Barbara M. Stafford, John La Puma and David L. Schiedermayer, 'One face of beauty, one picture of health: the hidden aesthetic of medical practice', *Journal of Medicine and Philosophy* (1989), 213–30. The authors note that Lavater's contemporary, Georg Christoph Lichenberg, opposed his theories, and suggest that 'Lichenberg's most profound insight was that, to be in relationship with anything, be it another person or the world, is by definition to be constantly deformed ... Life erodes geometrical perfection; it distorts edges and roughens contours ... a calibrated central form ... can be  maintained only in narcissistic isolation' (p. 224).

9.  Lavater, *Essays on Physiognomy*, I, p. 19.

10.  A. Walton Litz, '*Persuasion*: forms of estrangement' in J. Halperin (ed.), *Jane Austen: Bicentenary Essays* (Cambridge, 1975), p. 225.

11.  Litz, 'Forms of estrangement'. pp. 223, 228.

12.  I am indebted to my colleague, Ann Blake, for this phrase, as well as much else in this discussion of suffering in *Persuasion*.

13.  Claire Fagin and Donna Diers, 'Nursing as metaphor', *American Journal of Nursing* (September, 1983), 1362.

14.  Thomas Gisborne, *The Duties of the Female Sex*, second edition (1797), pp. 11, 12.

15.  Alistair M. Duckworth, *The Improvement of the Estate* (Baltimore, 1971), p. 188.

16.  Judy van Sickle Johnson, 'The bodily frame: learning romance in *Persuasion*', *Nineteenth Century Fiction*, 38 (June 1983), 43–61.

17.  Tony Tanner, *Jane Austen* (London, 1986), quotes (p. 237) Nora Crook in *The Times Literary Supplement*, 7 Oct. 1983.

18.  D.A. Miller, 'The late Jane Austen', *Raritan*, 10 (1990), 55–79, includes a witty analysis of this passage, pp. 60–2.

# 12

# Doubleness and Refrain in Jane Austen's *Persuasion*

*CHERYL ANN WEISSMAN*

Among the characters in Jane Austen's canon of fiction, the heroine of *Persuasion* is supremely mysterious. Anne Elliot suggests a residual depth of personality that eludes narrator as well as reader in this, Austen's last completed work. Yet even as character emerges with extraordinary subtlety, this novel's structure and language call themselves to our attention by virtue of their contrasting and conspicuous schematism. The wistful tone of *Persuasion* is informed by a bizarre and implacable emphasis on doubleness and refrains in diction, plot, themes, and even syntax.

Symmetric doubling is not intrinsically remarkable in Austen's fiction, of course. The titles *Pride and Prejudice* and *Sense and Sensibility* reflect the harmoniously epigrammatic rhythm of eighteenth-century prose. But in that tradition, as in Austen's earlier novels, structural symmetry suggests the dependable order of a stable, rational world. In *Persuasion*, names and events recur in a disturbingly irrational way, reflecting a transient, uneasy one.

It is a world keenly reminiscent of the stylised and gloomy milieu of fairy tales. Anne Elliot is a Cinderella figure dominated by a vain and unloving parent (Sir Walter) and two selfish sisters. In a mythical past, eight years prior to the novel's time frame, she was persuaded by a well-intentioned godmother (Lady Russell) to reject Frederick Wentworth, a suitor with modest financial expectations, and that submission to persuasion has proved to be the mistake of her life. Now Wentworth returns, having improbably made his fortune after all, and to Anne's profound anguish he courts both of her sisters-in-law; no Prince Charming was ever more misguided! Anne has become faded and impoverished, but she remains deeply in love with him. She regrets her decision, although she refuses to repent it; it was the correct choice under the circumstances, she insists, even though it chanced to be the wrong course of action.

Meanwhile, chance further contrives to present her with a second suitor, William Elliot. As heir to her father's estate, this man would offer her the unique opportunity to succeed her long-deceased mother in name, fortune, and even place of residence. With fairy tale symmetry, Anne could thus be restored to her home and in some measure be compensated for the wrongs done her by a god-mother's error in judgement and a natural mother's symbolic abandonment. We, as readers, can see that the legacy also includes her mother's terrible folly of marrying an unworthy man, but for a time Anne's perception of this remains uncertain.

Fortunately but not accidentally, she is *not* persuaded to be inconstant in favour of this specious continuity. The problematic options of sameness and difference do not double her vision; she recognises the opportunity for authentically changing the bleakness of her life by remaining faithful to Wentworth, her original and only lover. Consistency of character and of attachment prevail over the menacing forces of chance and confer a happy ending upon the revised fairy tale after all.

Inlaying this hauntingly elemental story are stylistic devices that emphasise its kinship with fairy tales; Austen appears to have gone out of her way to focus attention on the artifice of fiction. We find a surprising occurrence of coincidentally shared names, for example. In the plot, the dramatic turning point is foreshadowed by an earlier, strikingly similar contrivance. And both the narrator's and characters' diction are studded with arresting refrains. Presented from its outset as a sequel to an implicitly meaningful, unwritten earlier story, this novel is a puzzling play on the notion of doubleness.

Beginning with names, the first page contains a breezily irreverent reference to 'all the Marys and Elizabeths' that ancestral Elliots have married, alerting us to a quirk of repetitiveness that the coming story will vigorously display. In Anne's contemporary world, Charles Musgrove has both a son and a cousin (his brother-in-law-to-be) with the same Christian name, and Mrs Smith's deceased husband was a Charles as well. This is an oddly extravagant gesture, coming from an otherwise tautly economical crafter of novels. Ironically, Admiral Croft remarks that he wishes 'young ladies had not such a number of fine Christian names'; how much simpler 'if they were all Sophys, or something of the sort' (p. 181).

William Walter Elliot, heir to Sir Walter Elliot, incorporates a remarkable range of identities within his semi-original name. Morally duplicitous, he has been a false friend to Sir Walter and to Charles Smith. Narratively he is accorded an odd versatility as well. He appears first as an unidentified traveller, spontaneously smitten with Anne at Lyme, then later is shown to have had a calculated plan to court her. Yet, despite his characteristic deviousness, his admiration at the inn was genuine, arising in ignorance of her identity. It was simply a coincidence – a narrative doubleness.

A striking doubleness characterises the plot as well as the cast of characters. Anne's anticipated first meeting with her former lover, Wentworth, is scuttled by a domestic accident in the Musgrove household: little Charles is injured in a fall. And with a thud that is uncannily familiar, the turning point of the novel will occur when the boy's aunt, Louisa Musgrove, falls on the Cobb at Lyme. The symmetry is as significant as the similarity; as the child's fall heralds a courteous and cold reacquaintanceship, Louisa's precipitates Wentworth's recognition of love and his return to Anne.

Freud was intrigued by the congruence of chronological and spatial patterning in the grammar of dreams, observing that '*temporal repetition* of an act is regularly shown ... by the *numerical multiplication* of an object'.[1] Repetitions inform Louisa's accident with just such dreamlike ciphering. The company at Lyme are taking their second walk along the Cobb, owing to Louisa's determination, and she further, obstinately insists that Wentworth 'jump' her down the steps once, and then again. After she has fallen and her sister Henrietta has fainted from shock, we are told that the passersby are especially delighted with the entertainment of seeing not merely one, 'nay, two dead young ladies, for it proved twice as fine as the first report' (p. 131).

Along with such doubling in names and actions, a cadence of poetic refrain characterises much of the novel's diction. For example, an unusually long and spiralling sentence expresses Anne's piteous solitude in the wake of events following Louisa's accident:

> She was the last, excepting the little boys at the cot, she was the very last, the only remaining one of all that had filled and animated both houses, of all that had given Uppercross its cheerful character.

> (p. 138)

This nostalgic sentence echoes another description of lingering last-ness, the reference to the old nursery-maid who is delightedly rehabilitated by Louisa's fall:

> A chaise was sent for from Crewkherne, and Charles conveyed back a far more useful person in the old nursery-maid of the family, one who having brought up all the children, and seen the very last, the lingering and long-petted master Harry, sent to school after his brothers, was now living in her deserted nursery to mend stockings, and dress all the blains and bruises she could get near her, and who, consequently, was only too happy in being allowed to go and help nurse dear Miss Louisa.

> (pp. 137–8)

The sentence is a chanting, balladlike story; the image of the nursery is presented with the soothingly monotonous rhythm of a nursery rhyme, another variation on the theme of refrain.

And refrain *is* a theme. Implicit in the novel's premise is a double-ness of time, for *Persuasion* is constructed like a palimpsest, an overlay through which we must decipher an original. The dramatic action that occurred in the novel's implied past is reflected and reflected upon throughout the text. We need only consider the way in which Anne is presented; until the events at Lyme precipitate her 'second spring of youth and beauty', she belongs more to the ghostly past than to her dismal present circumstances (p. 139). She lives amid the resonant tension of simultaneous time periods.

The passage which most pivotally expresses this impossible doub-leness of time occurs just before the story's turning point. In the poised, held moment before Louisa jumps down the Cobb steps and sets in motion a tumultuous rearrangement of the characters' ro-mantic pair-bonds, Austen pauses in her story for a haunting reverie on the sea:

> The party from Uppercross passing down by the now deserted and melancholy looking rooms, and still descending, soon found them-selves on the sea shore, and lingering only, as all must linger and gaze on a first return to the sea, who ever deserve to look on it at all, proceeded towards the Cobb. ...

> (p. 117)

Anne's first view of the sea is paradoxically not her first view, it is a 'first return'. And all of the radical patterning in *Persuasion*'s plot structure and diction emphasises this tremulous union of beginnings and returns.

The motif of first returns opens the apparently closed story of Anne's life. It suggests the possibility for recovery of what was thought to have been irrevocably lost. And as the story of a misunderstanding that is revisited, the novel challenges the reader's convictions regarding his own perceptions. In the earlier Austen novels, the anticipation of the happy ending invests the whole with a promise of pleasing resolution. But the anticipated ending of *Persuasion* must provoke apprehension; we cannot be sure where this return will lead, or if it will have an ultimate destination at all.

Even Anne's dizzyingly narrow escape from a wasted life is not as properly satisfying as we expect fictional escapes to be. A painful residue of doubt clings to the ending, and we wince with ambivalent desires and beliefs when we are told that

> They returned into the past, more exquisitely happy perhaps, in their re-union, than when it had been first projected; more tender, more tried, more fixed in a knowledge of each other's character. ...
>
> (p. 243)

Analogue of a first return, here is a redeemed past. And Anne teasingly denies us our sigh of relief with her paradoxical insistence that Lady Russell had been wrong in her advice, yet she herself had been right to follow it. We want to agree, yet we are left frowning; like Dr Johnson's Rasselas, we are being asked to drink from the mouth of the Nile even as we drink from its source. Anne's defence of her terrible error feels like a flirtation with disaster even as the novel is about to close, grinding against her miraculous, precarious rescue.

It is the nature of storytelling to etch patterns and simultaneously to violate them. In *Persuasion* this aesthetic conflict is brought into the foreground; the will to conserve the patterns of the past inviolate abrades against the impulse to disrupt and reform them. As the 'imaginist' Emma Woodhouse in *Emma* wishes to preserve authority over her world and yet wishes to make matches (which must necessarily undermine her control over those matched), so the narrator of *Persuasion* expresses contradictory impulses toward enshrinement of the past and toward implacable progress.

Narrative ambivalence is apparent from the start. If the promised story of Anne Elliot is introduced as the wistful remnant of a lost past, then the scene with which that story commences farcically counterpoints the yearning to return there. We meet the fatuous Sir Walter gazing tirelessly at the two handsome duodecimo pages of the Baronetage upon which his family's historical existence is summarily acknowledged. He delights in beholding his own name, feeling an endless glow radiated by his ancestors' prestige. He favours the pursuit of no profession at all, any sort of employment being necessarily deleterious to one's original personal substance. Absurd as such a caricature of conservatism is, his compulsion to hold his story still brings into relief the narrator's and heroine's inclinations to cut Anne's losses, to deny the potentially dangerous possibilities of hope and change.

In change there is loss, of course, but there can be more than compensatory gain as well. On a thematic level, both characters and narrator frequently express faith in justice and the value of suffering. On another level, Anne's losses can be equated with the missing elements of the narrative. The story that overflows the banks of fictional knowledge is in a sense lost, but as with Anne's and Wentworth's lost days, absent features of the text are pledges of a greater richness to come.

The more information we are given about a character's inner life, the sparser that information seems. Who was Anne Elliot before the novel began, and how can we account for the eight years that transformed the persuadable girl of nineteen into the firm woman we are shown? And further, how has this narrator elicited from us such unconventional, seemingly inappropriate curiosity?

She has done so at least in part by contrasting a playfully contrived, non-mimetic fictional background with an earnestly realised, provocatively elusive central figure. Figure and ground resonate, creating a tension that invests the text with powerful emotional authenticity, and anticipating the direction taken by such later novelists as Proust and Joyce.

In place of the unobtrusive mimetic foundation that persuasively supports earlier Austen heroines, here is fictional scaffolding illuminated with narrative searchlights. Patterns of doubleness and refrain have taken the place of progressive momentum, creating a cadence exquisitely suited to this heroine's step. For she is no Elizabeth Bennet, coming of age and learning to distinguish between appearances and reality; Anne Elliot begins her narrative journey with maturity and discernment, and in her world such phenomenological distinctions are no longer possible. Here the focus has veered from character to the perception of character, and knowledge of another person's motives and idiosyncratic vision is always insufficient. Grounded by *Persuasion*'s schematically patterned narrative surface, personality emerges with a residual richness that extends beyond the borders of the text.

From *The Kenyon Review*, 10:4 (1988), 87–91.

## NOTES

[Cheryl Weissman's short but incisive essay starts by examining the schematic nature of *Persuasion* in terms of its structural patterning, and arguing for the novel's similarity to certain archetypal fictions, such as fairytales. Weissman identifies the fictive, self-conscious nature of the text, which appears to contain numerous internal references to other narrative forms. She suggests, however, that while such narrative patterns and expectations are established, they are simultaneously violated. The resulting tension functions to foreground ambivalence and elusiveness, and ultimately the reader is frustrated in the desire to arrive at any definite solutions or resolution. While adopting a radically different approach, Weissman's discussion shares with Julia Prewitt Brown's essay (essay 7) the interest in the evasive quality of the novel and the difficulties this poses for a reader in arriving at a definitive interpretation. References to *Persuasion* are to the edition by D.W. Harding (Harmondsworth, 1967). Ed.]

[All references to the novel are given in parentheses in the text. Ed.]

1.  Sigmund Freud, 'Chapter VI: The Dream Work', in *The Interpretation of Dreams*, ed. and trans. James Strachey (New York, 1965), p. 407.

# Further Reading

The following reading list does not attempt to provide a comprehensive survey of current work on Jane Austen. Rather it is intended to identify some of the main threads in contemporary Austen criticism and to help you find your way through the great mass of commentaries on Austen's work that are available – several hundred studies and articles published each year. In addition to discussions which focus specifically on *Mansfield Park* and *Persuasion*, the bibliography contains more general discussions of Jane Austen's writing which provide further insights into how the novels can be read. While the material is broadly divided into categories, it is important to note that these are not necessarily mutually exclusive. There is always a danger in trying to classify criticism too narrowly, and many of the critics whose work is recommended here show their debt to a wide variety of critical or theoretical approaches in arriving at their own interpretations of Austen's texts

## BIOGRAPHICAL AND HISTORICAL STUDIES

Despite the apparently limited amount of hard evidence about Jane Austen's life, biographical studies appear to be on the increase. The following titles all make valuable links between Austen's life, her writing and the historical and social conditions which informed her work. It is worth pointing out that at least two major new biographies, by David Nokes and by Claire Tomalin, are currently in production. These will undoubtedly be worth adding to the list below.

Jan Fergus, *Jane Austen: A Literary Life* (London: Macmillan, 1991).

John Halperin, *The Life of Jane Austen* (Baltimore: Johns Hopkins University Press, 1984).

Park Honan, *Jane Austen: Her Life* (London: Weidenfeld & Nicolson, 1987).

Terry Lovell, 'Jane Austen and Gentry Society', in Francis Barker (ed.), *Literature, Society and the Sociology of Literature: Proceedings of the Conference Held at the University of Essex, 1976* (University of Essex, 1977), pp. 118–32.

David Monaghan, *Jane Austen: Structure and Social Vision* (London: Macmillan, 1980).

David Monaghan (ed.), *Jane Austen in a Social Context* (London: Macmillan, 1981).

Warren Roberts, *Jane Austen and the French Revolution* (London: Macmillan, 1979).

Roger Sales, *Jane Austen and Representations of Regency England* (London and New York: Routledge, 1994).

## LITERARY AND IDEOLOGICAL CONTEXTS

Jane Austen was immersed in the cultural and ideological debates of her period. In order to appreciate the ideas and range of reference contained in her novels it is helpful to be able to locate them within their literary and intellectual context.

Isobel Armstrong, *Mansfield Park* (Harmondsworth: Penguin Books, 1988).

Nina Auerbach, 'O Brave New World: Evolution and Revolution in *Persuasion*', *English Literary History*, 39 (1972), 112–28.

Alistair Duckworth, *The Improvement of the Estate* (Baltimore: Johns Hopkins University Press, 1971).

Moira Ferguson, *Subject to Others: British Women Writers and Colonial Slavery, 1670–1834* (London and New York: Routledge, 1993).

Jocelyn Harris, *Jane Austen's Art of Memory* (Cambridge: Cambridge University Press, 1989).

Glenda A. Hudson, *Sibling Love & Incest in Jane Austen's Fiction* (London: Macmillan, 1992).

Elaine Jordan, 'Pulpit, Stage and Novel: *Mansfield Park* and Mrs Inchbald's *Lovers' Vows*', *Novel: A Forum on Fiction*, 20:2 (Winter 1987), 138–48.

Anne K. Mellor, *Romanticism and Gender* (London: Routledge, 1993).

Kenneth Moler, *Jane Austen's Art of Allusion* (Lincoln: University of Nebraska Press, 1968).

David Musselwhite, *Partings Welded Together: Politics and Desire in the Nineteenth-century English Novel* (London: Methuen, 1987).

James Thompson, *Between Self and World: The Novels of Jane Austen* (University Park: Pennsylvania State University Press, 1988).

Janet Todd, *Sensibility: An Introduction* (London: Methuen, 1986).

## FEMINIST STUDIES

Feminist criticism has made an enormous impact on Austen studies. In addition to those essays included in this volume, the works listed below provide a valuable introduction to discussions of gender in Austen's fiction. They include studies both of female authorship and of contemporary representations of the feminine. Two are collections of essays which offer a useful overview of the debates in feminist literary criticism as applied to the work of Austen and her contemporaries.

Mary Evans, *Jane Austen and the State* (London: Tavistock Publications, 1987).

Kate Fullbrook, 'Jane Austen and the Comic Negative', in Sue Roe (ed.), *Women's Reading Women's Writing* (Brighton: Harvester, 1987), pp. 39–57.

Deborah Kaplan, 'The Disappearance of the Woman Writer: Jane Austen and her Biographers', *Prose Studies*, 7:2 (1984), 129–47.

Margaret Kirkham, *Jane Austen: Feminism and Fiction* (Brighton: Harvester, 1984).

Ellen Moers, *Literary Women: The Great Writers* (London: The Women's Press, 1976).

Meenashki Mukherjee, *Jane Austen*, Macmillan Women Writers Series (Basingstoke: Macmillan, 1991).

Mary Anne Schofield and Cecilia Macheski, *Fetter'd or Free: British Women Novelists, 1670–1815* (Athens, GA: University of Ohio Press, 1986).

Leroy W. Smith, *Jane Austen and the Drama of Women* (London: Macmillan, 1983).

Alison G. Sulloway, *Jane Austen and the Province of Womanhood* (Philadelphia: University of Pennsylvania Press, 1989).

Kathryn Sutherland, '*Jane Eyre's* Literary History: The Case For *Mansfield Park*', *English Literary History*, 59 (1992), 409–40.

Janet Todd (ed.), *Jane Austen: New Perspectives, Women and Literature* (New Series) Vol. 3 (New York and London: Holmes & Meier, 1983).

## TECHNIQUE

Studies of the language and form of Jane Austen's novels no longer confine themselves to explications of her artistic method and its effects. Modern twentieth-century interest in reading practices accords significance as much to what is unsaid as with actual discourse, and is also concerned with ways in which linguistic analyses can provide psychoanalytic insights. Two of the studies below discuss constructions of meaning in Austen's fiction in the context of contemporary linguistic codes.

Louise Flavin, '*Mansfield Park*: Free Indirect Discourse and the Psychological Novel', *Studies in the Novel*, 19 (1987), 137–57.

Judy van Sickle Johnson, 'The Bodily Frame: Learning Romance in *Persuasion*', *Nineteenth-Century Fiction*, 38 (June 1983), 43–61.

James L. Kastely, '*Persuasion*: Jane Austen's Philosophical Rhetoric', *Philosophy and Literature*, 15 (1991), 74–88.

David Lodge, *Language of Fiction: Essays in Criticism and Verbal Analysis of the English Novel* (London: Routledge, 1966).

Norman Page, *The Language of Jane Austen* (Oxford: Basil Blackwell, 1972).

Roy Pascal, *The Dual Voice: Free Indirect Speech and its Functioning in the Nineteenth-century European Novel* (Manchester: Manchester University Press, 1977).

Myra Stokes, *The Language of Jane Austen: A Study of Some Aspects of her Vocabulary* (London: Macmillan, 1991).

Stuart M. Tave, *Some Words of Jane Austen* (Chicago: University of Chicago Press, 1973).
Michael Williams, *Jane Austen: Six Novels and their Methods* (London: Macmillan, 1986).

## GENERAL

There are many works of general criticism on Jane Austen. The four listed below are among the best recent studies. They include a collection of essays on *Persuasion* with a reprint of the 1817 edition of the text.

J. David Grey, A. Walton Litz and Brian Southam (eds), *The Jane Austen Companion* (London and New York: Macmillan, 1986).
Susan Morgan, *In the Meantime: Character and Perception in Jane Austen's Fiction* (Chicago and London: University of Chicago Press, 1980).
Patricia Meyer Spacks (ed.), *Persuasion: A Norton Critical Edition* (New York and London: W.W. Norton & Co, 1995).
Tony Tanner, *Jane Austen* (London: Macmillan, 1986).

# Notes on Contributors

**Nina Auerbach** is Professor of English at the University of Pennsylvania. She is the author of *Communities of Women: An Idea in Fiction* (Cambridge, MA, 1978); *Woman and the Demon: The Life of a Victorian Myth* (Cambridge, MA, 1982); *Romantic Imprisonment: Women and Other Glorified Outcasts* (Columbia, 1985); *Ellen Terry, Player in her Time* (New York, 1987); *Private Theatricals: The Lives of the Victorians* (Cambridge, MA, 1990); and *Our Vampires, Ourselves* (Chicago, 1995). She is co-editor of *Forbidden Journeys: Fairy Tales and Fantasies by Victorian Women Writers* (Chicago, 1992).

**Julia Prewitt Brown** is Associate Professor of English at Boston University. She is the author of *Jane Austen's Novels: Social Change and Literary Form* (Cambridge, MA, 1979) and *A Reader's Guide to the Nineteenth-Century English Novel* (London, 1985; Japanese translation, 1987). Her study of Oscar Wilde, *Cosmopolitan Criticism: Oscar Wilde's Philosophy of Art*, will be published by the University Press of Virginia in 1997.

**Marilyn Butler** is Rector of Exeter College at the University of Oxford. In addition to *Jane Austen and the War of Ideas* (Oxford, 1975, reprinted with a revised introduction 1987), her books include *Maria Edgeworth, a Literary Biography* (Cambridge, 1972); *Peacock Displayed: A Satirist in his Social Context* (London, 1979); *Romantics, Rebels and Reactionaries* (Oxford, 1981) and *Paine, Godwin and the Revolution Controversy* (Cambridge, 1984). She is also co-editor of *The Works of Mary Wollstonecraft* (London, 1989) and of *The Works of Maria Edgeworth* (London, 1996).

**Sandra M. Gilbert** is Professor of English at the University of California, Davis. **Susan Gubar** is Professor of English at Indiana University. Together they have co-authored *The Madwoman in the Attic: The Woman Writer and the Nineteenth-Century Literary Imagination* (New Haven and London, 1979); and *No Man's Land: The Place of the Woman Writer in the Twentieth Century, Vols 1, 2 and 3: The War of the Words, Sexchanges* and *Letters from the Front* (New Haven and London 1988, 1989 and 1994). In addition, Gilbert and Gubar have co-edited *Shakespeare's Sisters: Feminist Essays on Women Poets* (Indiana, 1979) and *The Norton Anthology of Literature by Women:*

*The Tradition in English* (New York, 1985). With Diana O'Heiir, a Professor Emeritus of English at Mills College, they have also edited *MotherSongs: Poems By, For, and About Mothers* (New York).

**Claudia L. Johnson** is Professor of English at Marquette University, Chicago. She is the author of *Jane Austen: Women, Politics and the Novel* (Chicago, 1988).

**D.A. Miller** is Professor of English and Comparative Literature at Columbia University in New York City. In addition to *Narrative and Its Discontents* (Princeton, NJ, 1981), he is the author of *The Novel and the Police* (Berkeley, CA, 1988) and *Bringing Out Roland Barthes* (Berkeley, CA, 1992).

**Mary Poovey** is Professor of English at the Johns Hopkins University, Baltimore. In addition to *The Proper Lady and the Woman Writer: Ideology as Style in the Works of Mary Wollstonecraft, Mary Shelley and Jane Austen* (Chicago, 1984), she is the author of *Uneven Developments: the Ideological Work of Gender in Mid-Victorian England* (London, 1989), and *Making a Social Body: British Cultural Formation 1830–1864* (London, 1995).

**Edward W. Said** is Parr Professor of English Literature at Columbia University, New York. His key publications include *Orientalism* (New York and London, 1978; reprinted 1985); *Covering Islam* (London, 1981); *The World, the Text and the Critic* (London, 1984); and *Culture and Imperialism* (London, 1993).

**Laura Mooneyham White** is Visiting Associate Professor of English and Assistant to the Dean of the College of Arts and Sciences at the University of Nebraska-Lincoln. She is the author of *Romance, Language and Education in Jane Austen's Novels* (London, 1988).

**John Wiltshire** lectures in English at La Trobe University, Melbourne. In addition to *Jane Austen and the body* (Cambridge, 1992), he is the author of *Samuel Johnson in the medical world: The Doctor and the patient*.

**Ruth Bernard Yeazell** is Chace Family Professor of English at Yale University. She is the author of books on Henry James (1976) and Alice James (1981). She has edited collections of essays on *Sex, Politics and Science in the 19th Century Novel* (1986) and on *Henry James* (1994). Her latest book is *Fictions of Modesty: Women and Courtship in the English Novel* (1991).

# Index

ADV-2771

Printed in the United States
951400002B